TAURUS

ALSO BY ERIC TAUB

Gaffers, Grips and Best Boys

TAURUS

THE MAKING OF THE CAR THAT SAVED FORD

ERIC TAUB

A DUTTON BOOK

To Audrey,
who always knew.

DUTTON
Published by the Penguin Group
Penguin Books USA Inc., 375 Hudson Street,
New York, New York 10014, U.S.A.
Penguin Books Ltd, 27 Wrights Lane,
London W8 5TZ, England
Penguin Books Australia Ltd, Ringwood,
Victoria, Australia
Penguin Books Canada Ltd, 10 Alcorn Avenue,
Toronto, Ontario, Canada M4V 3B2
Penguin Books (N.Z.) Ltd, 182–190 Wairau Road,
Auckland 10, New Zealand

Penguin Books Ltd, Registered Offices:
Harmondsworth, Middlesex, England

First published by Dutton, an imprint of New American Library,
a division of Penguin Books USA Inc.
Distributed in Canada by McClelland & Stewart Inc.

First Printing, November, 1991
10 9 8 7 6 5 4 3 2 1

LIBRARY OF CONGRESS CATOLOGING IN PUBLICATION DATA:

Taub, Eric.
    Taurus : the making of the car that saved Ford / Eric Taub.
        p. cm
    ISBN 0-525-93372-7
    1. Taurus automobile—History.   2. Ford Motor Company—History. I. Title.
TL215.T34T38 1991
629.222′2—dc20   91-16631
                                                                     CIP

Printed in the United States of America
Set in New Caledonia
Designed by Leonard Telesca

Taurus
Acknowledgments

This work began life over two years ago, when a long interest in automobiles led to a brief sketch for a possible book. My agent, Jane Dystel, enthusiastically guided and supported me through the development of each phase of the project. For all her essential work, I am deeply grateful. With great skill and intelligence, my editor, Kevin Mulroy, carefully analyzed the manuscript, offering suggestions that greatly contributed to the story of a group of men and women fighting to save their company. If this book succeeds in touching or enlightening the reader, it is due in no small measure to the labors of these two people.

The Public Affairs office of the Ford Motor Company, and its executive director, Jerry Sloan, showed its generosity and professionalism by providing access to key executives, employees, and documents. Chuck Gumushian was my point man at Ford; he cheerfully led me through the maze of this enormous corporation, and studiously arranged for interviews, tours, and demonstrations. Videotapes of key Ford events were quickly supplied by Carol Bonamici of Ford's broadcast news department, and Tom Foote of the corporate news department assisted my research into the company's financial position.

My many trips to Detroit were smoothed through the kindness, generosity and friendship of Reena, Peter, and Tal Nagourney. They helped me get my sea legs in a strange city, spending hours showing me the town and introducing me to some of the people I needed to meet. In addition, they opened up their home to me, welcoming a stranger into their lives. In the process, I became one of their family, and cemented an important, continuing relationship at a critical time.

The support from loving friends and relations across the country was an essential ingredient in the writing process. Richard Anobile's concern and publishing experience helped sustain my equilibrium. Ken Luber's funny daily telephone calls and empathy from a fellow writer reminded me that there were indeed people beyond my computer screen. Jay and Roann Rubin read parts of the manuscript and offered important ideas about its structure and content. Martha and Manny Bohrer heartily welcomed me on several trips to Chicago. Jan Hartman's communications from New York and London, as well those from Stuart Gordon, Norman Groves, Alice Jay, Barbara Kessel, Judith Taylor, Peter Wetherell, Carol Zulman, my parents Sonya and Dick Taub, as well as Andrew, Cheryl, Jason, and Jeremy Taub, all encouraged me in my work.

Many individuals agreed to be interviewed for this book. Those past and present Ford employees who kindly gave of their time and thoughts include: Ray Ablondi, Marilyn Aiken, Joseph Bobnar, Jake Chavers, Richard Feldman, Terri Glowacki, Charles Gumushian, Charles Houser, Thomas Howard, Richard Hutting, Bob Jacobson, Matt McLaughlin, Tom Page, Joel Pitcoff, John Risk, Louis Ross, Richard Ross, Jay Stanwich, Jack Telnack, John Tighe, Mimi Vandermolen, Lewis Veraldi, and Henry Wolpert.

Those interviewed not employed by Ford include: David Andrea, Chris Cedergren, David Cole, David Davis, Don Ephlin, Kinder Essington, Michael Flynn, Patrick Gaughan, Martin Goldfarb, Darwin Greenley, Gerald Hirshberg, Jeff Jani, William Jeanes, Dan Luria, Richard Marburger, Sean McAlinden, Thomas Mignanelli, Carl Olson, Alex Rhodes, Franklin Schoonover, Joseph Schulte,

Irene Veraldi, Joe Veraldi, William Veraldi, and Doug Wilson.

The automotive industry has bred a number of excellent business journalists. A number of them helped me learn the lay of Detroit's automotive land, and provided me with essential background information on the industry, including: Jim Higgins, Doron Levin, Paul Lienert, Dutch Mandel, Leon Mandel, James Risen, David Smith, David Versical, and Helen Vogel.

Contents

1

THE FALL

As soon as she saw her husband getting dressed, Irene Veraldi knew that things were not well.

Lewis Veraldi had always been a barrel of a man, a short, chubby Italian with a quick grin, twinkling eyes, a slap on the back, and a ready bear hug for anyone he liked. But Lew, now a retired Ford Motor Company vice president of engineering and manufacturing, wasn't a big hit with everyone at the firm. His tendency to inappropriately shoot off his mouth, his demanding perfectionism, his streetwise style, angered some of his fellow straightlaced vice presidents. Even if they had wanted to, there wasn't much they could do about him. While few liked to talk about it, many knew that it was Lew Veraldi, more than anybody else, who in the 1980s was responsible for saving Ford from destruction.

But today, the laughter and the jokes were gone. "He can't go, he won't make it," Lew's wife realized in despair, as she watched him struggle to put on the clothes he hadn't worn for months. As Irene helped Lew get into his wheelchair, she couldn't help notice the telltale sign. His suit was way too big. Over the last several months of his illness, he had lost a tremendous amount of weight. The man who always joked that he decided not to become a priest because he had no neck was now disappearing inside his suddenly oversized collar. Irene Veraldi knew that Lew's frail body, ashen face, sunken eyes, and horrible, desperate gasps for air were the unmistakable cues of approaching death.

Still, this was meant to be a joyous time. For Veraldi, July 16, 1990, was not only his sixtieth birthday, but a vindication of the last eleven years of his life. Today, the man who had headed up the program that developed the Ford Taurus, the car that radically changed American automobile design and helped return Ford from near bankruptcy, was donating one to the Henry Ford Museum. The Taurus would take its place in the museum's transportation collection alongside the Model T, the Mustang, the Dodge minivan, and other vehicles that have come to define American automotive art and industry.

Veraldi sat in his wheelchair and struggled through the ceremony. As the head of the Taurus project, this was supposed to be his day. He posed for photographs, shook hands, and politely answered the same questions from reporters that he had been asked hundreds of times before. Eleven years earlier, he had picked employees from all over the company and worked them into a team that would help bring Ford back from the brink and make it the most profitable car company in America. Today, weakened and pained by diabetes and an almost nonfunctioning heart, Lew Veraldi could no longer even lift himself into the bright red Taurus that was placed in front of him. His glassy stare hinted at his pain. Still, he did his best to cope. "What was it like to have worked on this car?" Veraldi was asked once again by a reporter. The hackneyed question nevertheless caused him to stir, to momentarily become the energetic executive he once had been. "It feels great to have done the Taurus," the emaciated man told the reporter, his eyes widening. "There was nothing like it. Nothing." For the first time all day, Veraldi managed to smile.

In 1978, Veraldi's health was still good. It was his disposition that was poor. The workaholic car engineer was rapidly going crazy from boredom. Veraldi had been back in the States since 1976, after a three-year stint in charge of the launch of Ford's successful new European subcompact, the Fiesta. The job had earned him a vice president's title, but he would have traded that in a second for something useful to do. Ford made him the head of its product planning and research division—a desk job supervising a group of people developing new cars. But once back in Dearborn, Veraldi discovered Ford's dirty little secret: the company wasn't really developing any new models at all.

Attempts were being made: Veraldi's group would go through the motions of preparing sketches, working out engineering problems, costing out components. But once it was time for Ford top management to give the go-ahead for a new project, they'd reject the idea, no matter what it was. After several false starts Veraldi finally found something he could get excited about: the Mini/max. A new type of vehicle, it would become America's first small van for families. Veraldi's team got to work on it, producing detailed sketches of the unique hybrid. Everyone loved it; they thought it was a great idea. Despite extraordinary sales projections for the new product, this, too, was shot down. The opposition to the vehicle came from none other than the chairman himself, Henry Ford. "The Mini/max is too expensive," he said. "We'd have to develop a completely new engine and drive train for the car, and we can't afford to do that."

Not only money prevented the development of the Mini/max. In the 1970s the company had no strategic direction. Nobody in charge seemed capable of figuring out how to respond to the changing market. "From 1974 until the day that I left that company four years later," said Matt McLaughlin, a former vice-president and general manager of the Ford Division, "my main concern was that we did not have a product lineup that would be acceptable during the 1980s. A cycle plan for new cars should last at least three months before it's reviewed. We had a new one every week. We could never make up our minds about what kinds of cars we wanted to build."

During the early part of the decade the company was still competing in a sheltered market with its two sole competitors, General Motors and Chrysler. But after the 1978 oil embargo forced a hike in gasoline prices, Ford was caught with its pants down, as people rushed to buy more economical cars. Ford had nothing to offer the consumer, so the consumer bought Japanese, European, and General Motors vehicles.

Even if Ford had wanted to attack its product problems, it was too preoccupied at the highest levels to do so. In the late 1970s the company was mired in internal disputes as its two top executives, Henry Ford and Lee Iacocca, battled for control of the company. Their disagreements had started in 1972, when Iacocca wanted his man, Hal Sperlich, to become the next head of Ford of Europe. Henry Ford was vehemently opposed to Iacocca's choice and appointed Philip Caldwell instead. Iacocca's political defeat only exacerbated the strong differences in social class and personal tastes that defined the two men. Whereas Henry was a member of America's royalty, Lee was the son of an immigrant hot dog vendor. Lee's style was gruff and earthy. He was the poor boy on the outside trying to get into the inner circle, but he just never seemed

to fit. Henry questioned the loyalty of Iacocca and his lieutenants, while he worried about Lee's quest for power. Iacocca believed that Ford's notorious drinking problems and
noble upbringing did not allow him to see the hard realities
the company was facing. In 1973, after the first oil embargo caused by the Yom Kippur War, Henry Ford cut $2
billion from the company's new car development program
in a shortsighted attempt to save money. Furious, Iacocca
openly broke from Ford. After further years of enmity,
Iacocca saw his stature as president reduced. In 1977,
Henry Ford elevated Phil Caldwell, the man that Iacocca
had not wanted to head Ford of Europe, to the newly created post of vice chairman, effectively diminishing Iacocca's power. In June 1978, Caldwell was made deputy vice
chairman, forcing Iacocca to report to Ford through him.
One month later, Henry Ford fired Iacocca, after his well-
publicized and strategically inappropriate appeal to the
corporation's board of directors for help in saving his position. In the fall of 1979 Caldwell replaced Iacocca as
president of the company.

Throughout this time, product decisions became political decisions, as the one titan favored or condemned a
project based on the position of the other. Henry Ford
knew that Lew Veraldi's Mini/max project was going to be
a winner. His chief designer, Gene Bordinat, had even told
him that the van had all the makings of another Ford Mustang, the phenomenally successful car that Lee Iacocca was
credited with creating in the 1960s. "Who *needs* another
Mustang?" Ford wanted to know.[1] It was the Iacocca connection that sealed the project's fate.

Veraldi was furious over the Mini/max's demise, because the vehicle had a clear shot at success. Coming into
work day after day to twiddle his thumbs was not Veraldi's
idea of satisfying work. After three years on the fast track
in Europe, Veraldi, a thirty-year Ford employee, was now
getting to the point where he was wondering if he should
just retire.

Throughout the period of inner turmoil Ford stockholders would have been surprised to learn that anything at Ford was amiss. The 1978 annual report told a happy story. In the United States, Ford had sold 2.6 million cars and trucks, slightly more than the previous year. Sales had increased worldwide to 6.46 million units. After-tax profits were $1.5 billion, the majority of it coming from the United States. Its 23 percent U.S. market share had even risen slightly. "The company continued its strong performance worldwide in 1978," the report stated, "as new records were achieved for dollar sales, factory unit sales, and employment." Profits were down compared to 1977, but that was "attributable to continued escalation in the cost of labor and materials worldwide and higher costs associated with the company's new-model programs in North America."

The gloss put on the Ford annual report extended far beyond its cover. Whatever resources Ford had committed to develop new vehicles for the eighties were insufficient. Henry Ford was not willing to make the hard decision to cut back on profits in the short term in order to devote more capital to future development. It was as if all that mattered was "making the numbers," having something good to tell the stockholders rather than creating policies that would ensure the long-term health of the company.

But the ruse could not last forever. While the company continued to debate the best way to reduce the size of its cars in response to government fuel-economy standards and emissions regulations, its major competitor, General Motors, had already started to downsize its American product line. GM's all-new X-cars were now going to market, a series of higher-mileage Oldsmobiles, Buicks, Pontiacs, and Chevrolets that featured front-wheel drive and larger than expected interiors. These cars were designed to appeal to energy-conscious American families. Ford had nothing similar ready to go, and it had no plans to produce anything in the foreseeable future.

If the world had remained stable, perhaps the company could have muddled through for a few more years with its somewhat smaller, fuel-inefficient, boxy cars. But in mid-1978, the nations that belonged to the Organization of Petroleum Exporting Countries (OPEC) hiked oil prices again. In 1979, two months after California instituted odd-and-even-day gas rationing to prevent panic buying, GM introduced the X-cars. Worried about the return of gasoline lines, consumers turned to these as well as Japanese vehicles.

The surge in import sales was greeted with derision by many American auto executives. It was beyond them why anybody would want to buy a foreign car. The sheer preponderance of American automobiles driven in Detroit was proof to the provincial Motor City executive that foreign car sales were an aberration. American cars looked and handled the way they did, executives believed, because American buyers liked them that way.

"I've heard so many Detroit car men look at a Japanese car and then ask me, 'How could you drive up to the country club in a thing looking like that?' " a former Chrysler designer recalled. "That question has been put to me so many times that to attribute it to any one person would be ridiculous."

But most people in America were not driving to the country club. They were using their cars to go to work, to haul their kids, and carry their groceries. In a period of economic uncertainty, they wanted reliable, comfortable, and cheap transportation. They were drawn to imports just as their parents and grandparents had been to Ford's Model T several generations before.

The 1978 OPEC price rise, the introduction of General Motors' new vehicles, and the availability of more fuel-efficient cars from overseas had a devastating effect on the company. The new X-cars were immediate successes, stealing sales from Ford. In its first year of production GM sold over 300,000 Chevrolet Citations, close to the same number of Ford's established Fairmont. In 1980, Citation sales jumped over 20 percent, while Fairmont sales dropped. Thanks to rising gasoline prices, Toyota sales were up by

20 percent while Datsun's rose over 30 percent. Over half a million more high-mileage imported vehicles were sold in 1979 than the year before. Twelve months after an ostensibly healthy Ford Motor Company reported strong gross revenues and profits, the company's fortunes sank. In 1979 Ford's U.S. car sales dropped 23 percent, an extraordinary 597,000 units. Only the steadiness of the foreign market, in which Ford competed with smaller, more fuel-efficient cars and lower labor costs, allowed the company to show an overall after-tax profit. In America, however, the company saw 1978's $800 million profit transformed the following year into a nearly $200 million loss.

With the grim economic news, even Ford's next annual report took on a sober tone. In place of the report's regular "Message to Stockholders," a spot in which corporations usually offer self-congratulatory praise and overlook their failings, management decided to offer answers to the public's "most frequently asked questions."

"All things considered, I would say we had a pretty good year" was Phil Caldwell's blindly optimistic response to the first printed query. "Our car business in North America was a disappointment, and we must improve our results there." In case the reader hadn't been thinking about it yet, Caldwell mentioned that, no, "we do not need government financial assistance and are not looking for any handouts." Yes, things had been bad in 1979, but they would only be getting better in 1980, Caldwell reassured his shareholders. "As the year progresses, we expect sales to increase. Overall, I expect 1980 to be a year in which people in the United States will be able to see for themselves the results of what I like to term a new American industrial revolution—the rapid, major change to smaller, more fuel-efficient cars and trucks."

The American public took a look at Ford's new lineup, and they didn't like it. For the 1980 model year Ford's bread-and-butter cars, the Fairmont, Granada, and Mustang, remained the same. The huge Lincoln Continental lost two feet and eight hundred pounds. And the compa-

ny's image car, the famous Thunderbird, now came in a
shorter model. While it was somewhat smaller, the new
T-Bird's styling continued the bulky, rectangular, angular
look of its predecessor, and bore absolutely no resemblance
to the 1950s sports coupe of the same name.

Ford's response to the demands of the marketplace for
more efficient cars only proved that the company was in
worse trouble than anyone had thought. No one at Ford
seemed to have any idea what to do to compete. The new
Thunderbird was a terrible car; sales of the model soon
would virtually disappear. Chris Cedergren, a well-known
auto-industry analyst for J. D. Powers and Associates, said,
"The 1980 Thunderbird had to have been the worst domestic car ever introduced in the 1970s and '80s. That car
was awful design-wise, quality-wise, precision-wise. It was
just an abortion. If I was the head of Ford, I would have
canned everybody associated with the project. I would
have said, 'you gotta be kidding, get out of the building.' "

By the end of 1980, Ford's woes had become substantially worse. Its total U.S. car sales declined even more
than the previous year's. The company was now selling
half the number of cars in America it had only two years
earlier. Ford's share of the U.S. market fell an additional
3.4 percent, while imports gained ground again. As usual,
the bulk of their gain could be traced to Ford. The company's $199 million U.S. loss in 1979 plummeted to over
$2 billion the following year.

Ford's financial implosion affected every aspect of its
operation. With drastically reduced sales the company had
no need for as many employees. In June, Ford fired 80,000
of them. Then the company started "outsourcing" its work,
contracting with overseas firms—like its partner Mazda, to
manufacture transmissions in Japan instead of its own U.S.
plants—to save money. Just when the company desper-
ately needed to improve the quality of its cars, the firings
and outsourcing further weakened assembly-line morale
and increased the factory workers' distrust of management. "This was a very serious problem for us," said Don

Ephlin, then the head of the United Auto Workers' Ford Department. "Before 1979 we had never been faced with a permanent loss of jobs. We'd been in a highly profitable, highly productive industry. How could anybody believe that the Ford Motor Company could seriously be in financial trouble? I mean, that was just beyond people's imagination. Until then the American auto industry had never had any competition." Now, the competition was getting worse.

Consumers had discovered that imports offered them amenities that Detroit never seemed to think of, like cup and change holders, split folding rear seats, easy servicing and, most important, reliability. As the imports began to move to more aerodynamic shapes, Ford continued to build large, boxy automobiles. In their size and conservative design, these cars looked like no others in the world.

Even when brand new, the quality and reliability of Ford cars were atrocious. A Ford owner could never be sure his car would start, even if it was fresh from the factory. Testing the new models, *Consumer Reports* wrote, "The five-liter, V8 Granada/Monarch often stalled after a cold start. The automatic transmission shifted somewhat abruptly. The power steering is numb." The car is "sluggish and sloppy in emergency maneuvers." As for the Fairmont, *CR* found: "The 200-cubic-inch V6 usually stalled several times before it would run steadily. The Fairmont scored far below the Chevrolet Citation on our tests."

By the late 1970s, all of Ford's quality problems came to a head. In 1979 the Hertz Corporation showed Ford its maintenance records, which indicated that its Japanese fleet had half as many repairs as Fords. In 1981 *Consumer Reports* wrote that the predicted repair rates for the downsized 1980 Lincoln Continental, Mark VI, and the Lincoln Town Car were "much worse than average in the first year." Ford's behemoth Thunderbird and its twin Mercury Cougar "emphasize style and fancy features rather than usefulness. Predicted repair: worse than average."

The company's overall sales sank as customers continued to look elsewhere for better-quality cars. Beginning in 1979, Thunderbird orders began to disappear. The 297,000 units sold in 1978 dropped 30 percent in 1979. In 1980 sales declined an additional 39 percent, and then another 47 percent the following year. In 1982 Thunderbird sales bottomed out at just 14 percent of its volume four years earlier.

Overall, Ford's share of the U.S. market declined almost three points, with most of Ford's loss becoming the importers' gains. By the end of 1979, 22.7 percent of the country was now purchasing cars made somewhere else. And two times out of three, somewhere else meant Japan.

In March 1980, Henry Ford, his health declining, resigned the chairmanship of the company founded by his grandfather almost eight decades before. Phil Caldwell, now the head of Ford, began to assemble the next generation of Ford management, internationally experienced men who could see beyond the likes and dislikes of the country club set, men who had different ideas about how cars should look, handle, and operate. The new group included president Don Petersen; Lou Ross, the head of car product development; Jack Telnack, one of Ford's top designers; and Lewis Veraldi, responsible for the launch of the Fiesta, one of Ford of Europe's most successful cars ever.

These executives had all spent considerable time working for Ford overseas. Caldwell had been head of International, and Telnack had headed up design in Australia and worked with Veraldi on the Fiesta in Europe. Both had returned to Detroit filled with a new perspective on how good automobiles could be. Two years earlier, Lou Ross had finished a stint as vice president of the company's Brazilian operations. Suddenly he, too, had a whole different outlook on his company's American products. "I came back from Brazil and thought, 'Gee, I hate to say this, but there isn't enough in our cars that interests me. We don't have enough to appeal to people.' There just wasn't anything that we sold in America that I wanted to drive. I would never drive a Lincoln Town Car. It was too big, too heavy. It wasn't responsive. In Brazil, whatever you drove had manual transmission, and it was sporty. And in Europe you really enjoyed driving, you could be turned on by driving. It's kind of hard to be turned on by a four-thousand-pound wallowing American thing."

The new management team had seen firsthand that Europeans were making major strides in design, in aerodynamics, and in ride unlike anything in the States. They realized that cars could handle better than the typical American mammoth and still be as comfortable. And they believed both that their engineers could design and that American workers could build a product as good as the Japanese if only they were encouraged and respected. The biggest question in Phil Caldwell's mind was whether they could move fast enough to save the company before it bled to death.

Time was, unfortunately, very short. With Ford's continuing enormous dollar losses and declining market share, a crash program was needed that would create a lineup of dramatically new vehicles. At best, his executives figured, they had until the middle of the decade to turn the company around before the Ford Motor Company would have to call it quits.

To show the public that Ford was changing, Lou Ross had to get some new models developed and brought to market quickly. In addition to the short-term fixes, a long-term strategy was needed, one that would introduce cars to the American market that people wanted rather than cars that Ford executives decided they should have. The baby boomers were growing older and starting families; this new generation had little loyalty to American car manufacturers. If Ford was going to hold onto them, it had to make cars that were as reliable and of as high a quality as the Japanese did. Now, Caldwell knew, was the time to sit down with Lew Veraldi and see what ideas his people had.

Veraldi's group had already been playing with a replacement for the company's midsize lineup, code-named

"Sigma." Preliminary sketches for it were rather radical looking, but that was nothing unusual. Designers always drew wild-looking cars, only to see them rejected once they reached management level. As far as Veraldi knew, this concept would soon be thrown into the trash just like all the other projects he had worked on since returning from Europe.

This time it was different. The company was ready to make the leap, Caldwell told Veraldi. Ford was ready to commit itself to a "world-class" car, one in league with the best sold anywhere. Caldwell knew Veraldi from Europe and decided to have him head up the development of this new vehicle.

"Lew, there are two questions I want you to ask yourself while you're working on this project," Caldwell told him. "First, you've got to find some way to figure out what people don't have in their present car that they would want on this one. And more important, I want to know why I should bother to cross the road from another dealer's to buy this car. Lew, if you can convince me why I should, I'll support you all the way."

After the meeting, Veraldi descended the twelve flights from Caldwell's office on the executive floor and walked across the tile lobby of the Skidmore, Owings, Merrill, Ford World Headquarters building, past the permanent display of the best and newest vehicles Ford made, to the parking lot. In front of it, facing The American Road, a line of twenty-seven poles stretched across the lawn, displaying flags of the United States and all the other nations around the world in which Ford manufactured and assembled vehicles. The parking lot was, as always, filled with employees' cars: Granadas, Monarchs, Thunderbirds, and the other Ford automobiles that were contributing to Ford's destruction.

This program sounded different, Veraldi thought, as he got into his car. This one sounded exciting. After two years of spinning his wheels, it looked like he finally was going to get a chance to show what this company could do, if just given the opportunity. If he was successful, he knew, then the Ford Motor Company might still have a fighting chance to survive.

"How was your day, Lew?" his wife asked as he arrived home late from work.

"Great, terrific," Lew said. Irene's ears perked up. She hadn't heard him this chipper in months.

"I've got a new assignment," he told his wife. "I'm going to be building the perfect car."

2

THE RISE OF FORD

If Lew Veraldi succeeded in his quest for perfection, it would not be the first time that the Ford Motor Company changed the nature of American transport. The company founded by Henry Ford was once the biggest, best-known, and most influential automobile manufacturer on the face of the earth. Ford prospered not because he invented the automobile; that had been done by others years before. The Ford Motor Company struck it rich because Henry Ford perfected the methods of manufacturing and marketing cars that changed their stature from a rich person's luxury to a low-cost necessity, available to anyone with a few hundred dollars to spare. When General Motors was but a pup, when Horace and John Dodge were still supplying engines to Henry Ford rather than building their own vehicles, inexpensive Ford cars were plying the dirt roads of America, playing a critical role in the radical transformation of the United States from a rural to an urban, mobile, transportation-dependent society.

By today's standards, Henry Ford arrived relatively late to car manufacturing; he began selling cars to the public in 1903, fourteen years after Charles and Frank Duryea had produced the first American car, a high, huge, bulky machine. Before Ford even started working on cars full time, Gottlieb Daimler was already producing automobiles in Germany, Peugeots had been available for eleven years in France, and cars made by Franklin, Pierce, Locomobile, Packard, and Stanley were being sold in the United States. By 1899 there were 4,000 automobiles in the U.S., most of them powered by steam or electric engines; the Vanderbilts were already driving theirs out to their Long Island estates. In the first three years of this century, over 150 car companies began operation in America; four years later, most of them had failed.[1]

Henry Ford was born in 1863, the son of Irish Protestants who moved to the United States from County Cork during the 1847 potato famine. Rather than settling in New York like many immigrants, they went to Detroit to join their successful farmer cousins, Samuel and George Ford, who had arrived in America almost twenty years earlier. Establishing a farm in nearby Dearborn, William and his wife, Mary Litogot Ford, soon became well-to-do. In the 1876 Illustrated Historical Atlas of Wayne County, the Ford farm was the featured drawing, a settlement with well-tended lawns, orchards, farm buildings, and a white picket fence.[2]

William was a country boy who relished the values of rural life. He would repeatedly tell his son Henry about its virtues: as compared to the city, villages offered a life without fear, filth, or depravity, an atmosphere in which traditional American and Protestant values could flourish. Although Henry would not remain on the farm, eventually moving to Detroit, it was his conflict between urban and rural ways of life, between change and conservatism, between taking unheard-of risks and pulling in the reins, that would come to fuel his company's greatest successes and ultimately lead to policies that would precipitate its near collapse.

Henry Ford was mesmerized by machines from the very beginning. He loved to take apart watches. He grilled his father upon his return from Philadelphia's Centennial Exposition in 1876 about the steam engines, power lathes, and locomotives on display. At the end of the nineteenth century, steam engines were common sights in rural America. When Henry saw his first one as a boy, attached to the rear wheels of a cart and used for threshing, he rushed out to the field, questioning the farmer about its mechanics and capabilities. At home, he built a model of the engine he had seen, using wood to create its body and a five-gallon oilcan as the boiler. As he grew, Henry's goal became the development of a practical gasoline engine. But if he was to succeed he needed easier access to raw materials and technology. In spite of his father's wishes, Henry and his new wife, Clara, decided to move to Detroit. On September 25, 1888, Henry took a job as a night-shift supervisor at the Detroit Edison Company, a plant that supplied electricity to the several thousand Detroit homes wired for the new technology. The position allowed Ford access to the tools he needed for his work. And once in the city his attention turned from farm machinery to automobiles.

Three years after his only son, Edsel, was born in 1893, Henry Ford succeeded in producing his first car. After months of work and two final sleepless nights, the Quadricycle rolled out of Ford's Bagley Avenue garage. The Quadricycle was a primitive machine, with a tiller for a steering wheel, bicycle tires, a bicycle seat, and a bicycle chain to transfer the power of the engine to the wheels. Engine-manufacturing plants didn't exist, so Ford's car was constructed entirely by hand, with common parts recycled

into new uses. A house doorbell was the horn. The two
cylinders were made from scrap pipe rescued from an old
steam engine, honed and then cut in half.[3]

Unlike the virtual limousine simultaneously built by
his friend, Charles King, in March 1896, Ford had constructed a compact. King figured that cars should truly be
horseless carriages, elegant conveyances for the wealthy.
Ford had, perhaps unconsciously, taken the opposite route,
creating a stripped-down vehicle that weighed just 500
pounds, barely one-third the weight of King's 1,300-pound
behemoth. Whereas King's car could just make five miles
per hour—the speed of a brisk walk—Ford's reached 20
miles per hour.

In 1899, a successor to the Quadricycle was so im-
pressive, Ford obtained backing for Detroit's first car manufacturer, the Detroit Automobile Company. But Ford was
out of his element. He knew how to build one-off models,
but he had no factory experience. Complaining that he was
being financially exploited by his backers, he rarely showed
up for meetings and often ducked out of sight when crucial
decisions needed to be made. The company folded before
a single car was produced.

The convincing win of one of his cars in the 1901
Grosse Pointe auto race swayed a new group of backers
that Ford still could be successful in the auto business. With
$50,000 in capitalization, they set up the Henry Ford
Company. But Ford couldn't set his mind to designing and
building the low-cost cars in which he claimed he was interested. Instead he had his friends work on racers. When
his backers found out, just four months into the venture,
they kicked him out of the company, re-forming it around
the talents of Henry Leland, brought in to the company as
a troubleshooter. After Ford's firing, Leland renamed the
firm the Cadillac Automobile Company. The company
which Ford had founded would eventually become the first
element in the future General Motors Corporation.

By 1903, Ford had designed another car. The Model
A came with a two-cylinder engine developing eight horse-

power, capable of speeds up to 30 miles per hour. Ford was now able to attract new financing. The Ford Motor Company was born.

Rather than build their own engines, the company had them manufactured to their specifications by the Dodge Brothers. (The Dodges had been making motors for the rival Oldsmobile, but decided to pick up the Ford work when they realized he paid faster. Ford's partner, Alex Malcolmson, had such poor credit that the Dodges were able to demand cash on delivery for the first one hundred units.)[4] The engines were then brought to Ford's new Mack Avenue plant, where workers were paid $1.50 per day to assemble the various parts. Four models were planned: the Model A was priced at $850, while the most luxurious, the four-cylinder Model B, was offered at $2,000. Each sported Ford's name written in fanciful script designed by Childe Wills, a Ford engineer who decided to embellish the style of the *F* in Henry's signature and place the name in an oval logo.

Ford liked the Model A, but it was still not quite right. His vision was to build even more affordable cars for the masses. This stemmed not from a selfless desire to bring transportation to the people. It was a question of business. Henry Ford understood that by sacrificing the profit margin on individual cars, he could price them cheaply enough to increase the product's market share and overall revenues. In a statement that foreshadowed the problems Ford would face sixty years later, he proclaimed that cars would be the coming thing "if the manufacturer does his part and makes the cars practically free of trouble and lowers the price so more people can buy them."[5] In order to achieve those economies of scale, cars could no longer be built as individual, hand-assembled machines, with mechanics forced to bang each part into shape. Instead a process had to be developed whereby every piece was identical to its sibling, enabling complete interchangeability of parts and a reduction in the time needed to put a car together. "The way to make an automobile," Ford said, "is to make one

automobile like another automobile, to make them all alike
. . . just as one pin is like another pin when it comes from
a pin factory."[6]

In January 1906, Ford revealed his new Model N, a
car derived from the models A, C, and F and using high-
strength vanadium steel for the first time. The car was the
only $600 vehicle with a four-cylinder engine. Ford sold
over 8,000 units in the twelve months ending in September
1907, five times their previous annual totals. Spin-off versions created a model R and S. By the end of 1907, the
company had made over $1 million in profit on sales of
$4.7 million. In just four years Ford cars were selling in
Great Britain and Canada. The company was doing so well
that Henry's salary climbed to $36,000 per year.

The Model T was introduced in October 1908. Initially priced at $825 (the salary of an average teacher), the
car offered innovations and features never before seen in
an automobile. The four-cylinder engine had a removable
head, allowing for easy servicing. The car had a primitive
automatic transmission, a magneto that allowed the car to
be started without dry-cell batteries, and axles and drive
shafts encased in steel and sheltered from the elements.

Henry Ford decided that the Model T "would be constructed of the best materials, by the best men to be hired,
[and] offer the simplest designs that modern engineering
can devise. But it will be so low in price that no man making a good salary will be unable to own one, and enjoy
with his family the blessings of hours of pleasure in God's
great open spaces."[7]

So many orders were taken for the car that the company had to shut its books by the end of the year, as production had been scheduled through the next August. By
September, 10,000 cars were sold, bringing in a record $9
million in sales.[8]

Although Henry Ford was brilliant in engineering, he
was a terrible failure as a social scientist. He became so
convinced of the potential of the Model T that in 1909 he
ceased production of all his other models. The Model T,

he decided with his typical stubbornness and grandiosity, was the perfect car.

For years the market agreed with him. The Model T became the American people's car. It was the first car that won wide appeal with farmers, who used it to haul goods and animals. Panel truck versions were created for commercial use. The car was affectionately nicknamed Tin Lizzie and Flivver. Wild stunts were devised to promote the car: to show its sturdiness, a Model T was driven up Mount Wilson in 1912. Another was photographed driving up the steps of the YMCA in Columbus, Nebraska. One person drove back and forth on a seesaw for five hours to illustrate the car's control. In the Model T Rodeo in Las Vegas, cowboys jumped from the car's running boards to wrestle bulls to the ground.

In 1910, Ford produced 19,000 Model Ts. One year later, that figure almost doubled to 34,500. And the year after that, they more than doubled again, to 78,440. Orders were so great that Ford couldn't keep up with demand. He had to figure out how to speed up production. In the spring of 1913, Ford first experimented with changing the method used to put together the Model T's flywheel magneto. When one man assembled the entire unit, it took him twenty minutes to finish. But once the assembly was divided into its twenty-nine component steps, with each man doing only one of those twenty-nine tasks over and over, assembly time dropped to five minutes.

During the first assembly-line experiments at the company's new Highland Park plant, teams of men moved along the floor, pushing the car from one station to the next, where piles of parts awaited installation. By August 1913, cars were being assembled in six hours, but that still wasn't fast enough. Ford took a cue from the overhead motorized line used by Chicago meat packers; rather than the men moving with the cars, the cars would move while the workers remained stationary, performing the same job over and over again as each car passed. Assembly time dropped immediately to just one hour and thirty-three minutes. "The man who places a part does not fasten it. The man who puts in a bolt does not put on the nut; the man who puts on the nut does not tighten it," Ford bragged about his new process.

What Ford gained in manufacturing, though, he lost in employee relations. Assembly-line work was monotonous and oppressive. Workers were laid off when machinery was changed; though they did not work on holidays, they also were not paid. Employee turnover was so excessive that by 1913 the company was hiring 963 workers for every 100 it kept on the payroll. Ford lost $3 million a year on training costs for workers who quit. In that year only 640 of 15,000 men had worked at the plant three years or more.[9]

In January 1914, Ford doubled wages from $2.50 to an unheard of $5 per day. He was immediately idolized as a saint by some newspapers, reviled as a traitor to capitalism by others. The five-dollar day was "a blinding rocket through the dark clouds of the present industrial depression," said the *Cleveland Plain Dealer*. A headline in the *Algonac Courier* proclaimed, "God Bless Henry Ford," who was "one of God's Noblemen." The *New York Times* said it was a bad idea and would cause nothing but upheaval. The raise was "distinctly Utopian and dead against all experience." The *Wall Street Journal* argued that Ford committed economic blunders and crimes which would "return to plague him and the industry he represents, as well as organized society."[10]

Overnight, worker absenteeism dropped from 10 percent to 0.5 percent. Hearing of the new wage, unemployed workers from around the country descended on his Detroit factory. The very day after his announcement, 10,000 men gathered in ten-degree weather looking for work. There was no work to be had, but the workers didn't leave until the police sprayed them with freezing water.

The strategy was a brilliant business move. While portrayed as a populist, Henry Ford was basically a pragmatist. The wage increase not only reduced labor costs, but tremendously increased Ford's stature around the world. As a side benefit, it even raised the possibility that his better paid employees would finally be able to afford the very car that they were making.

The extra dollars came only if the worker could prove that the money would be "of permanent benefit to himself and his family." To certify that workers abided by Henry Ford's aberrant and paternalistic concept of clean living, inspectors from the newly created Ford Sociological Department checked up on them. Workers were asked questions about their marital status, savings, life insurance, recreation, and the amount of their mortgage. Taking in boarders, excessive drinking, and a bad diet were grounds for losing the additional salary. In six months the case could be reconsidered. To aid workers in the right attitude toward life, the Ford Motor Company issued illustrated pamphlets with photographs of "profit-sharing" and "non-profit-sharing" dining rooms, along with other examples of proper deportment.

Despite his professed concern over the fate of the workingman, he treated his employees and his son, Edsel, as vassals. Ford's idea of fun was to keep workers wondering when they'd be fired. He enjoyed giving two employees, without their knowledge, the same job title and then watching them fight it out. Walking through his accounting department, he would periodically ask his aides, "What do these people do?" Told that they kept the books, he would regularly dismiss the lot of them. Faced with a tyrannical father, Edsel chose not to fight. With few exceptions, he deferred to his father in company matters despite the fact that Edsel was president.

Ford's belief that he knew best how his workers should run their lives was part of a grander notion that he knew best how the world should run. He was a stubborn man and, like most stubborn people, he never let his ignorance stop him from voicing his beliefs. His semiliterate writing style and intolerance of minorities would have been laughable had he been an inconsequential man. As one of the world's most powerful industrialists, people listened to his prattle.

He knew nothing about history and saw no need to. During his 1919 libel trial against the *Chicago Tribune*, in which he sued the paper for calling him an "ignorant idealist," Ford claimed that Benedict Arnold was a writer and that the American Revolution had been fought in 1812. "History is more or less bunk. It's tradition. We don't want tradition," Henry Ford told the *Tribune* in 1916. "Bankers, munitions makers, alcoholic drink, kings and their henchmen, and school books" were the cause of the world's problems, he said to the *New York World* in 1919.

The German Jewish international bankers were responsible for starting World War I, he asserted. As bankers financing the war, they won no matter which side lost. He purchased his local newspaper, the *Dearborn Independent*, and turned it into a nationally distributed publication advocating racism and anti-Semitism. Over 750,000 copies of each issue were printed, and Ford forced his car dealers to distribute them to their customers. The *Independent* printed one of the first English translations of *The Protocols of the Elders of Zion*, a fictional anti-Semitic document that accused a Jewish group of Learned Elders of plotting to take over the world for their own people. Ford even had his personal secretary, Ernest G. Liebold, set up a New York detective agency to ferret out dirt about prominent Jews, and then expose them in the *Independent*.[11]

The collected writings in the newspaper were later published as *The International Jew: The World's Problem*. "The Jews are the conscious enemies of all that Anglo-Saxons mean by civilization," the pamphlet declared. It was widely read throughout Germany, Russia, Portugal, and Brazil. Whether racism or ignorance was the reason for Ford's bigoted beliefs is irrelevant, for he contributed to damaging race relations throughout the world. Adolf Hitler was said to have a picture of Henry Ford on his desk, and Ford holds the distinction of being the only American to be lauded in Hitler's autobiography, *Mein*

Kampf. Baldur von Schirach, the Third Reich's Youth Leader, stated that he became an anti-Semite after reading *The International Jew.*

Henry's son Edsel implored him to renounce his statements, if only because his anti-Semitism was beginning to hurt the sale of Ford vehicles. Henry at first refused to do so. "If the public wants our product, it will buy it."

It started to look as if the public didn't want it. The Model T that spread throughout America during the second decade of this century began to lose its appeal at the beginning of the third. In 1922, Ford salesmen wanted the car line updated, but Ford refused. Henry was convinced that there was nothing wrong with the Model T. He had built the perfect car, and he would not change it. "Well, gentlemen," Ford told the dealers, "as far as I can see, the only trouble with the Ford car is that we can't make them fast enough." Between 1920 and 1924, the company cut the price of the car eight times, but by the middle of the decade the vehicle that had defined automobile transportation in the United States began to lose sales to its rival, Chevrolet.

While the Ford Motor Company was still touting its utilitarian, and now anachronistic, slogan, "It gets you there and brings you back," its rivals were stealing market share, offering different styles, more comfort, and colors other than Ford's famous basic black. In 1923, Ford sold an amazing 57 percent of all the cars in the United States. But just two years later that number dropped to 45 percent. Chevrolet sales were on the upswing, rising from 280,000 in 1924 to 470,000 just one year later. By 1926, 730,000 Chevys were sold.

Rather than develop a new car line, the elder Ford once again took the high road, and became obsessed with developing a radical new "X" engine that all tests showed would fail. But Henry persisted in working on it.

Ford sales were decreasing, and dealers, fed up with selling an outdated product—along with Ford fertilizer and the *Dearborn Independent*—were switching to General

Motors cars. A six-page memo written by Ford employee and Edsel's brother-in-law, Ernest Kanzler, took issue with Henry's business philosophy. "We have not gone ahead in the last few years," Kanzler said in the memo that just as easily could have been written in 1979 as in 1926. Ford was "barely holding our own, whereas the competition has made great strides. You have always said you either go forward or backward, you can't stand still. . . . We know we've been defeated and licked in England. And we are being caught up with in the U.S. With every additional car our competitors sell, they get stronger and we get weaker. . . . Our Ford customers . . . are going to other manufacturers, and our best dealers are low in morale."[12] He ended the letter with what may well have been the worst thing he could say: "It is one of the handicaps of the power of your personality, which you perhaps, least of all, realize, but most people when with you, hesitate to say what they think."[13] The memo did not sit well with Henry. Six months later, while Edsel was on a European trip, Henry fired Kanzler. Edsel did nothing to prevent it.

By 1927, Henry Ford finally understood that the Model T had to be replaced. With General Motors incorporating such innovations as self-starters and hydraulic brakes, Ford's car seemed antiquated in comparison. While he was excruciatingly slow in making changes there remained a strong attachment among the public to Ford cars. On the first day that the new Model A (named after Henry's original car) debuted, people began lining up in New York at 3 A.M. to see it. Over 50,000 cash deposits were placed on the car that day, mostly by people who hadn't had a chance to drive one. Across the United States, ten million people saw the new model in its first thirty-six hours, 8.5 percent of the nation's population. The Model A launch was "one of the great national events of 1927, rivalling the delirium with which Charles Lindbergh was greeted that year after his transatlantic flight."[14] The new model was successful because it sold for $495, $100 less than the Chevrolet, and came with a self-starter, balloon tires, and a safety glass windshield. And, just as important, it was a Ford.

The Model T now passed into history, but its impact on the United States is difficult to exaggerate. In its nineteen years of production, 15.5 million Model Ts were sold in America, one million in Canada, and 250,000 in Great Britain. Ford's total Model T production accounted for fully one-half of all the cars made in the world. The shift from horses to cars as primary transportation was largely fueled by the Model T. The move happened so rapidly, in just twenty years, that many farmers had to quickly change from hay to other crops in order to stay in business.

Henry Ford was not content with just selling the most popular car in the world. He also wanted to control all the means of production that allowed the car to be manufactured. By controlling the car's componentry, from its sheet metal to its glass, Ford could keep costs low. He decided to build a huge manufacturing facility that could create a car from start to finish. Completed in 1927, the Rouge plant was a massive complex, one and a half miles long and three-quarters of a mile wide. It occupied 1,100 acres with 93 buildings and 93 miles of railroad track. The plant employed 75,000 workers, 5,000 of whom simply kept the place clean. The Rouge had a $35 million steel plant and its own glass-manufacturing facility, cutting the cost of Ford's windows from $1.50 to 20 cents per foot.

Once a barge arrived at the Rouge steel mill with ore, it took just 28 hours before that ore was turned into a finished car. With its carefully synchronized delivery of raw materials and parts to the assembly line, the Rouge was instrumental in introducing the "just in time" delivery system that the Japanese would perfect in their facilities sixty years later. "There is no secret to how we learned what to do," Eiji Toyoda, the president of Toyota, would tell a Ford official in the 1970s. "We learned it at the Rouge."[15]

Although Henry Ford was now the single most powerful industrialist in the world, his power came at the price of his company. His refusal to share command, his adamant, obsessive pursuit of ideas, illustrated by his beliefs in a Jewish cabal, soybeans as a miracle crop, his relentless work on the useless X-engine, and the firm conviction that smoking cigarettes caused criminal activity, eventually led to the near destruction of his company. When he should have listened to his subordinates, he dismissed them. When he should have shared power, he gathered more power and hired subordinates who followed his orders explicitly. And when he had the chance to expand his car model lineup, he sabotaged his own opportunities.

Two years after the Model A was introduced, the Ford Motor Company was selling close to two million units per year. It now held a 34 percent market share, compared to Chevrolet's 20 percent. But by 1931 the General Motors Corporation outsold Ford 31 percent to 28 percent. Even Chrysler's Plymouth was now outselling the Model A. The car that had been designed to be the successor to the legendary Model T was discontinued that year.

Virtually whatever Edsel suggested to revive the company, Henry was against. When the son convinced the father to purchase the Zephyr car from another manufacturer in 1933 and produce it as a car for the middle class, Henry agreed but demanded that the car be produced on the recently purchased Lincoln assembly line, knowing that that would keep sales low. When Edsel suggested that the company go public to raise capital, Henry wouldn't hear of it. "I'll take every factory down brick-by-brick before I let any of those Jew speculators get stock in the company," he told his son.[16]

The firing of his brother-in-law, Ernest Kanzler, resulted in the loss of Edsel's base of support. And his involvement with Kanzler in the 1930s finally ensured that Edsel's star at the Ford Motor Company continued spiraling downward.

In 1927, Kanzler began a banking career, helped substantially with investments from Edsel. By 1929 Kanzler's Guardian Group had become the largest financial entity in

Michigan. Edsel Ford, in turn, was the group's single largest shareholder. A subsidiary handled its biggest client: the Ford Motor Company. In launching the Model A, Henry had finally agreed to allow people to buy cars on the installment plan, and Guardian became Ford's lender.

Guardian's success began to falter with the October 1929 stock market crash. Share prices fell, depressing Guardian's value, and thousands of its customers defaulted on their loans. To boost the solvency of Guardian, Edsel transferred $14 million of his own and Ford Motor funds to the bank, but this was not enough to save the Group. Soon the bank began to lend itself its own money, by transferring millions of dollars to its officers and then issuing its own shares as security. In order to survive, the company had decided to eat itself.

By 1932, the Guardian had loaned itself 34 percent of its own capital, and the only thing that would save the bank from insolvency was a federal bailout—or a massive loan from Henry Ford. Henry refused to help the company, but he saved his disgraced son from financial disaster by transferring several million dollars to Edsel's personal account.[17] Edsel was terribly humiliated by the bailout. In his one attempt to strike out from his father's oppressive hold, he failed.

Henry never turned to Edsel for support and advice. Instead he began to look to a man named Harry Bennett for comfort. Ford liked Bennett because, unlike Edsel, he was a yes-man and a bully, a thug who knew nothing about cars but did know how to please his boss: by simply never questioning him. Ford would ask, "Harry, can you take care of that?" and the deed, however dirty, would be done. By fulfilling Henry's every desire without complaint, Bennett helped Henry believe in his own omnipotence.[18] "I became Henry Ford's most intimate companion," Bennett wrote at the beginning of his autobiography, "closer to him even than his only son."

To the five foot, six inch tall Bennett, violence was a way of life. He boasted that he wore bow ties instead of straight ones because if he got in a fight, it would be more difficult for his opponent to strangle him. Starting in Ford's photography department, he rose in the company in spite of the fact that he was neither an engineer, designer, accountant, nor lawyer. His job was not carefully defined; he was there to do Henry's bidding.

For instance, when Ford wanted an engineer, Frank Kulick, fired, Bennett—then chief of security—asked Kulick to step over to his car to listen to the magneto. While Kulick was standing on the running board, Bennett roared out of the yard and quickly turned, throwing Kulick to the ground. Bennett then raced back into the yard and locked the gates.

The United Auto Workers union was anxious to gain representation at Ford, a goal Henry vehemently opposed. Once again Edsel was on the wrong side. Instead of trying to destroy the UAW, Edsel counciled negotiations with them. The union cited Edsel in its radio commercials as a friend of labor,[19] even while his father was its archenemy. Henry told Edsel to stay out of the way. Edsel was told not to meet with union officials, talk to the press, or discuss labor issues at all with anyone. Instead, Harry Bennett would handle everything.

On May 26, 1937, UAW organizers Walter Reuther, Richard Frankensteen, Richard Merriweather, and others drove to the Rouge, ready to pass out leaflets to the workers as they changed shifts in the afternoon. Reuther and Frankensteen split off from the group and walked to the overpass near the street. Waiting for them there were a group of thugs assembled by Bennett: the head of a Detroit gang, several professional wrestlers and boxers. They set upon the union men, severely beating them. Reuther was kicked repeatedly in his face and body, and thrown over the railing of the overpass. Frankensteen had his arms pinned back while he was kicked in the head, kidneys, and stomach. Merriweather's back was broken.

Photographs taken by reporters at the scene of the "Battle of the Overpass" were enough for the National Labor Relations Board to take the Ford Motor Company to court, charging them with actions meant to disrupt workers' rights to collective bargaining. The courts found the company guilty and ordered Ford to allow union organizing to continue. Despite the evidence, Henry Ford, who had personally put Bennett in charge of stopping the union, refused to admit guilt. "Anybody who knows the Ford Motor Company knows the things the Board charged never happened and could not happen here."[20]

Over the next few years Edsel continued to fight Bennett. He hated and distrusted the man, his tactics, and his close relationship to his father. In the struggle to control the Ford Motor Company once Henry died, Edsel was losing.

When he learned from his sales manager, John Davis, that one of Bennett's aides, Harry Mack, had broken up a Ford sales meeting and started a fight, he ordered Mack fired. Bennett went to Henry, turned the story completely around, and claimed that it was Davis who started the fracas. Henry, always taking sides with Bennett in any dispute with his son, ordered Edsel to fire Davis. For once Edsel refused. "Get the man out of my sight," Henry ordered. Davis was not fired, but Edsel was still forced to have Davis relocate to the hinterlands of California. "This is the saddest day of my life," Edsel told Davis.

The relationship between father and son deteriorated to the point that Henry ordered spies to keep watch on his son's activities. Nor did Ford think anything of ridiculing Edsel in public. During a party at Henry's estate, he saw his son drinking, a practice of which he disapproved. Henry told the band to speed up the music and watched as Edsel made a fool of himself trying to keep pace with the tempo. "Afterward," said Bennett, "Mr. Ford would report with glee how he had danced Edsel and his friends until they were all in, and how 'they sweated until they stank.' " "Who is this man who has so much control over my husband and is ruining my son's health?" Edsel's mother, Clara, once cried out in her dismay with Bennett.[21] In

1942, already suffering for years with severe stomach ulcers brought on by his tumultuous relationship with his father, Edsel died of stomach cancer. He was forty-nine years old.

Edsel's death allowed seventy-nine-year-old Henry to consolidate his power and remold the company in his own, increasingly bizarre image. Before the start of World War I, the company had ruled the American automotive industry, with a 60 percent share of the market. By the beginning of World War II, that share had shrunk to less than 20 percent. Ford quickly elevated Harry Bennett to his heir apparent, while purging the company of his son's protégés, including car designer Eugene Gregorie and Fred Black, the man responsible for creating Ford's massive exhibit at the 1939 New York World's Fair. Edsel's dream of developing a small economy car that would be attractive during the postwar recovery period was quashed. Also stopped were plans for a front-wheel drive vehicle with independent suspension. The problem with the Ford Motor Company, Henry decided, was that it had lost its roots. It had succeeded at the beginning of the century when it was a simple company producing just one automobile, and that is the philosophy to which it should return. "We've got to go back to the Model T days," he told an employee. "We've got to build only one car. There won't be any Mercury, no Lincoln, no other car."[22]

Bennett convinced Ford to add a codicil to his will stating that after Henry's death, the Ford Motor Company would be run for ten years by a trust, of which Bennett would be the secretary. By doing so, Bennett ensured that Edsel's children, Henry II and Benson, would be shut out of the company. Ford would not listen to criticism of the man who stood closer to him than his own son. "The Jew and Communists have been working on poor Harry until he's almost out of his mind," he told colleagues.[23]

Once again the company was being brought down by a lack of vision and day-to-day management. Bennett was running the company like a banana republic. The company had been in the red for close to fifteen years. Thousands of unnecessary workers staffed the factories, while the company remained dangerously short of engineers to work on new models. There was no cost-control mechanism in place, materials delivery was not being properly scheduled, and the company's finances were kept from most executives. When asked why, a Bennett lieutenant stated, "You never know what someone will do with one of those financial statements."

The government gave permission for young Henry Ford to muster out of the navy and return to Ford to try to save it. Although Henry II had worked briefly in a low-level position in the engineering department, he admitted that he knew virtually nothing about how to run an automobile company. He quickly assembled a team of assistants to fight Bennett for power. For reasons never explained, Bennett decided to tear up the codicil with which he could have retained control over Ford.

Henry Ford II was named executive vice-president of Ford at the beginning of 1945. But only by becoming chairman could he control the company and return it to solvency. On September 21, 1945, Henry Ford, now eighty-two years old, agreed to relinquish control to his grandson. The decision was forced upon him both by his wife, Clara, and daughter-in-law Eleanor, who could not stand to see the company destroyed by an old man who had spent his last few years tottering on the brink of reality. They were able to sway Henry to give it up after they threatened to sell their substantial holdings of company stock, which would have ended the family's control of the company. "He killed my husband [Edsel], and he's not going to kill my son," Eleanor Ford said. "I'll take the job," Henry told his grandfather, "only if I have a completely free hand to make any changes I want to make. We argued about that, but he didn't withdraw his offer."[24] One day after assuming the chairmanship, Henry Ford II walked down the hall and unceremoniously fired Harry Bennett.

The great patriarch died eighteen months later. During his life he had manufactured as many cars as there were people in the United States at the time of his birth. By providing the first practical, affordable means of motorized transportation, he, more than anyone else, was responsible for turning the United States from a rural to an urban society. In an oft-quoted statistic, when Ford left his father's Dearborn farm for Detroit, one in five Americans lived in cities. At the time of his death, four of five Americans did.

Henry moved quickly to undo the deeds of his grandfather. Within months he had one thousand Bennett appointees fired. He conducted pep rallies with Ford dealerships, asking them to hold on, telling them changes were coming, and the company would be number one again. And he instituted the company's first college-graduate training program, in which Lee Iacocca would be one of the first participants.

Still, Henry needed help running the company. In 1946, he received an intriguing, brash telegram from an unknown individual. "I represent a group of associates who have served under me and the Office of Statistical Control," it stated. "We would like to discuss with you personally a matter of management importance and request early meeting." The wire was from Charles Thornton, an aide to undersecretary of war Robert Lovett.

Thornton, Lovett, Arjay Miller, J. Edward Lundy, Robert McNamara, and six other air force colleagues decided after the war was over to cast their fate together. This brash group of young men was convinced they had something to offer a major corporation. Ford was impressed enough with their energy and competence to immediately hire them as the nucleus of the company's future management. But the Whiz Kids, as they later became known, were not ready to take control because they knew nothing about cars or the car business. As an interim step Ford hired Ernest Breech, a General Motors executive, to run the company.

Henry's finance men, finally able to inspect the books,

found that there were none to inspect. The company's finances were a shambles. In 1949, hundreds of thousands of dollars were being lost each year through sheer stupidity. Millions of dollars were being kept in non-interest-bearing bank accounts. Ford accountants estimated the amount of money that the company owed vendors by measuring the height of the pile of bills sitting on their desks, and then multiplying that number by what they determined was the average amount of each bill recently paid. Workers continued to be paid in cash because the elder Ford had discovered that when workers were paid by check, many employees cashed them in bars.

In what would become the most famous speech of his career, one that put Ford on the cover of *Time* magazine in 1946, the pragmatic grandson called for a truce in the battle between management and labor. With the company's severe problems, it was obvious that the elder Henry Ford's adversarial approach to unions was useless. What was needed, Henry II said, was "industrial statesmanship, from both management and labor. There is no reason why a union contract could not be written and agreed upon with the same efficiency and good temper that marks the negotiation of a commercial contract between two companies."[25]

In May 1949, the company introduced its next Ford, only the fourth completely new model Ford ever produced.[26] The new car drew 50,000 fans to New York to see it. The company sold over 800,000 of them that year, but that still kept Ford in third place in sales, behind Chrysler, by 5,000 units. Despite strong sales the quality of the car was terrible. "This car is a piece of junk," Ernie Breech said. "Water and dust always get in." He counted over one thousand separate defects on the car. Part of the problem was the design process itself. The engineers, designers, and marketers never spoke to each other, each group instead working in isolation. When one specialty finished its task, it handed its work "over the wall" to the next team. As a result, the designers didn't know if the car that they had sketched could be easily engineered. The engineers didn't know if the brake system they had designed could be easily manufactured. And the manufacturers didn't convey their problems back to the other two groups until changes became costly to make.

Chevrolet meanwhile had introduced its 1950 Bel Air, a "hardtop convertible." Realizing that they needed a fast remake for their car, company officials quickly put together a face-lifted version for the following model year, the Crestliner. It was available in three different colors and came with some cosmetic styling changes. The pent-up demand for cars after the war helped Ford sales. The company sold 1.5 million of its new model, beating Chrysler but still coming shy of Chevrolet.

In 1952, Ford introduced an all-new model, its first car with a one-piece windshield. Fortunately, neither GM nor Chrysler brought out new models that year, giving Ford the field to itself. The company captured 17.6 percent of the market, just shy of Chevrolet's 20.5 percent. At the same time the company began to enlarge its available car lines. From two in 1949, four separate car lines and fourteen different models were available by 1953. There were more cars available because studies showed that when people could afford to buy more expensive cars, they abandoned Ford and moved on to Buick and Pontiac, its GM competitors. "We're just growing customers for General Motors," one Ford executive lamented.[27]

By 1955, Ford was selling 43 percent of all low-priced automobiles in the United States, but only 13 percent of higher-priced models. Robert McNamara, recently promoted from comptroller to president of the Ford Division, proposed broadening the company by creating separate divisions for Mercury, Lincoln, and Continental, analagous to General Motors' separate divisions for Chevrolet, Buick, Oldsmobile, Pontiac, and Cadillac. In addition, a new group would be created solely to build and market the E-car, an upscale vehicle that would have no interchangeable parts with any other Ford.

The E-car project was headed up by Dick Krafve, and entailed such high secrecy that if one key to the E-car design center was lost, all of the locks were changed. In the meantime, Mercury was building its own entry in the higher-priced niche, and McNamara's Ford Division was creating a "luxury" Ford, larger even than any Mercury. Rather than develop a corporate-wide plan to attack its GM and Chrysler competitors, the three Ford divisions were busy fighting among themselves. The company became its own worst enemy, creating internal competitors for their own vehicles and ultimately contributing to their weakening market position. But Ford officials didn't see that. Instead, family members and executives were basking in their enormous windfalls thanks to the company's decision to go public in 1956. It was the largest share offering in the history of the United States.

The first casualty of the internal struggle for divisional supremacy was the E-car, now named the Edsel, after Henry's father. When the car was put on the market, it faced competition from GM, McNamara's bigger Fairlane, and a recession. Sales were disastrous. Despite projections that 200,000 would be sold within the first year, just 84,000 were sold after two.

Meanwhile, as a result of poor Mercury sales, McNamara fired the head of the division and recombined it with Lincoln. He then fired Krafve and put the Edsel division into the new Lincoln-Mercury as well. Once again the company had just two marketing groups. In November 1959, Edsel production was ended, leaving Ford with a $350 million loss. By the mid-fifties, with the costly failure of the Edsel, the lower than expected sales in the Mercury Division, and the fateful decision to price the new Continental Mark II 35 percent higher than its rival Cadillac, Ford's challenge to General Motors for American sales supremacy had come to nought.

Robert McNamara was named president of Ford in June 1960, replacing Ernest Breech. Whatever McNamara may have planned never had a chance to be put into action. Months after he assumed the presidency of Ford, John Kennedy asked him to become his secretary of defense. Weeks after his rise to the top of the Ford Motor Company, McNamara left for Washington.

One year later, one of McNamara's protégés, Lee Iacocca, was appointed to head up the company's Ford Division. The son of Italian immigrants, Lee's upbringing was radically different from that of his boss, Henry. Because of his lack of privilege, Lee was more concerned with the trappings of luxury than Henry. Iacocca began his career with Ford when he was recruited out of college. He was trained as an engineer but soon switched to sales. Iacocca became known as the consummate salesman, a man who knew all about cars, a trait borne out by his later marketing efforts on behalf of the Chrysler Corporation in the 1980s.

Encouraged by Henry's search for a "poor man's Thunderbird for the working girl," Iacocca oversaw the development of the Mustang, a new sporty coupe. Recycling the Ford Falcon's engine, transmission, and axles to save money, the Mustang became Iacocca's greatest hit. Selling over 400,000 units its first year, Iacocca predicted that the car would be "the start of a new golden age for Ford that will make the peaks of the past look like anthills."

While Iacocca was gaining control of Ford, Henry was losing it. He began to drink heavily, spend considerable amounts of time vacationing in Europe, and pursue other women. In 1964, after an obsessive, embarrassingly public love affair with Cristina Austin, he divorced his wife, Anne.

After McNamara's departure the company wallowed through several different versions of management that Henry would later admit were all mistakes. Finally, in 1968, he succeeded in hiring Semon E. "Bunkie" Knudsen, a top General Motors executive, to become president. The move infuriated Iacocca, who couldn't believe that Ford had gone outside the company for its top executive when Iacocca was clearly the next insider in line. "The day Bunkie was hired, Lee declared war," said former product planner Donald Frey. Iacocca set out on a campaign to get rid of Knudsen. When Knudsen argued for importing a low-cost compact from Europe, Iacocca said he wanted to build one in the United States. The new car would be "two thousand pounds for two thousand dollars." Iacocca's plan won, and the company produced the Ford Pinto. Lee made it plain to his colleagues that he, not anybody else, was the top product person at the company. His new car, the Maverick, was selling well, almost as well as both his Mustang and the Falcon. He hinted to his supporters that he might be forced to take a job with an outside firm if things didn't go right—and if that happened, who knew how Ford would fare with him gone? On September 3, 1969, after a year of feuding between his two top executives, Henry Ford fired Knudsen.

Ford was becoming wary of Iacocca, and had no intention of naming him president, even though he needed him at the company. He recoiled at Lee's arrogance, gruff personal manner, and empire building. To cut him off, Ford created a management troika, dividing the company's operations into three areas: Diversified Operations, International, and North American Operations, to which Lee was named chairman. It failed, and in 1970 Henry finally appointed Iacocca president of the company.

The 1973 oil embargo motivated Americans to buy fuel-efficient cars. Both Ford and General Motors had such models, but the Ford Pinto and Chevy Vega were poor competitors, both mechanically and stylistically, to Japanese and European imports. The Pinto had uncomfortable seating, poor exterior visibility, and anemic power. The Vega was cramped and unreliable. Adding an air conditioner—almost a requirement in many parts of the country—drained so much of the weak four-cylinder engine's power that the car could barely move at all. As Americans shifted their attention to foreign cars, Ford's profits dropped from $240 million in the fourth quarter of 1972 to $57 million a year later.

The struggle for power at the company continued. Iacocca made his own man, Hal Sperlich, a vice president at International, in an effort to position him as the future head of the division. Henry Ford appointed Phil Caldwell as president to block Iacocca's move. As a result of the animosity between the two men, product development suffered. With a recession looming in 1972, Henry ordered that $2 billion be removed from the company's product-development program, a move that angered Iacocca. Iacocca saw Ford's actions as an attempt to usurp his own power. The strategy was also shortsighted, decreasing the company's chances of keeping abreast of the competition at a time when dramatic changes were happening within the industry.

To save money Ford lobbied against the development of the Mini/max minivan. Company research indicated that this new marketing niche could be wildly successful. Numbers showed that Ford could expect to sell 800,000 units the first year. The Mustang had sold half that number; if the Mini/max figures were even as much as 75 percent off, a 200,000-unit vehicle was still worth developing. Ford argued that the company couldn't afford the costs, not with its plans to build the new Escort. To the dismay of many executives, the project was killed, only to be resurrected by Iacocca once he became head of Chrysler.[28] "I'm sure [former Ford executive] Harold Sperlich or Iacocca took our design after they left Ford," said John Risk, a Ford vice-president. "I saw early prototypes of the Chrysler minivan, and it was almost a duplicate of ours." It was that minivan, now known as the Plymouth Voyager and Dodge Caravan, that saved the Chrysler Corporation from bankruptcy.

Although the power struggle within the company remained largely unnoticed outside Detroit, the internal feuding was dissipating energy that should have been spent developing new vehicles. Corporate executives would continually submit ideas for smaller, fuel-efficient vehicles for the 1980s, but then no action was taken.

Matt McLaughlin, a Ford sales vice-president, warned his fellow executives that their constantly changing ideas for new products was going to seriously hurt the company. They had to stop dickering around with possibilities and come to a decision on their future product strategy. "As in the past," McLaughlin said in a prophetic 1976 paper addressed to the board, "it is almost a certainty that sometime in the next five to six years, the industry will experience a traumatic period, be it another oil crisis or economic downturn. Nevertheless, our competitors appear to have decided on their basic product strategies to cover the market, and are proceeding to implement them on a timely basis. . . . It is extremely important that Ford offer viable product entries in each market segment to protect against significant customer demand shifts."

This memo, as well as others presented by his colleagues, was ignored. In the late 1970s federal government regulations for increased fuel economy and decreased exhaust emissions meant that cars had to shrink. "Everything—engines, powertrains—had to change, top to bottom," Lou Ross said. "These are enormous expenditures, and they created enormous conflicts and differences of opinion. But they were compounded by Henry Ford lacking confidence in Lee Iacocca. "It was embarrassing to be in those meetings with Ford and Iacocca," McLaughlin added, more to the point. "Virtually anything that Iacocca brought up, Henry was against."

As plans languished, both Henry Ford and his company suffered a series of embarrassing revelations. Henry's second marriage to Cristina was ending, due in part to his well-known affair with Kathryn DuRoss. A drunk-driving arrest with DuRoss as passenger brought Ford ridicule and public humiliation. Then the company was fined $7 million for falsifying auto-emissions data submitted to the Environmental Protection Agency.

With Henry's health failing because of severe angina, Iacocca expected to soon grab the chairmanship. He was once again blocked by Ford, who created yet another troika, this time with Phil Caldwell in second position, above Iacocca.

In April 1978, attorney Roy Cohn filed suit on the behalf of the Ford shareholders against Henry for taking bribes, improperly employing relatives, and misusing company funds. It was a less than objective action, as Cohn was an old friend of an Iacocca associate. Fearing that his position was now in jeopardy, Iacocca appealed to the corporation's board of directors to help him save his job. By going above Henry, Iacocca had sealed his fate. Three months later, Henry Ford finally fired Lee. In March 1980, with Henry ailing, Phil Caldwell was elevated to the position of chairman, the first nonfamily member ever to run the Ford Motor Company.

When Henry began working for his grandfather 34 years earlier, Ford was producing 80 percent of the world's vehicles. By the time of his departure and Phil Caldwell's appointment, that figure had dropped to 28 percent. In the United States, Ford's market share had plummeted from more than 30 to 16.5 percent during Henry II's tenure. The company that had literally created the American automobile industry and, by so doing, radically changed this country's way of life, was now enmeshed in internal management struggles, stuck with outdated car product lines, and having no clear plans for the future.

Phil Caldwell may have been the first non-Ford to become chairman of what was once the world's greatest automobile manufacturer. But from the very first day of his new job, he was already wondering how much longer there would be a Ford Motor Company for him to run.

3

THE TEAM

By choosing Lew Veraldi to head up the Sigma program, Phil Caldwell picked one of Ford's most capable engineers for the job. The question in some people's minds wasn't why Veraldi was ultimately chosen, but how he ever advanced as far as he did in the first place.

His qualifications were never in doubt: a strong engineering background, thirty years' experience, and the recent launch of one of Ford's most important European vehicles. What troubled some at Ford was Veraldi's erratic personality. There were only the two *F*s in Veraldi's life— Ford and family—and he acted the same way with both. He could hug an employee one moment and scream at him until his face turned beet red the next. At home, he was so moody that his children skirted around him until they knew how he was feeling. He was a working-class vice-president who hated desk jobs, someone who preferred to stick his nose under the hood of a car with his engineering buddies at Ford than to go to a meeting. Yet he was devoted to work and home; during the day his life centered around fulfilling the needs of the company; in his ever shorter evenings his wife and children received all his attention.

He would bully an opponent into submission and then apologize for his arrogance. He hated papers and paperwork, but he couldn't throw away a thirty-year-old furniture receipt. He wanted everyone on the Sigma project to work together, but when he had an opinion he would pigheadedly demand that things be done his way.

"One time Lew started going through a list of bad traits that he thought he might have," Frank Olsen, a former engineering colleague said. "He told me to stop him when he had gone too far. He kept on running down the list, but I kept letting him go. 'Aren't you going to say stop?' he asked me. I just let him go on and on."

If Veraldi succeeded as an engineer, he failed as a politician. Unlike most of his fellow Ford vice-presidents, who could wheedle and cajole, keep their mouths shut when they could be hurt, Veraldi had no tact. If he felt strongly about something, he hammered away at his opponent, friend or foe, until he broke him down. "He was often right, but his strategy was usually wrong," said his project partner, John Risk. "When we first started working together, I presented him with a Sigma position paper that I wrote, with various financial analyses and conclusions about the project. Lew reviewed it and then the paper evolved. I got better information and changed the numbers and substantially altered the conclusion of the whole thing. He looked at the new version and said, 'This is different from what you presented before.' 'That's right,' I said. He was furious. He started yelling at me, banging on the table, and I had enough of that. I slammed the door and went back to my office. The problem was, I was a product planner and he didn't like product planners—he thought we were nothing but paper pushers. And he let me know it. People respected him for his product knowledge and his sincerity, but he wasn't a political animal. He could have risen further at Ford, but he alienated himself from people."

Yet he endeared himself to others. Every Christmas he had his secretary call Detroit's nuns and priests to find out the names of families in need. Then he and his wife spent two weeks buying and delivering presents to people he didn't even know. His secretary started calling him "Lewis Claus." In another example, one of his employees started falling behind in his work because his wife was ill with cancer; he was about to be laid off when Veraldi interceded. When his chief engineer was dying of Lou Gehrig's disease, he spent two long meetings pushing personnel to increase his retirement benefits way beyond the norm. "You either loved him, respected him, or hated him, there was no in-between," said an employee who worked closely with him.

Lewis G. Veraldi was born in 1930, the second eldest of eight children of unskilled Italian immigrants who settled in Pennsylvania. Lew's father eventually moved the family to the boomtown of Detroit to get a job in the auto industry. Already in his late fifties when Lew was born, Veraldi's father was a demanding parent who pushed his kids to do what he thought was right. Lew, like everybody else, was forced to learn to cooperate with his siblings to prevent the household from falling into chaos. Devotion and commitment to the group was paramount.

Lew's first dream was to attend a seminary and become a priest. But his father wouldn't have it. "The priesthood can wait," he told Lew. "First, you've got to get a trade. You can always become a priest later." His father ordered all of his sons to attend the Henry Ford Trade School. Lew studied drafting and by his early twenties was working at Ford.

Despite his poverty, he was impetuous and irresponsible with money. When he had some, he just as quickly lost it gambling at the track or by giving it away to some-body he thought needed it more. He was constantly having his cars repossessed. Feeling flush one time, he bought his mother a washing machine. After he made the first pay-ment, though, he ran out of money, and his older brother had to bail him out.

After getting the drafting job at Ford, Lew seemed to be heading upward, but he remained the black sheep of the family. They worried about his devil-may-care atti-tude, and they didn't think he'd change. Matters came to a head when Lew's elder brother, employed for several years at Ford, learned that his secretary had been secretly dating Lew. He had already bought her a watch for Christmas, a significant present for someone so threadbare. "Do you realize what you're doing?" the brother asked Lew's future wife, Irene, when he found out. "Do you realize who you're getting involved with? My brother's a bum. I'm telling you, Irene, don't marry him or you'll be taking in washing the rest of your life." Irene ignored his advice.

Once wed, he began to settle down. He was an opti-mist, always reassuring his wife that somehow he'd get the money they needed. In order to do so, however, he had to put in long hours. Just months into the marriage, he began mechanical-engineering night classes at Lawrence Institute of Technology, and did not get home until eleven o'clock.

After thirteen years of part-time schooling he finally became a mechanical engineer. He loved the field, and he loved working for Ford just as much. His 11 P.M. arrivals were over; now that he was a full-time Ford engineer, he had shorter hours. He managed to usually get home by eight, having left for work at six-thirty in the morning.

After a succession of engineering positions in Dear-born, Phil Caldwell asked Veraldi in 1973 to move to En-gland to head up the launch of the new Fiesta. With narrower roads and smaller pocketbooks, the minicar in Europe was not the sole province of teenagers and first-time car buyers, as in the United States. In the mid-1970s, the company had earmarked $1 billion to produce a brand-new car, a European vehicle that brought Ford into the hemisphere's all-important subcompact segment.

Quality problems plagued many European manufacturers in the 1970s; car owners were resigned to the fact that a brand-new Peugeot, Alfa Romeo, or most other European cars often left a pool of oil on their garage floor every morning. Quality was so poor at Ford's British plants that in 1971 Henry Ford had threatened to close them and move operations to the Continent if things did not improve.[1]

A major reason for the problem, Veraldi realized, was that departments didn't talk to one another. The attitude of Ford's British executives amazed him; despite his position as an engineer, Lew was used to hanging out with the boys. He had never forgot about his friends in drafting after he was promoted to a management spot. But at Ford's Brentwood headquarters, top management ignored people in inferior positions. It appalled Lew; he didn't understand how people could function that way. In his family, everybody had helped out. Teamwork made things happen, Veraldi knew, whether at home or at work.

In Europe, not only divisions failed to talk to each other, but nobody from one country spoke to Ford people in another. As a result, operations constantly missed their objectives and production-start dates. Lost production meant lost sales and lower profits.

Veraldi learned about the communications problems firsthand when he toured the German assembly plant that manufactured the Ford Capri and was assigned to produce the upcoming Fiesta. Based on the quality of the Capris that the plant was turning out, the new Fiestas were bound to have problems. Both cars were two-door models with a hatchback door in the rear. Whenever the plant water-tested the Capri's hatch, it always leaked. As with many European cars, nothing was done to fix the leak. Customers just had to put up with it. Management knew about it, but the cars were going out the door anyway because the engineers had never come up with a solution.

"I hope you guys are going to do better on the Fiesta than you've done on the Capri," the plant's manager said to Veraldi. "The Capri's door always leaks."

"Herr Jedermann," Veraldi responded, "I'll go you one better. I'm gonna let you design it so it doesn't leak."

"No, I can't do that, Mr. Veraldi. I manufacture cars, not design them," Jedermann responded. "I don't know how to fix a problem like that."

"Come on," Veraldi said impatiently, "you know what leaks and what doesn't leak, right? You redesign the door seal. When I come back in a few weeks, I want to see what you've come up with."

Jedermann got to work with production and together they devised a possible solution. On his next visit, Jedermann showed Veraldi their sketches. Veraldi approved the design and had it incorporated into Fiesta's manufacture.

This incident had a profound effect on Veraldi. It made him realize what people could do when forced to solve a problem. He had pushed the plant manager because the manager was on the front lines. If the quality of the car was better, more cars would be sold, and the plant would stay in operation. If the workers were given more responsibility, they'd feel more committed to the job. In the end, absenteeism, sick costs, and employee turnover would decrease. Anything that lessened the threat of labor unrest had to be good for management.

"That incident taught me that if you give the worker, the person that has the most equity in the process, the chance to get his or her oar in the water, it's gonna work better. They'll be more enthused and they'll do a better job in the project because they'll have their own ideas in it rather than being brought into the project after everything's been decided."

Launched at the end of 1976, the Fiesta became one of Ford of Europe's big successes. The car was ready four months prior to its scheduled date and sold 50,000 units above its target number.[2]

Veraldi was pleased with the car's success, but after three years his family had had enough of living abroad, and they pressured him to get permission to return home. Caldwell agreed with Veraldi's request, but no jobs were available in Dearborn at the end of 1976. Heading up the advanced-vehicle development group was the only job Ford could give him, and Veraldi soon hated it. Even though he was now a vice-president, he was a hands-on guy, and the desk job made him miserable. A loyal Ford employee, he stuck it out for three years, until Caldwell asked him to pick up the leadership of the Sigma project. The offer came in the nick of time.

"Let's pick up from this Fiesta experience," Veraldi suggested to Caldwell. "This time we'll integrate not just engineering and manufacturing, but all divisions of the car's production process: sales, marketing, design, public relations, even dealer relations."

Veraldi decided that everyone involved with Sigma would be in on the project from the beginning. Regular meetings would be held between all areas of the production process, so that every discipline would understand how the car was taking shape and what the problems in the process were. Each division would elect an individual to represent that discipline at the meetings. For some areas, its representative would work part-time on Sigma; for others, the commitment would be total.

"Throwing it over the wall" was now out. Manufacturers could no longer claim that an engineer had wasted months designing an engine no one could build, because the manufacturer would be present during the design. Marketers could not argue that the public hated a car, because research would be carried out on every stage of the design process and reported back to the entire group before a vehicle was finally approved. "Public relations staff would come up to an engineer five weeks before production and ask, 'What have you got for me to promote?' "

Veraldi remembered, "You know, it was chaos." Now they wouldn't need to do that because they'd be working on the project years ahead of introduction.

All areas of the production process were used to working in isolation. It was not in an American worker's vocabulary to voluntarily say, "I'm sorry," or "I made a mistake." "It's hard to get people to come out in the open and say, 'This is what I'm doing wrong,' because they feel that they're going to be criticized," Veraldi said. "But once they trust you and understand that all we want to do is make the best product we know how to make, then it's easier."

The company had common objectives: to be profitable, to make cars that people wanted, to establish and preserve customer loyalty, but often those objectives were forgotten in internecine battles between opposing work groups. Veraldi, however, had worked as both a manufacturer and an engineer, and had in addition worked closely with marketing people. When he pitched this new program, he had some validity. Furthermore, the time was ripe for such an experiment. With the company in serious financial trouble, people were looking for a cure. "There's no better way of getting people to rally together toward a common goal," Veraldi said, "than to all be massacred at the same time."

Still, the conversion was not easy. "Most of the old-timers were trained to be specialists in their own chimneys," Veraldi recalled. "The mind-set had always been, 'Stay out of trouble, it's the other guy's fault.' "

John Risk was one of the first people Veraldi brought into the program. They had been working together on advanced-vehicle programs and were just beginning to get to know each other. Risk would be Sigma's product planner, Veraldi's right-hand man. He had put together the project's original business plan, and would now be the liaison among the engineering, marketing, design, and financial divisions.

The product planner had to be the tough guy. He had

to tell the engineer that the cost of a suspension was too high, to inform the designer that a headlight switch could not be illuminated because it would add fifty cents to the cost, that the curved rear window was too expensive and elaborate to manufacture. "An automobile is five thousand compromises," Joel Pitcoff, a Ford manager, loved to point out, "because there are five thousand parts in an automobile."

Veraldi and Risk had similar temperaments. Both men were capable of putting up a good fight, although Risk had a cooler head. Physically, though, they couldn't have been more different. The lanky Risk stood a good head taller than the rotund Veraldi. It took Lew two steps for every one of John's just to keep pace with him. "There go Mutt and Jeff," secretaries would whisper as the two walked down the halls.

Veraldi visited each division contributing people to Sigma to explain the project and appeal for their support. "Look," he said, "I've got to have one of your men on my team—permanently. He'll be your liaison. But they have to be stationed over there with me, not here in your division. And they won't answer to you anymore. For the duration of their time on this project, they'll be reporting to me."

Traditionally, one worker would rotate among work units to help out on several projects simultaneously. For example, a body-and-assembly executive normally consulted with designers working on a Ford truck one week, a Ford station wagon the next, and a Lincoln sedan the third.

Veraldi ran into tremendous resistance with this new scheme. The team approach had been decreed by Caldwell, but still, the idea of giving up a top person for a project that would last for four years did not sit well with many Ford managers. Even colleagues who in theory agreed with the plan had needs of their own to be met.

"I screamed at Veraldi a few times," Tom Page, a strong supporter of the team approach, recalled. As executive vice-president for diversified products, Page was in charge of manufacturing components for Ford subsidiaries worldwide. "If I had a guy who was good at something, I might have had only one. Veraldi would ask to have him. I had to go to Lew and say, 'Look, I'd like to put him on your team permanently, but I may have to take him back every two weeks and send him to Europe.' So we'd try to compromise."

Veraldi agreed, letting Page divide some of his team representatives between the project and his other obligations. But one point was clear: even if a team member was given leave to attend to other duties, his responsibility to Sigma would never waver. If he was diversified products' emissary from the glass plant, then he would always be the person that the team would turn to if problems emerged with the manufacture of the rear window.

Power-train engineers and development executives rounded out the core group. "They all functioned as members of the symphony, under my direct supervision," Veraldi said. "Component engineering, manufacturing, service, dealer organizations, public relations, design, safety, all these people were the cellos, trumpets, and tubas."

Veraldi was thrilled to be working on Sigma, but in the back of his mind he feared the project was jinxed. Other advanced projects had recently been axed by the company, and nobody wanted that to happen again, especially with a vehicle as technologically advanced as this one. Executives had watched the board vote down the Monica, a small car that competed with the Tempo for approval, and then the Mini/max. John Risk and Veraldi were sitting in the design center when the subject turned to the recent vehicles that the company had killed. All in all, six advanced projects had been terminated.

"Boy, let's make sure we give this project a strong working name so it doesn't get canceled," Veraldi said half seriously. The two began brainstorming code names. By chance the conversation eventually turned to astrology.

"What month was Jerry born?" Veraldi asked Risk about his wife.

"May," he said.

"So was Irene. So they're both Tauruses," Veraldi replied.

"Let's call the car that. We'll call it Taurus," said Veraldi. "It's good enough—at least until research comes up with a better name."

The project was formally known as DN5. In this alphanumeric system, the first letter designated the class of car under development; the second letter, the country in which it was being developed; the digit indicated the rank in the development series. Taurus, a *D* class car developed in North America, was the fifth project in this new nomenclature, hence DN5.[3]

Preliminary engineering work on the car began early in 1980. The decision to make this vehicle front-wheel drive meant that hundreds of millions of dollars in development and manufacturing costs had to be added to the budget. A transmission that could work with front-wheel drive also did not exist; it alone would require six years to develop. Also, front-wheel-drive cars were assembled and painted in a different order than rear-drive models. So the two assembly plants that would eventually make the Taurus would have to be shut down for at least two months to be retooled to accommodate a front-drive system.

Before they would approve the project, top management wanted proof that front-wheel drive would be as technologically sound as the proven rear-wheel drive system, because the costs of developing the new system were enormous. Upward of $1 billion, close to one-third of the cost of the entire program, would be spent just on front-drive development. If the cost had been smaller, even as much as $50 million, then the debate would never have taken place.

This development was vigorously fought by some veteran vice-presidents. Harold McDonald, the head of the engineering staff, also pushed for rear-wheel drive. In a paper he argued that because of the weight of the vehicle, rear-wheel drive would provide a better package.

One complaint about front-wheel drive was that upon initial acceleration, the car tended to pull either to the left or right. Veraldi suspected that the condition was caused by the use of non-uniform-sized power-transmission arms, the traditional way of engineering front-wheel-drive cars. But it didn't have to be this way. Once equal-length transmission arms were used, the torque-steer problem disappeared.

During the early stages of development, virtually every permutation of engine and drive train were considered. Like the schoolroom adage that "there is no such thing as a stupid question," the idea of starting with a clean sheet, as Sigma was doing, meant that no technological consideration, however inappropriate and ill-conceived, was overlooked.

The sheer number of schemes began to annoy Veraldi. "I fought with some old vice-presidents at the start of the program on the car's configuration," he said. "We had eleven different power-train configurations under discussion. We had front-wheel, rear-wheel, mid-wheel, we had the power train doing everything but standing on end.

"By the time this car is completed," Veraldi warned them, "nobody will be able to tell whether it's a front- or rear-wheel drive, or where the engine is. You can develop either configuration into a very acceptable car, or you can develop either into a pretty seedy car. It's all in the program's execution."

It was difficult to predict accurately the state of the economy at the time the car would be introduced in 1985. With the price of fuel continuing to rise, product planners assumed that the public would want smaller cars with greater fuel efficiency. That meant that four-cylinder engines would be in great demand. Eight-cylinder power plants, synonymous with traditional big American cars, would not be offered; the car's engine compartment was going to be too small for it to fit. If the car was enlarged to accommodate an eight, it would cost still another $500 million to design and manufacture the new engine.

Even six-cylinder models, it was assumed, would be perceived by many Americans as inefficient. Eighty percent of Taurus buyers would therefore want a higher-mileage four-cylinder engine, it was predicted.[4] But that engine would not be designed in-house. With the company having just lost $1 billion in 1979, the decision was made to drop out of the costly business of engine design for the Taurus altogether. Whatever engines were used would be purchased from outside suppliers.

Within the next few months, the car's exterior dimensions continued to change. From its established dimensions, the car's overall length and wheelbase increased thirty days later. But as the size increased, the higher price of gasoline motivated John Risk to recommend that the size of the four-cylinder engine be cut from 2.5 to 2.0 liters to increase fuel economy.

In August, early engineering tests revealed that with a car of these dimensions, only two inches of legroom would be available for rear-seat passengers. That might be adequate for sports cars or subcompacts, but not for a car billing itself as a family sedan. As a result, the overall length of the car was increased again.

Because of this, by the autumn of 1980, it was decided that the proposed 2.0 liter, four-cylinder engine was going to be inadequate to power a car of this size properly. Engine displacement was upped to 2.3 liters, with a 2.8 liter V-6 added to the lineup. In-house development work continued on the engines, even though it was still assumed that they would actually be purchased from a supplier. The contingency was necessary—if management changed its mind about outside purchases, Ford had to be prepared to step in.

Chairman Caldwell was confident that he could sell the board on the plans, but he needed ammunition to bolster his position. "Why should I buy a Taurus?" Caldwell asked Veraldi and his team over and over. It was a question that could not be answered this early into the program. But Veraldi felt he was on the right track. "Whenever we do something unique, we succeed," he mused. "It's only when we follow the rest of the industry that we get in bad shape." He thought of cars like the Mustang, a vehicle that had become a part of American automotive folklore, and his own Fiesta, receiving strong reviews and sales, to bolster his belief. "If we do a world-class project, nobody will be able to touch us," he told his staff.

World class, to Veraldi, meant a car that followed and improved upon worldwide trends in engineering and design. He wanted a vehicle that could be sold in any country. As far as he was concerned, the concept of an insulated American car company was dead. No longer could manufacturers in the States design cars that looked and drove like no others in the world. With an ever increasing number of imports flooding America, consumers were receptive to alternative approaches to automotive design and engineering.

If this car was going to be world-class, it had to be broken down into its components and analyzed. The philosophy was called "Best in Class." Team Taurus members identified certain cars that performed various tasks better than any others, and then they figured out how to improve on that performance for Taurus.

Comparison cars were selected from all over the world, including some never intended to be sold in the United States. Engineers received a temporary federal license to drive and evaluate them on American streets, even though the vehicles did not meet safety or air-pollution standards. Mustangs, Lincolns, and LTDs soon began to share space at Ford's Dearborn parking lots with the Audi 100, Germany's Opel Senator, the Honda Accord, BMW 528e, Toyota's Cressida and Supra, and the Mazda 626 models.

Best in Class was in large part a subjective concept. What was best for one person could be average or even worse for another. The goal was to meet or surpass every item on the list. Shortcomings would be inevitable, since structural restraints, the Taurus's size, and engineering costs prevented the car from coming out on top in every category.

To aid Veraldi's Best in Class efforts, the company's research group surveyed owners of Ford and competitive makes. Interviewers took consumers through a series of questions that appeared on a computer display screen. Answers were entered onto the screen with a light pen. Depending on the particular response, the questioner would then give a predetermined follow-up query; if all went well, the consumer perceived the conversation as natural and unstilted.

Owners were asked about their car's transmission and electrical system, its body and chassis. From the responses Ford executives came to understand what concerned its new customers.

Veraldi was not looking for specific suggestions from consumers as to what they wanted on new automobile models. Consumers were not car designers—their ideas could be unrealistic, impractical, or financially difficult to achieve. Veraldi wanted to learn what problems consumers were experiencing, so that the team could come up with the solutions.

Over the next two years the Best in Class inventory grew to include more than four hundred items. Included were indices for forward and rear visibility, the quality of the sound system, speedometer readability during the day and night, glove-compartment size, seat comfort, the number of turns required to lower a window, and the effort required to open and close the hood.

"Look, I'm a perfectionist," Veraldi told his team. "I want the best of everything. I don't care where it comes from. If the best ashtray is in a Honda Civic, then I want to know about it. If you're going to work for me, I expect you to try to reach perfection. You'll find out that I've got a passion for perfection. There's no point in trying to reach for mediocrity, because then you'll just fall short of mediocrity. And don't tell me you can't do something. Everything's possible. Just figure out a way to do it. On this project, you'll be doing some pretty common things. But our success will come only if you do those common things uncommonly well."

4

TEN IMPOSSIBLE THOUGHTS BEFORE BREAKFAST

Lew Veraldi's oft-stated quest for perfection fired up his team, but it was his insistence on ridding the project of the old corporate structures that gave the Taurus project a chance. Pulling off a plan of this magnitude required total communication. There would be no time for extended bickering and empire-building. Veraldi had to keep the team members focused on the car rather than their careers.

It made no sense for Veraldi's work to proceed in a vacuum. The point of the Taurus project was not to create an isolated success, but to be one of many experiments that would fundamentally alter the way the company worked. While Veraldi was proceeding on Taurus, disparate elements of the company were already engaged in unconnected efforts.

No matter how good any car project turned out to be, it would be a failure if a revolution did not occur in the process of manufacturing as well as planning. Plants needed to become more efficient. Assembly-line workers had to be made a greater part of the process if they were to believe that they, too, had an investment in improving quality.

Don Petersen supported Veraldi in the need for change company-wide, but he wanted it done in stages. As president, he had to figure out how to move forward. A test bed was needed, he thought, and some of Ford's smaller plants were the place to start. Petersen summoned Tom Page, the head of diversified operations, to his office. Page's smaller eleven businesses provided the right environment for the experiments. A slightly built man, Page was not an aggressive corporate executive. He was unusually soft-spoken, polite, and courteous. "Tom, we have to lower our costs. We have to reduce our work force and become more efficient. We have to try out a new way of working. Which of your plants do you want to experiment with?"

"You really couldn't start one of these tests in a huge assembly plant with ten thousand employees," Page said later. "We had to start in a plant with two hundred employees, try them out and perfect them there, and then spread them to the rest of the company. I didn't buck Petersen, I was very interested in his ideas. I wanted to find out if these would work because it was a way of keeping my operations alive. Some of them would have died if we hadn't found a way to be more efficient in production."

Page was greatly impressed with the ability of Japanese industry to give the individual on the shop floor the right to make decisions. From what he knew about Japan, workers had a much greater say in their day-to-day working environment. The procedure improved productivity because it gave the worker a psychological stake in the operation. "We wanted to learn how to achieve improvements in efficiency and quality," Page said, "by not having to run all the way up the management structure for approval, and then come back and say okay."

Two programs were developed: employee involvement and participative management. The first gave hourly workers a say in running their jobs; the second allowed low-level managers to make essential decisions without having every one approved by a higher-up.

Change was needed because Ford's factories provided no outlet for grievances. If you spoke out, you risked punishment. You kept quiet because you needed to keep your job. If you tried to go around a despotic manager to appeal to a more sympathetic superior, you were quashed. You just did your job, however unpleasant.

"The supervisors were the all-mighty rulers," said Jake Chavers, a body-shop worker in Ford's Chicago assembly plant. "They just wanted to get the numbers out. And you got to be a supervisor because you had a friend who did the job. If you went to the supervisor to complain about bad parts, or if you thought there was a problem with the machinery making those parts, the supervisor didn't give a damn. All he wanted was for you to fix it."

"The attitude was 'I'm the boss and you just work,' " Bob Jacobson, a twenty-three-year veteran, agreed. If suggestions were brought to management, they were routinely ignored. "I had a problem one time in the body shop. The center post on the left side of a car was off. The engineers were banging away with hammers on the doors and window frames to get them to fit. I told them the problem was not in the part, it was in the gauges they were using to measure the part. But they wouldn't listen to me. I took a piece of masking tape and measured with that and showed them I was right. There they were, tearing up those doors and busting those window frames for no reason. They were engineers and they knew everything, and you didn't know nothing."

"If something wasn't going right in assembly," Chavers said, "you'd hope the next guy would catch it. You'd only spot-check cars, one of every fifteen or twenty. The attitude was 'Get as many out as you can.' "

"The supervisor said, 'Do this,' " recalled Marilyn Aiken, a worker in the interior trim department. "And if it didn't get done well, it was out the door anyway."

Even when lower-level management wanted to be conscientious, they were often thwarted by colleagues who didn't want to be made to look foolish. "I hired in at Chicago in 1967 as an inspector," Bob Jacobson said. "I had people say to me, 'You better lie about the quality of these cars. If you don't, I'll break your arm.' All they cared about was numbers."

Most shop floor managers, those at the lowest level of management, were not ready for change. They had spent their working lives in the old structure. They had clawed their way up the ladder from worker to management. The idea that they would suddenly have to take suggestions from their underlings rather than just dish out orders angered them. But it was a chance that Page and Petersen were prepared to take. Because the company was performing so poorly in 1980, they knew the financial problems bolstered their position. The company's fiscal crisis finally gave management what it had long sought: credibility with its workers.

One of the first experiments in the new management style was conducted at Ford's Ypsilanti plant, manufacturer of the company's generators and alternators. Product quality was atrocious: 25 percent of the alternators were unusable and rejected as soon as they came off the line. Alternator quality was judged by two inspectors on an eight-man assembly line. The workers, all paid on an hourly basis, resented their inspectors, who were salaried managers. They didn't like the power that they held or the fact that they were the ones who decided which units should be used and which rejected.

Tom Page approached the head of the Ford Division of the United Auto Workers, Don Ephlin, and proposed an experiment. "Let's get rid of the inspectors, Don," Page suggested. "Instead, each person on the assembly line will be responsible for inspecting their own work. They'll do their own rejecting. And they'll feel better about the job because they'll have a direct say in the final product."

"I'll explain your proposal to the workers," Ephlin replied, "but I don't know what the response will be." Indeed, the suggestion was immediately met with suspicion. "It's just another attempt by Ford to exploit us," many workers said. "Now we'll not only have to make the product, but we'll have to spend extra time inspecting it too. You want us to inspect? Well, how much more money are we going to get for this extra work?" they wanted to know.

"Let's not get into the game of more money," Page said to Ephlin. "Let's talk about pride in their work. They're not getting paid to be inspectors. But they are getting paid to turn out good pieces."

To get them to comply, Page offered the workers additional inducements. "We'll give you the right to stop the line if you see that bad components are being used in the assembly process. You can decide yourselves to reject components and send them back to the manufacturer if they're unusable. You can even bring in your own tools to measure component tolerances, so you can be assured that they meet standards before they're assembled."

Page had a stick as well, though. Ford had no ultimate loyalty to its in-house suppliers like Ypsilanti. If the factory couldn't supply what was needed at a competitive price, an outside company always could. In fact, a Japanese company had just offered to supply alternators for less than Ford paid to build them itself. If quality did not improve and costs were not reduced, the company was more than ready to out-source to Japan. In fact, workers at two other Ford plants had already lost bids to supply windshield-wiper motors and air-conditioner compressors to the parent company. With many Ypsilanti workers making forty thousand dollars per year, they did not want to sacrifice their jobs to Japanese firms.

Employees were encouraged both to clean up the factory and to rearrange the machinery if they felt it wasn't in the most efficient place for manufacturing. Bathrooms were repainted, relaxation rooms were refitted. As a final gesture of good faith, time clocks, the bane of hourly workers, were banned. "You don't have to clock in anymore," workers were told. "But your team leader needs eight people here, so you better show up." The program worked. Alternator-reject rates dropped from 25 percent to 1 percent.

Since Petersen was a hands-off manager, he didn't keep tight control over Page. Instead he met with Page every few weeks, listening as the diversified products chief pulled out his usual stack of three-by-five cards and reviewed progress.

Petersen gave Page the authority to institute operational changes worldwide, but they both agreed that he had to be mindful of cultural differences in other nations. In the United States, Page knew he could lay people off without a fight from the unions. UAW officials had historically left job security out of their contract negotiations. There had always been plenty of work. As a result, there was no job security in the United States.

In Europe and Latin America, personnel reductions would not come so easily. Other countries had tight restrictions on forced layoffs. Still, Page figured that some of the programs he had instituted in the U.S. would work well in other countries. He invited managers from Ford plants in Australia, Germany, and Great Britain to spend a week in Michigan to see his experiments firsthand and to implement them if they thought they'd work. The foreign managers were no more anxious for change than their American counterparts. If good was going to come from his experiments, Page would have to institute changes himself.

"Get them involved in things that don't center on the product. Get them involved in improving their work experience," Nancy Devore kept on telling Page in the early 1980s. An industrial psychologist once employed by ALCOA, Devore had gained her stripes by venturing down a Guyanese bauxite mine to learn how to keep miners happy in that oppressive atmosphere. Devore played a key role in helping Ford management get a better understanding how to improve worker morale. Until her arrival, executives just did not understand workers. Management knew that a good salary alone was not enough to make an employee happy, but they didn't know what else was needed.

One of Page's first stops was at the company's electrical-parts assembly plant in Enfield, England. When it had been under the management of Ford of Europe, he had had no reason to visit. But after 1981, control had been transferred to his division. A year later, Page finally had time to inspect.

"The first time I went through the plant, I was appalled," he said. "It was so dirty inside it was atrocious. The ceilings and walls hadn't been painted probably in fifty years—at least not since World War II. And on top of that, production quality at the plant was not good.

"When I walked through the plant, I must have been shocked, because the people there told me later that I was upset with them." This time his usual courtesy broke down. "I gathered them together at the end of the day, and I really raked them over the coals. 'You know, it's really no wonder you can't produce top-quality work when you've got such appalling conditions here in this plant.' "

"I agree," the newly appointed plant manager confessed, "but I asked for some help from Ford of Europe people to do some things in the plant, and nobody would give me any money, so I'm just sort of limping along here."

"I'm telling you right now," Page recalled saying, "that I'm giving you a hundred thousand to spend just to clean this place up. You don't have to ask anybody for it. I'm just giving it to you, plus anything you need beyond that to make this place a model plant. I'm coming back in two months to see the results."

Page realized that the manager was in an impossible position. "It was only because I was touring these European plants that he got the money. If he had appealed directly to Ford headquarters in Worley [England], he would have had his head cut off."

Upon his return, Page was as shocked as the first time around. "I'd never seen so much transformation in one place in all my life," he said. "The black ceilings had been cleaned with some sort of solvent and painted white. The walls were painted flashy colors, highly unusual for a plant." The cafeteria, which had been so disgusting that Page felt ill setting foot in the place, was now completely different. "The tables had been painted, some of the women had brought in plants, and a bay window had been built to let in more light. It was almost like a McDonald's glass entry. They were so proud of what they had done that they held an open house for the first time. The plant was fifty years old, and the families of the workers had never been let in before."

Page encouraged Enfield management to be more forthright with the workers. "We started a whole feedback system. Workers were now told what kinds of warranty problems were occurring because of their parts. They'd never been told that before. The manager had put them in his bottom drawer. Then we started putting in some better automated equipment and they started getting more work, so we hired more people. This little town had been going downhill and we created some more jobs there."

Page tried to export his notion of industrial democracy to other countries as well. In one Brazil factory, workers were allowed to paint their factory and cafeteria any color and design that they chose. They were also allowed to set their own lunch menus, to add or remove items at will.

In Toronto, workers consulted with the architects designing a new plant in the suburb of Markham. The workers, not the architects, picked the best location for the rest rooms. The workers said where they wanted the assembly machinery placed. And they decided what colors to paint the plant. Though it would quickly become dirty, Markham became the only facility in the Ford empire with a white factory floor. In addition, the workers started to clean up after themselves, and they mounted pictures of their families at their work stations in an attempt to bring a bit of humanity onto the shop floor.

Building worker morale wasn't enough, however. American cars had a reputation for being shoddy, and the quality of the product suffered at every stage of the process. Workers were encouraged by managers to accept construction defects that the Japanese rejected. And the quality of the parts used to assemble those cars was also often suspect. The level of workmanship had to increase. Too much time and too many people were involved in checking others' work. Once Ypsilanti rid its work force of inspectors, Phil Caldwell wanted to rid the entire company of them.

In particular, he didn't want to employ people to check the quality of parts that had been manufactured by third-party suppliers. But that's the way it had always been done at Ford. Suppliers were given a list of specifications for a particular job. Once a piece arrived at a Ford plant, it ran through a quality check to guarantee that it fit its tolerances. If it didn't, it was immediately shipped back to the supplier at his expense. It was the supplier's responsibility to come up with a new batch that would pass. To ensure against shoddy parts, a multitude of suppliers was used, operating on one-year contracts. Competition, it was thought, would keep quality levels high.

The concept was terribly flawed and produced the opposite results. Because suppliers knew that they would have their work double-checked upon arrival, they did not push themselves to produce the best possible pieces. Ford wasted time, money, and manpower trying to catch the material that didn't meet its specifications. The supplier wasted money in shipping fees and labor every time that work had to be sent back to its plant. There had to be a better way.

"We have to make the original manufacturers responsible for their own work," Caldwell announced to management. "That's the best possible way to streamline supplier operations." In return for producing quality goods, they were designated "Q-1" companies. Operating in a corporate version of the federal government's most-favored-nation program, firms that qualified for Q-1 would not have their work double-checked once it arrived at Ford. Rather, they alone were responsible for keeping quality high.

Becoming part of the program was a tedious process. Q-1 qualification took three to four years. Ford personnel worked with the suppliers, even giving them the tools and gauges needed to ensure product viability. If the supplier's manufacturing methods were faulty, they had to correct them if they hoped to qualify.

In return for that trust, Q-1 suppliers received a three-to-five-year contract rather than the one year that had been the norm. The number of suppliers was reduced from a multitude to two, giving each company a bigger share of the business.

Suppliers were required to post a full-time company representative in the Ford plant. If quality problems arose, the supplier's rep made any necessary changes or substitutions. The program worked because the supplier's neck was on the line. Poor quality meant the end of the supplier's lucrative contract. In addition, if poorly manufactured parts reached dealers and the public, the supplier was contractually obligated to pay damages to Ford for any recalls.

Suppliers owned by Ford also had to qualify to become part of the program, and not all were successful. Motorola gained some electronic-component manufacturing business when Tom Page's factories could not deliver the goods. Metal-stamping operations were also awarded to outside contractors who did a better job than Ford plants.

Improving the worth of their vehicles was now one of Ford's primary tasks. The lack of product integrity had become so bad in the 1970s that management had decided not to have its corporate name sully the one product that still had a positive image: the Thunderbird. A decision was made that the name *Ford* would be put in only one place on the car—on the inside step, hidden from view except for a fleeting instant when the door was opened.

Extolling the virtues of quality was a strategy that top Ford management prayed would become self-fulfilling. "The workers knew that we weren't the best in the world in quality," Tom Page said. "And until Phil Caldwell really started putting some teeth into that program, by outsourcing some things and rejecting things and putting a lot of heat on people about it, there was a perception that 'they talk about quality but what they really want is increased production.'

"When we shut the line down a few times, and when we told people we were not going to ship things anymore that didn't meet our standards, the workers began to understand what we were talking about. Then, when we went one step further and said, 'Anytime you people feel we're not producing quality parts, you can shut the line down,' that suddenly transferred the power from the guy at the end of the line to the guy on the line. And it didn't take workers long to figure out that they had a stronger position than they had had before."

Ford's new slogan for the 1980s, "Quality Is Job One," began to appear in print ads and television commercials. Page was excited by the new commercials coming out of J. Walter Thompson, the company's ad agency. Oddly, it took hype to quell the belief that Ford was interested only in hype. The agency decided to drop its spokesman, Telly Savalas, and use real workers in their television spots instead. JWT sorted through scores of employees until it had the right mix of sincerity, believability, sexual and racial characteristics. Assembly-line workers, regular Joes, popped up on screen, extolling Ford's commitment to quality.

"Using our own employees was a magical touch," Page felt. "That was one of the most electric things that went through our plants. The people on the line would talk about the ads and ask when they'd see more, and who'd be on them. The ads helped us communicate to Ford workers what we meant when we talked about quality. The commercials were a stroke of genius."

The idea was to get people to work more closely together for a common good: their survival. To make employees understand that this was a long-term philosophy, top management needed a credo to rally the troops, to make them feel part of a team. Seizing a set of criteria originally developed by a truck-division executive, Petersen instructed staff writers to come up with a set of rules by which all company personnel would live by.

This was hardly the first time that Ford had attempted to raise morale. Videotapes were regularly circulated in the fall of each year, stating that season's challenges and the need for quality. The campaign had always fallen on deaf ears because employees knew it was nonsensical jargon.

Now Petersen was devoted to this project. The search for the golden rules of behavior became known as Ford's "company mission, values, and guiding principles." He met often with top executives to help hone the criteria that would become the light all Ford employees would be instructed to follow. The tome would be easily written, complete, yet narrow enough to be instructive. No simple but ultimately useless platitudes would be included.

"Geez, is this one of those typical plans of the month?" Ray Ablondi, director of marketing research, wondered.

"Petersen's nuts," Lou Ross thought after one of the many meetings held to discuss the tract. "All those little things, what difference does it make? It'll be like everything else we do, you put it out and it'll be like the videotape and you'll never pay attention to it."

"Company mission, values, and guiding principles" became, in the early 1980s, Ford's religion. The statement was printed onto plastic-coated index cards that employees carried around in their suit pockets. Larger versions, suitable for framing, hung in top executives' offices.

The company's mission, the card stated, was "to improve continually our products and services to meet our customers' needs, allowing us to prosper as a business and to provide a reasonable return for our stockholders, the owners of our business.

"Our people are the source of our strength" began the section on values. "Quality comes first" stated the first of the six guiding principles. "To achieve customer satisfaction, the quality of our products and services must be our number one priority."

Ray Ablondi became one of those who carried a copy of the statement in his suit. The company began to preach incessantly about quality. Employees saw the CMVP as the dispensation they needed to pressure executives to uphold their standards.

After years of following in the footsteps of General Motors, the company was moving in its own direction. Speaking to a gathering of Ford dealers, Don Petersen gave a hint of things to come:

"It's going to be a revolutionary job to change things around. It's going to take years and this is why I'm so struck with the need for single-mindedness about what we do. I'm convinced the sooner we can drop the old and get on with the new, the more we can identify ourselves in a very new and different way.

"I know a few things I don't want to be," Petersen told the guests. "I don't want to be anywhere near the GM lineup or the Chrysler lineup. The more we look different from them, the better I think we're going to be."

This statement of principles reflected a corporate philosophy never before practiced at Ford, one that would take the company down an entirely unknown path.

"We were panicked, trying to do everything and get it all done," Lou Ross remembered. "We had 256,000 employees in North America in June 1978. For starters, we knew we had to get rid of forty percent of our work force and improve our quality by one hundred percent. I was really worried, and fortunately, the whole organization was worried, too. To succeed, I knew we had to be like Alice in Wonderland. If this company was going to make it, we had to have ten impossible thoughts before breakfast."

5

CREATING THE LINEUP

While Veraldi was assembling his Sigma team, his senior executives were busy trying to put the entire corporate house in order. The problems at Ford extended far beyond the need to develop one new mid-sized car. The solutions to them would set the scene for all future product development.

By 1979 the Ford Motor Company was in a state of panic. So many things had to get done that at times the problems seemed insurmountable. To bring things under control, Lou Ross, in charge of reshaping the company's product lineup, and Don Petersen began one-on-one weekly meetings, with Petersen updating Caldwell on progress. Petersen had always been keenly interested in new product development, but now, necessitated by the crisis, his involvement with it increased. Petersen barraged Ross with questions. "What are the latest vehicle ideas? Why aren't we working on multi-valve engines? When do you think we should bring out a replacement for the Thunderbird?" were typical of the queries. Petersen was an executive known for his honesty. Rather than put on a happy face in front of his employees or the public, he let them know how he felt. Just because he was the president of Ford, he did not feel he had to extol every one of its products without reservation.

Both Ross and Petersen had a healthy skepticism about the quality and continued marketability of Ford's American products. Like Ross, Petersen had had extensive overseas experience, having just finished a three-year stint as head of Ford's International Operations before becoming president. Both men knew what foreign cars were like, and they knew that American cars often didn't compare to vehicles even their own company was making overseas.

Ross, a tall, thin, carefully groomed man, tended to speak in rapid-fire phrases, shooting out his ideas as they occurred. As long as he could remember, he had wanted to be in the car business. "Cars were mobility, freedom, someplace to go with a girl. My first auto was a 1937 Plymouth for $75 that needed a new clutch and a headlamp and a cylinder gasket. And in those days that was something you fixed yourself.

"I was good at science and math in high school. I figured I'd become an accountant or an engineer; in the end, I decided it would be engineering. But I couldn't decide what kind of engineering to get involved in. I thought about mechanical or aeronautical, but if it was aeronautical, I'd have to go live on the West Coast. The West Coast? That's alien territory. Here I am living in the automotive center of America. I've got to go in the car business. So I went to Wayne State in Detroit to study mechanical engineering, because I couldn't afford to go anywhere else.

"After graduation, I went to work for General Motors.

I really wanted to work for Ford—I grew up in Dearborn, and Ford grows in the veins. But Ford wasn't hiring. My father, who was a Detroit policeman, always wanted to drive a Ford police car, because he said they were the only ones that would hold up. Of course, that wasn't exactly so. None of the cars held up then."

Ross's superiors were a study in contrasts. Although Chairman Phil Caldwell wasn't known as someone deeply involved in cars, as Don Petersen was, he needed to know everything that was going on in the company. "Pete," on the other hand, was a delegator, expecting subordinates to fulfill his requests once he made them. Whereas Caldwell was aloof, Petersen was the genial sort.

Despite his casual air, Petersen could be Machiavellian. He was known by corporate employees as the "Smiling Cobra," a man who made high demands on his staff. If Petersen asked for a marketing plan, he expected one to be delivered with full details. His managerial style eschewed memos and other paperwork. Communication was often casual; Tom Page kept him up to date by dropping off index cards scribbled with just one line of information. "If he wants to know anything else," Page said, "he's got my telephone number."

Because of Petersen's delegating style, the day-to-day running of the product programs was ordinarily left to the product-planning committee, composed of Ross and the heads of various divisions within Ford, including manufacturing, sales, purchasing, and power train. Meeting once or twice a month, the chair would inform the corporate-planning committee of advances in the company's new cars.

Each new vehicle was supervised by a product planner. The liaison among the various divisions of the company responsible for manufacturing a new vehicle, the product planner also set the criteria to be met by a particular vehicle. Based on the population segment to which the vehicle was expected to appeal, the planner then charted what size the new vehicle should be, how many passengers it should seat, and its rough dimensions. Working with sales and marketing people, the product planner helped define the price range of the car. Once that was established, the allowable cost of each component—the seats, glass, sheet metal—could be set. All of the technical and pricing data was then sent on to the design team.

Lou Ross and his product-planning group's first job was to review the entire new-vehicle development that had stagnated during the Ford/Iacocca years. In the late 1970s, demands for increased fuel economy and decreased exhaust emissions meant that cars had to shrink. "Everything— engines, power trains—had to change, top to bottom," said Ross. When he received his first detailed glimpse of the company's future product plans, though voluminous, he found little to give him hope.

"When I came on the job in 1979," Ross said, "I asked for a copy of the company's cycle plan reviews we had in the last two years. I expected to get a one-inch loose-leaf that covered all presentations to the formal corporate product-planning committee. They gave me two six-inch binders. That's about ten inches of paper! The new vehicle plans had been reviewed virtually every month all through this time frame."

Ross and his group had to devise a rational, comprehensive scheme to modernize its product lineup quickly. First he took a look at the subcompact segment. Japanese companies had been very successful with their small cars, and the only comparably sized model that Ford had was the discredited Pinto, which just the year before, Ford had recalled to retrofit gas tanks. With predictions of gasoline rising to three dollars per gallon by the middle of the 1980s, a competitive, fuel-efficient subcompact was an important part of the product mix. Fortunately, Henry Ford had signed off on a new car, code-named "Erika," the year before. This vehicle was intended as a front-wheel-drive subcompact that could be sold not just in the United States but throughout the world.

The Escort, as it was renamed prior to launch, was

what marketing executives billed as Ford's first "World Car." Adopting a name that had been in use for years by Ford of Europe for a now well-heeled rear-wheel-drive vehicle, the new Escort (along with its Mercury counterpart, the Lynx) was planned as something completely different: a small front-wheel-drive hatchback that would be introduced simultaneously in both North America and Europe. In commercials touting its introduction, Ford's stress on its World Car classification distinctly implied that the vehicle was so good, it could even be sold outside of the United States.

Although the Escort represented the most popular segment in Europe, it would be considered too small by many Americans, who had grown up with vehicles considerably larger. Thus, Ross and the product-planning group needed to revamp its larger cars, currently represented by the just introduced, traditionally boxy Ford Fairmont and its twin, the Mercury Zephyr, as well as the full-sized Ford Granada and its Mercury equivalent, the Monarch.

Since the company needed to reduce the size of its cars, the problem for Ross was to figure out which car would fill the gap in the early 1980s between the Escort and the relatively compact Ford Fairmont/Mercury Zephyr. And then a few years later, some model had to replace the upcoming midsize Ford LTD/Mercury Marquis.

In the late 1970s it took Ford six years to develop and produce a totally new car. To save money, a company would often "reskin" or "face-lift" an existing model rather than starting from scratch. The makeover could be a simple instrument-cluster remodel or a complex reshaping of body panels. What didn't change in a reskin was the car's frame, engine and transmission. All designs eventually became stale. Face-lifts prolonged the life of a car. Marketers hoped that customers would perceive the revised version as new, even if it really wasn't.

In 1978, before Ross had taken over, Ford's planning group had decided to develop two new vehicles for the mid-1980s, one medium- and one large-size car. With larger, fuel-inefficient cars in its stable, Ford not only had to design new models to maintain interest in its products, but had to ensure that their new cars were both small enough to raise their overall fuel economy and also attractive enough to be popular. Only if their new line of small cars sold would Ford then be able to sell its larger gas-guzzlers, the cars that really held the profits for the company, and still meet the government's Corporate Average Fuel Economy (CAFE) requirements.

Several variations were considered for the midsize car that would replace the Fairmont/Zephyr. Eleven variations were considered for the larger-size vehicle, including a front-wheel-drive model with the engine mounted "transversely," or sideways, a rear-wheel-drive model, and a front-wheel-drive model with an engine mounted in the traditional longitudinal direction.

Work on the larger LTD/Marquis replacement had already begun: it was Lew Veraldi's Sigma project. The first sketches were very preliminary, but the product planner knew the desired target length, wheelbase, and weight. These dimensions would allow the proposed vehicle to achieve fuel economy of 22 miles city/25 mpg highway, with a 0–60 acceleration of 13–15 seconds, fairly high for a car this size. Since this car was designed to appeal to American families, a station wagon would also be developed, but no coupe. Instead planners hoped that customers looking for a two-door car could be encouraged to consider Ford's sportier Thunderbird/Cougar models. This new family car would be powered by one of several engines, including a four- and a six-cylinder power plant, a diesel, and the new low-emission PROCO engine that was actively under development at the company. With agreement on these basic points, the engineers and designers could begin to fashion a vehicle that would fit.

Lou Ross and his committee now considered their short-term options for the Fairmont model: they had to get something new out, and quickly, but they didn't have the luxury of spending time and money to develop a new set of engines and transmissions. Importing a currently produced small Ford vehicle from an overseas plant was also out of the question because with the decision to go to front-wheel drive, they had no comparably sized cars available that could be imported as is or even quickly modified for American tastes.

The combination of front-wheel drive and a transverse-mounted engine had been first popularized by Britain's twin Austin Seven and Morris Mini Minor models in the early 1960s. Conceived by Sir Alec Issigonis and available as a plain Jane or a souped-up Austin/Morris Cooper version, the Mini showed the world that a car could offer larger than expected space in a tiny package. Front-wheel drive grew in popularity in Europe during the 1970s. The Swedish manufacturer Saab was manufacturing nothing but front-wheel-drive models before Ford even had one on the road.

Front-wheel drive did have certain advantages over rear-wheel drive, which until then had been de rigueur in America. By having the engine turn the front wheels rather than the rear, the car was pulled rather than pushed through rain, snow, and ice, providing better traction. With the engine over the front-drive wheels, there was no long mechanism connecting the engine to the transmission, and the center hump characteristic of rear-drive vehicles could be eliminated. And by mounting the engine transversely over the front wheels, the engine compartment could be shortened.

Some Ford officials, like Lew Veraldi's onetime boss, engineer Harold McDonald, were skeptical about front-drive technology. What was the rush to front-wheel drive? McDonald wanted to know. The Europeans continued to favor rear-wheel drive, even in their fastest sedans. Besides, early efforts did not work well. Large cars that used front-wheel drive tended to lose responsiveness. Turning the steering wheel produced little effect, but turning it a bit more gave dramatic results.

Regardless of its true benefits, Americans perceived

front-wheel drive as a cutting-edge technology. Therefore, many consumers decided that they had to have it, even though they had no idea what it could do. Because of this, developing a line of rear-wheel-drive vehicles would not have made marketing sense. It would only have garnered negative press, showing Ford to be behind the times. "People want front-wheel drive," Lou Ross said. "They don't even know what it means, but they want it."

Ross realized their only solution was to build a variation of the upcoming Escort. Adapting its front structure to this new, larger vehicle—code-named Derby and later named the Ford Tempo and Mercury Topaz—meant that designers and engineers would be dealing with knowns. Prototype models would not have to be built and tested. "Let's design a vehicle that picks up the Escort's front structure," Ross said to his colleagues. "That way we know it'll pass government crashability guidelines. We'll use the same engine family, give it a unique rear suspension, a different length and a different width. And we'll be able to do it fast."

The future-product plans were finally gelling, at least on paper. By the beginning of 1980, this is what Ford's North American Automotive Operations had: a new small car, the Escort, ready for production; the replacement of the Fairmont—the Tempo—had been approved and would arrive in three years. And most important, the replacement for the company's bread-and-butter family car—code-named Sigma—was now under way.

When Ross and Petersen reviewed the product cycle, it was clear to them that the new downsized cars being developed for the 1980s could shape up as significant departures from existing products. They would be able to compete with whatever General Motors had on tap, in every segment of the market. But the question of the company's atrociously poor product reliability still remained. Japanese manufacturers were winning huge numbers of converts from consumers who were fed up with their Fords that were lucky to start on a cold morning.

"You know, Lou," Pete said to Ross, "we have to do something different with these new cars. We're not doing a good job of listening to the customer. It's obvious—all you have to do is look at the products we have. We've got a bunch of turkeys out there! We've got to do a better job of listening to the customer. We've got to figure out some way of being driven *by* the customer."

6

GOING OUT IN STYLE

The future-product plans gave hope to Ross and Petersen, but as far as most of the public was concerned, Ford was nothing but a stodgy operation with outdated, ugly, and unreliable cars. After years of building shoddy machines, Ford's goodwill was plummeting faster than its cash reserves. The old joke that the Ford name actually stood for "Fix or Repair Daily" seemed all too true.

Ford's declining sales were especially disturbing to Ray Ablondi, newly promoted North American director of marketing research. Because Ablondi's job was to monitor consumer perceptions, he knew better than anyone how poorly the company was perceived.

A distinguished man with a heavy Boston accent and a quiet demeanor, Ablondi had risen through the managerial ranks, serving as Iacocca's administrative assistant during the 1960s launch of the Mustang. He and Petersen were part of the same corporate generation and had known each other for over fifteen years, as Ablondi held various middle-level jobs in sales, marketing, and advertising. After years as a Ford advertising manager, Ablondi had jumped back into research at the end of 1979, just as the company was beginning to revamp its product line for the next decade.

Soon after Ablondi arrived at his new market-research job, Petersen called him into his office to talk to him about his "customer-driven" ideas. Ablondi had to become one of his allies in the effort to change corporate thinking. "That was a huge decision for an autocratic company like us," Ablondi said. "To be customer-driven imposes a tremendous burden on you, because then you have to listen to what customers want." Listening would be a new thing for Ford management. The company had not been paying any attention to the customer. The goal was not to give the customer what he or she wanted; it was to force-feed cars down their throats, giving them what Ford management felt comfortable owning themselves as they drove to their suburban homes.

The company had always done research, but they had been quantitative studies: a compilation of the number of responses given to a particular question. But now Ablondi felt compelled to add a qualitative aspect to the research. He wanted to ask people, in an informal way, what they thought about Ford and its products, not so they could tally up a score sheet listing the number of people who liked or didn't like a particular car, but to get a sense of people's feelings that could not be uncovered in a strictly quantitative survey.

Despite Ford's sorry financial state, Ablondi clung to the hope that the answer would be positive. He knew of a report, prepared by Mary Wells, of the Wells, Rich, Greene advertising agency, that had found that the public, for whatever illogical reasons, still had a large reservoir of goodwill toward Ford. Even if disputes between Henry Ford and Lee Iacocca were the stuff of Detroit's newspaper headlines, the feuding had not reached the rest of America. The Ford mystique, the myth of the mighty family-run car company that had put cars in the hands of the masses, the company that created three of America's seminal vehicles, the Model T, Mustang, and Thunderbird, still seemed to draw.

Even if consumers still felt good about Ford, though, Ablondi didn't. In 1979 Ford was a bad place to work, a company filled with backbiting males fearful about losing their place on the career ladder to another colleague. The way to preserve one's job was to avoid making waves, to follow the accepted way of doing things.

As a result, cooperation was an unknown concept. "There was no teamwork, no cross-fertilization, no cross-functional assistance, like we have today across disciplines," Ablondi said. "People were not sharing information; we just had chimneys. You had the body-and-assembly chimney, the sales chimney, the purchasing chimney—you know, there was no real teamwork in this company. Back in the late 1970s, with Lee Iacocca getting fired and not speaking to Henry Ford for two to three years, how the hell do you run a company that way? So that whole attitude permeated this company. And you just weren't really a company. Just a bunch of chimneys."

Ablondi spent his earliest days as research director searching for a nugget, any nugget that would give Ford some hope. He felt he had found some in Mary Wells's research, but Petersen wanted the study confirmed. "Ray, let's go out and see how bad we are—or how good we are," he said.

Ablondi enlisted the aid of Martin Goldfarb, head of a Toronto-based market-research firm that had been hired by Ford previously to explore new advertising themes for some of its cars. Goldfarb was different from most Ford executives Ablondi had worked with. A tall, lean, bouncy man with wiry, frizzy hair, Goldfarb was immediately identifiable as an academic. He was a thinker, someone who not only knew how to observe a situation but to interpret it, to understand its larger implications as well. He was an outsider—as a Canadian and a Jew (both rare in the WASP-dominated higher echelons of the American automobile business) he stood apart from the dominant culture and was more dispassionate in analyzing it. He did not work at Ford but for Ford. Consequently, he was free of internal corporate power politics. His success depended solely on the quality of his work.

"I came from teaching into this business," Goldfarb said. "I taught marketing, and I also taught a course called Man in Society. It was a combination of psychology, sociology, and anthropology.

"Our expertise is to study behavior, and we use an anthropological approach to do so. We study cars or soft drinks. We look at almost any commodity in culture and try to understand how that artifact functions in that culture. Within those artifacts, what are the qualities that make sense for the culture to buy? Some shapes, for example, are not acceptable. Shape dictates the 'personality' of a vehicle. So you, as a car manufacturer, need to make sure that you choose a shape that society is prepared to buy, in terms of what it says about the individual who drives it.

"Cars represent the most emotional purchase a human ever makes," Goldfarb believed. That's why he was drawn to studying automobiles and their relationship to society. "Nothing counts in an individual's life as much as a car. Not even a home. A car is freedom, mobility, it's accessible, everybody can get one. You do things to a car. You give it a nickname. People don't have nicknames for houses, they have nicknames for cars. They're reluctant to leave it sometimes, there's almost bereavement when it breaks down. When it does break down, there's a terrible resentment: 'You're letting me down.' It's still a mechanical device, but they treat it in almost a humanistic way. It becomes a friend of the family.

"The essence of freedom represented by the car is a powerful concept in American culture, because it is synonymous with the overriding myth of American society: the idea that in the U.S. the individual comes first, that the needs of the person override the needs of the state."

The goals of the U.S. were antithetical to those of Canada. "The U.S. is an interesting country. It was born of revolution. And no country cares about the individual like the United States. Where the U.S. venerates life, liberty, and the pursuit of happiness—individual goals—Canada's motto calls for peace, order, and good government—societal goals," Goldfarb said. "Early U.S. pioneers partially succeeded because they were able to be mobile. It was mobility that made this country, and mobility remains one of its most cherished rights.

"The freedom of the individual is the true religion of the United States," Goldfarb believed. "Automobiles, as a tool and expression of that freedom, become an important element of that belief. And individualism, the ability to express oneself, either in speech, print, or even in the types of vehicles owned and the right to drive them at will, is a corollary of that religion.

"What we're trying to do is understand how behavior changes over time. We relate it to visual taste. We can't predict the future. What you can do is demonstrate how difficult it will be for individuals to accept ideas that you're prepared to expose them to in the future. What are the roadblocks in overcoming those ideas? What are the fears, the excitement? And then you market against those fears, or for that excitement."

For all the complaints that Ray Ablondi had about Ford's previous lack of interest in its customers, he did have respect for his predecessors in research. "They prided themselves on listening. The new element that we brought in was a qualitative capability, and we called it 'market pulse.' So we combined the two, quantitative with qualitative studies. We had a piece of paper with answers to questions we had asked the focus group participants. And then on the last night we'd invite management to come in and listen to the customers. And we videotaped it." With the video the research people could reevaluate customers' opinions that at first seemed evasive and imprecise.

Ablondi and Goldfarb devised a structure to gauge this market pulse. A group of people were shown both Ford's and its competitors' current and future vehicles. Over several days thousands of people were run through the show rooms. Researchers wanted to know what everybody thought about the cars, the company's marketing plans, its advertising, its reputation.

Goldfarb had developed a reputation in the automobile industry as one of the few people who could understand as much of what was left unsaid as what was said. If only one person out of twenty said something positive about a car, that did not necessarily mean that everyone else couldn't stand it. Before one could draw that conclusion, everybody had to be given the chance to speak their mind, without intimidation.

Goldfarb never accepted the first answer he heard during these pulse studies. He was not interested in knowing whether or not somebody loved or hated Ford; he only wanted to know why. He forced participants, who were paid fifty dollars or less for their cooperation, to defend themselves. When a consumer had overwhelmingly negative feelings about a car, Goldfarb often said, "Now that you've got your emotions out on the table, tell me what you like about Ford. Tell me what you do like or don't like about that car. Forget about who made it."

Goldfarb's purpose was to understand the public's positive and negative feelings about Ford products. "By the time participants finish a session with me," Goldfarb said, "they're exhausted. They have to defend themselves. Because I'm going to draw them out. I'm going to probe to reach their hidden thoughts about a product."

By mid-1980, six months after Ablondi had started, Goldfarb and he began to meet with groups of consumers across America. From Texas and Chicago in that year, the studies moved to Marin County, California, in November and December of 1981.

Marin was a special milieu, a white, educated, upper-middle-class area north of San Francisco. As a sophisticated West Coast enclave, the community owned many foreign cars. Given this resistance to American vehicles, Ablondi figured Marin would be a good place to learn what people thought of Ford.

The results of the study were much worse than anyone expected. The reactions of the participants to the Ford Motor Company ranged from indifference to extreme dislike.

"You guys have sat back and continued to feed the same crap down the American public's throats," fumed one prospective General Motors buyer. "When the imports were putting the little things on their cars like remote trunk openers and adjustable seats, you just ignored it and said, 'That's a fad, that won't last.' "

"I'm tired of the big, cocky, mighty motor industry in the U.S. which went its way year in and year out saying, 'So goes General Motors, so goes the world,' " said the president of the Marin County Soroptomists, a professional women's organization. "That's the worst remark they could have ever made. That whole attitude permeated a lot of your thinking. Now I don't feel a bit guilty in going out and buying a foreign car."

"Detroit had a good reputation once, but it's going to take some time to get it back," added a materials-service manager from a high-tech company. "People want to buy American cars, but I don't want to be the first to buy one. I want my neighbor, friend, or relative to do it. Then word of mouth will get around. But that's going to take years. You've lost your reputation. Now it's going to be awfully hard to get it back."

"My parents have always driven Fords," added a young woman sporting Paloma Picasso earrings. "I learned to drive in a Ford. I've had a Ford before and my father's had one, and we've had problems with them. I've never owned one again. I'd look at them again if I had confidence that I'd be buying a quality product, but I don't have that confidence."

The response was the same in every place that they set up shop. From Chicago to California, people did not like Ford. Was the "reservoir of goodwill" that Mary Wells had reported to corporate staff several months earlier a statistical mirage?

"My parents have owned three or four foreign cars, and I've never driven a Ford," one young man said.

"Well, what did you think of it when you rode in a Ford?" Goldfarb asked.

"I've never ridden in one," was the reply.

Ablondi was flabbergasted. He had gone into these focus groups expecting to hear some sort of goodwill toward the company he had worked for, for most of his life. Instead he heard nothing but abuse. "These were frightening things we were hearing, when you think that this guy who's never been in a Ford is twenty-two years old." Ablondi was scared because if young people in the most progressive state in the union saw Fords as irrelevant, what did that mean for the future of the company?

What was even more frightening was Ford's surprise at the findings. It wasn't as if Marin County was on the moon; any company executive could have researched there years before. But for Ford executives, the United States began and ended in Detroit; what worked in Detroit naturally worked in the rest of the country. It was as if the idea of regional differences was incomprehensible.

"Damn, you people were light-years ahead of everybody else, and competition caught you, surpassed you," another participant told Goldfarb. "You're not appealing to our age group, and me and my children have to be your future, there's no doubt about it. But I don't see any cars out there that appeal to me. If you've got nothing for us, that's fine, we'll just move onto another manufacturer."

Ablondi returned to Detroit. "I was absolutely devastated," he said. "It was so bad, I started smoking again." He had captured the entire session on videotape, and he brought it back to show management. Company executives were not used to seeing potential customers telling them how Ford had let them down.

"The customers aren't mad at us, Pete," Ablondi told Petersen. "They just don't give a damn about us."

Ablondi knew that, for all intents and purposes, Ford did not have an owner body on which it could rely, at least certainly not in California. And California was the nation's trendsetter. What happened there was bound to rapidly spread across the country. After years of being misled and lied to, loyalty to Ford was collapsing, or had already disappeared.

It was a potentially disastrous situation. Without owner loyalty, Ford would not be able to count on repeat business for its products. The classic notion spawned by General Motors, that people would remain their customers for life, trading up from Chevrolet to Buick to Cadillac as they matured, had become an absurdity. With market share plummeting from 23.6 percent in 1978 to 17.3 percent in 1980, company officials were wringing their hands for ways to stem the outflow of customers.

The press continually battered Ford executives about the decline in sales. The abuse became so expected that Petersen had his staff prepare a book for him containing photographs and illustrations of upcoming products. Petersen carried the thick book whenever he gave an interview. After he endured the reporter's questioning, he'd pull out his volume.

"I agree with what you're saying," Petersen would say to the journalist. "But let me just give you a peek at what's coming," he said as he quickly flipped the secret pictures before the writer's prying eyes. The photos of the new models were so different from the company's lineup that few believed Petersen's claim that these cars would be made.

"That's really just a concept car, isn't it?" one reporter asked when he was shown a sketch of the upcoming, aerodynamic 1983 Thunderbird, a car that looked nothing like its overchromed, angular 1982 version.

"Pete's got to pull the book out and show them what's coming," said one of his lieutenants. "It's the only way he can keep his sanity."

In 1981, as the first pulse-group research was analyzed, Ablondi and his staff began to churn out reports to senior management. The studies pushed for a new way of doing business at Ford. "If this company is going to achieve greatness again, integrity must never be compromised. We must have integrity in everything we do, in our advertising, in our dealer relations."

As elementary a concept of sound business practices as this was, it struck many at Ford as a radical notion, certainly nothing that anyone would want to subscribe to. It was a utopian idea; to even attempt to institute it meant that Ford management would actually have to engage in self-reflection. Introspection seemed to be a concept alien to traditional corporate men; they weren't used to looking inside themselves for answers. They were more comfortable asking others for their opinions.

"Tough automobile men didn't use words like *integrity*," Ablondi said. "Integrity, God, that sounds like a sissy word. You couldn't say you believed in that, couldn't talk about love and your fellow workers and employee involvement. They'd have laughed you silly if you talked like that around here in the late 1970s."

Associates also weren't used to having research reports come back with what Ablondi called his "sledgehammer philosophy." Research studies had normally issued vague platitudes that could be ignored. But people had to get used to hearing confrontational statements, Ablondi felt, if the company was going to survive. The cocoon mentality of Detroit had to end. In Motor City, with the small number of foreign cars prowling the streets, one could easily imagine there was no Japanese threat, but outside of Detroit, foreign, especially Japanese, cars were capturing

Americans' imagination. Until the early 1970s, annual sheet metal, paint, and trim changes were all that was needed to stay even in the business. Alterations were made not because of technological advances but because a new body style meant increased sales. The era when every American boy could tell the difference between a 1955, '56, and '57 Chevrolet from two blocks away, though, had passed.

American drivers were beginning to demand a different kind of experience in their automobiles. They did not want to feel as isolated from the road, and to get that feeling, they had to buy foreign cars. But the American companies sluffed off those buyers as fringe consumers. "Detroit's blind insistence at looking at every BMW owner as a cult person driving a cult car is nuts," Lou Ross said. "Certainly, the good old-fashioned American car is not the one that people now want to drive."

In California, the nation's biggest state, foreign-car ownership was already over 25 percent in some cities and would later grow to 40 percent by the end of the 1980s. When research-team members had driven their Fords in Marin County, they felt like oddities as they watched the imports pass them on the freeway. In places such as the upper-middle-class West Side of Los Angeles, American cars were hard to find.

It was an ironic conclusion to a sordid tale of U.S. corporate greed. During the 1940s, Los Angeles' extensive and efficient streetcar system was dismantled and replaced by buses manufactured solely by General Motors. A government investigation revealed that GM, Firestone, Standard Oil of California, and other major industrial companies held minority interests in National City Lines, the rail system's parent company. By purchasing only GM buses, National was found guilty of antitrust violations, including anticompetitive business practices and restraint of trade.[1] By the 1960s, Los Angeles' extensive public rail system had disappeared, replaced by an inferior bus network and a vast number of freeways carrying hundreds of thousands of American cars. The city that had grown up around the automobile, whose streets were planned to accommodate large American vehicles, was now lost to GM, Ford, and Chrysler.[2] Ray Ablondi began spending more time in California, attempting to understand the market that was on the leading edge of American trends. On his trips he watched drivers in their vehicles and saw how they used them, as compared to citizens in the East. The idea that people would one day live in their cars, as prophesied by the 1960s' Charlton Heston film *Soylent Green*, had, in a fashion, come to pass. With fifty-mile commutes commonplace, people not only listened to the news but ate their breakfast while driving. They put on makeup, read newspapers, and even brushed their teeth while inching forward to work.

The dissatisfaction with Ford that had been illuminated by the pulse studies caused top management to wonder if they were trying to reach too large a share of the market. They had always emulated General Motors in offering a vehicle for every segment of the marketplace, but the reality was that large segments had no interest whatsoever in Ford cars.

Lou Ross and Don Petersen came to the conclusion that they were making a fundamental error in their marketing strategy. "We decided that there was no point in trying to appeal to the whole market, or take on General Motors. That was always our direction, and we were constantly trying to take GM into account when we came up with our product plans. In 1979 Petersen and I thought, 'Why not try to appeal to a different market?' We could put cars on a continuum. On one end are those with a tight feeling and a good steering response. On the other are cars that are loosy-goosy. Fans of one kind won't think much of the other. Petersen or I said, 'Wouldn't we be better off, since we only have 16 percent of the market, that we appeal to 33 percent of the market, and the other 66 percent don't like us at all?' Didn't like you at all. That was the key. So when you go out and do customer research, I'll listen only to the people who I'm aiming for, and I'm not going to pay attention to anybody else."

It had always been hoped that any given model would attract a very wide spectrum of the populace. "The Falcon, Fairmont, and Granada appealed to the whole market of small cars, of little bigger, and of medium-sized cars, respectively," said Ross. "But they were really trying to appeal to everyone from your aunt Sally to the sports enthusiast. So you put on some decals and stripes, and that was your sporty model. And a vinyl roof for granddad. That's why our market share went down. It wasn't directed, it wasn't defined."

Ross, Petersen, and Caldwell decided to try a new approach. "From now on, market research will survey only those people who might be interested in Ford vehicles," Ross said. "It makes no sense to survey GM owners as to their thoughts about Ford cars if they have no intention of ever buying them." Ross didn't think that GM owners would *never* buy Fords, just that their opinions were not as valuable as those predisposed to buy.

"We've been stodgy, and we've been square," Ross said. "We've been appealing to a market of grandmothers to sixteen-year-olds, and it's not working. Now [with the Sigma] it's time to appeal instead to people who like to drive vehicles, not people who liked to be driven by them." Ross knew that with this approach they'd be turning off many potential customers. "But I want to go after that 25 percent of the marketplace that would like this kind of car, those that would rate it eight to ten, not the 40 percent that would hate the car or just tolerate it." In this highly competitive market, with a growing Japanese presence, toleration wouldn't sell enough cars.

The traditional strategy was not abandoned altogether. It could work for some of Ford's upcoming expensive models. In addition, the Escort, with its low profit margins, needed large volume sales and had to be marketed toward a wide consumer base. Sigma, however, would be positioned as a family vehicle that would appeal to the nation's trendsetters.

Ford executives realized that they needed to design Sigma to bring in younger age groups. Its previous family-sized vehicles had attracted customers with median ages in the high fifties and low sixties, but the company had to lower that if it was going to reach a large population. What was needed was an adventurous design attractive to customers used to the smoother shapes pioneered by Audi and other European makes. This car would not appeal to every buyer of a midsize sedan, but would pull in the "opinion makers," the country's better-educated populace.

"We knew that there would be regional differences in market-research results between California and Atlanta or Dallas," Ross said." Which market should you design for? I'll give up on Iowa, they score low. I will give up on Texas and the Southeast. I expect to be strong in California—I will be strong in all five Pacific states—I'll be acceptable in the Midwest. You don't tell your dealers this, because the dealers in Texas would say, 'I don't want the car in that situation.' Instead you tell your dealers, 'I'll have the vehicle for you, but it's not this one. We're going to define this vehicle for other areas.' But we'll tell them that the new Lincoln Continental and Thunderbird will be for them."

The market-pulse studies, the company's plummeting financial condition, its poorly constructed cars, convinced executives that radical steps had to be taken with the design and manufacture of its new products. Its cars could no longer follow General Motors in styling. After fearing for years that it wasn't big enough to strike out on its own, Phil Caldwell, Don Petersen, and Lou Ross all knew that striking out was Ford's only chance for survival. "If we're going to go out of business," Lou Ross thought, "let's at least go out in grand style. Let's go to the poorhouse in a Rolls. Let's go out with the kinds of cars we want to drive. What's there to lose?"

7

STANCE IN SPADES

"What the hell am I doing here?" Jack Telnack wondered as he walked through the woods. This was certainly one of the strangest things he had ever done as an adult. He didn't like the whole silly business.

To the other Ford employees with him, he must have looked quite a sight. Usually attired in European-styled suits and boldly colored ties, here was Telnack, one of Ford's top designers, looking more like he was ready for maneuvers than a board meeting.

Telnack stopped walking and looked up. In the branches forty feet above him were a series of narrow boards placed across several trees. He noticed that the planks formed a sort of precarious walkway. Several men were already up there, attempting to cross the divide.

First a harness and then a tether were placed over Telnack's neck. He was hoisted into the tree, making his way up onto the boards. He looked down at the ground, at the other men and women below him, at the treetops in this wood surrounding Dearborn. "This whole thing is a crazy idea," Telnack said as he was about to step off the tree. He knew that he'd be safe, that the tether and harness would protect him. "I don't have time for this," he thought defensively. "I've got to design cars."

Once aloft, he readied himself to edge across the boards that bridged the trees. As he looked down to the ground, where his friends waited grasping the tether, he realized that he was truly afraid.

"I hadn't felt this kind of fear since I was five years old," Telnack remembered. "I knew, or hoped, my buddies were going to protect me when I walked across the plank. Still, I wondered about it." When he finally stepped onto the last plank and safely made it to the other side, he calmed down. "Maybe this was not such a crazy idea after all. Perhaps this is the kind of thing we need to do."

His ordeal was called the Ropes Course, an exercise designed to alter the working habits of Ford's key employees. The goal was to rid the company of its "over the wall" work ethic. No longer could one group toss their part of a car project onto the next division, to solve in isolation and without assistance. All workers, management decreed, had to trust and rely on each other.

The Ropes Course was one in a series of confidence-building games that was a favorite of Silicon Valley executives in the 1980s. Ford executives took strongly to them as well. As a result, weeks were spent on similar exercises in an effort to break down departmental barriers. These walls, Telnack knew, had to be broken if the Taurus designers, engineers, and marketers were going to truly function as a team.

Every industry has its glamorous occupations. In the automobile industry, design holds that title. For years the design people at Ford had operated autonomously, aloof from the rest of the company. Designers were the corporate elite, the artists, the creative dreamers. These people envisioned what could be rather than what was. Too often, management now felt, the Ford designer was a utopian, a dreamer of shapes who cared little or not at all about the practicality or feasibility of a new car.

This attitude, Telnack and Lew Veraldi knew, had to change. "Before we put pencil to paper," Telnack said, "we had to be in there with Lew and his people, saying to marketing and sales, manufacturing, engineering, product planning, finance: 'What are your needs? What kind of market is this?'

"We've got to talk to people. You might say, 'Well, what have you guys been doing all these years?' The answer is, we weren't talking to each other in the company. Hell, we weren't even talking to the guys like Veraldi next door in engineering. They were our enemy, we were their enemy. We were coming up with these designs that nobody could build. The manufacturing people hated our guts."

With the formation of Team Taurus, it was decreed that that attitude would change. "This may sound crazy," Telnack said, "but we'd been building cars for seventy-five years with a process that was never defined. We finally developed a process of developing a car that everybody could subscribe to."

It was called the Design Approval Process, later known as Concept to Customer, a set of rules that ensured that the creative process was thrown open to all. Procedures had been seat-of-the-pants operations that developed spontaneously until they became the status quo. Communication was to be the new way of working.

"We just opened up and said, 'Hey, how can we eliminate this adversarial relationship and really reach a more collaborative process in-house?' We went through years of corporate therapy—all those team-building exercises and learning how to get along better with each other. Basic stuff, but I think it paid off."

With the Team Taurus approach, engineers were able

to voice their concerns about the feasibility of a particular part of a design early on. If they foresaw problems in manufacturing a multiply curved rear window, for instance, the new corporate philosophy said that designers should know about it before the project became too advanced.

It was nothing short of a revolution. For years the design center had been off limits to most other departments. With work progressing on models that might not be built for another ten years, security was tighter even than that found at Ford World Headquarters a few miles away. Locked doors were opened only to those with passes. Admission was granted only after a telephoned confirmation with appropriate parties. Visitors were forbidden to walk the corridors alone. Public relations staff, among others, were strictly banned, despite the fact that they had to drum up interest in the company's new models. The reasoning was that with their close relationships to the automotive press, p.r. people might spill some secrets in a fit of corporate enthusiasm.

The structure itself exuded an attention to aesthetics not found in other divisions. The hallways to the design center's executive suites were bathed in soft low-voltage lighting, the offices decorated in fashionable tones of black and gray. In contrast, offices of many Ford divisions were plain and practical and ugly. Long corridors flooded in glaring fluorescent light led to warrens of identical prefabricated offices.

Telnack could never have worked in such a dehumanizing environment. When he assumed his new post as chief design executive in 1980, he immediately replaced the blond 1950s-style wood walls with darker tones. He brought in stylish furniture and threw out the utilitarian pieces. He added a classic black Italian Tizio lamp to his desk.

Like Lew Veraldi, Telnack had spent considerable time working overseas. In the late 1960s he had headed up design at Ford's Australian division. Both he and Veraldi moved to Ford of Europe in 1973 and worked on the Fiesta. A handsome man with a sharp angular face, Telnack favored fashionable, highly styled Italian suits and ties. These were not the clothes of Detroit corporate managers. Despite the glamour used to market an automobile, auto executives by and large tended to wear conservatively cut, traditional clothing. If they wore glasses, they favored standard-issue metal aviator frames. Only designers could be tolerated to look different, because only designers were getting paid to dream.

By this point Telnack was tired of having his dreams constantly crushed. He and his teammates were always reaching for new design ideas—as they had been encouraged to do by their bosses. But virtually every time they later found their ideas shelved by executives wary of new concepts.

"We just responded to internal suggestions and whims," Telnack said, "and it was a hell of a way to work. That's why our cars never really had the kind of personality or total look they needed. I swore if I ever got into a position where I could do anything, I'd try to turn that part of it around." In fact, working at Ford was so debilitating that in the 1960s, Telnack had taken a second job designing boats to keep himself sane.[1]

While in Europe, Telnack became enthused with the idea of the "globalization" of design, the idea that the look of a product could attract people in diverse cultures. "The world has become too small to believe that every country has its own tastes," Telnack believed. "You can see a kid on a skateboard in Red Square with an Ohio State sweatshirt and Nike shoes, and you can see that in Singapore. The minute an idea happens in this world, anyplace, it's traveling around the world with the speed of an electron. Givenchy could come up with a whole new line of dresses in Paris this morning, they'd be talking about it in New York at lunch, and some guy out in Texas would be making cheap imitations that they'd have in K-Mart in a week."

By the 1980s, classes, not countries defined cultures, Telnack thought. Upper-class men around the world wore the same types of suits and ties. Even Americans were moving away from the traditional shapeless, baggy look. Young middle-class people danced to the same groups and watched the same music videos. "My Tizio desk lamp can just as easily be found in an office in Minneapolis as in Milan," Telnack said.

His latest frustration had come with the design of the new Escort. Originally positioned as a "world car," the vehicle quickly took on distinctly different looks for Europe and the U.S. Promoted in television commercials as the world's best-selling car, the reality was that the European and American versions shared virtually no parts in common.

"I said from day one that I would have preferred to have the European version of the Escort sold in this country," Telnack remembered. "It was a car that just had more personality to it. But we 'proved' through market research that there were certain unique characteristics that were design requirements in both areas that we had to address. Which I think is a lot of baloney. I know the European Escort would have sold here. Every time I drive one around Detroit, people stop me and want to know what it is and where they can get one."

The costs of developing country-specific models were insupportable, Telnack believed. With a world car, development expenses could be drastically cut and parts would be cheaper, since buying would be on a massive scale. But the goal of world cars was hindered by the jealousies and xenophobia of each division's executives.

"One of our biggest barriers," Telnack said, "was this 'not invented here' factor, this 'us vs. them' factor within the company. There's probably more pride of authorship between [Ford of] England and [Ford of] Germany than there is between the U.S. and Germany or England or anybody else." Telnack fought to overcome this parochialism by constantly moving his design team. "I have from five to ten percent of our people from Dearborn out on foreign assignments. Whether it's Australia or Japan, South America, Italy, England, Germany, California—we consider that another country—our people are just continually moving. We're cross-pollinating. This will help eliminate the 'not invented here' factor."

When Telnack gained a senior position in the Detroit design staff, he hoped to increase the power of the designer. For years he had toiled in a system that was not interested in his ideas. Though designers were responsible for making a car look good, they were not allowed to think independently; management didn't want to know about their way-out concepts and strange-looking design exercises. The futuristic models known as "concept cars" were useful public relations tools, hauled out for another car show as proof positive of Ford's great strides in design, but they were rarely transformed into new models. Top executives knew those automobiles would never be built, because they had no interest in building them.

Ford designers were disenchanted with the characteristics of the standard American car. Most U.S. vehicles possessed what the industry called a soft, "boulevard" ride. The operating engineering principle was: the mushier the ride, the better. When a driver hit a bump, the car moved with the punches. "The whole body would roll and lean a lot when you went into the turns," Telnack pointed out. "It was okay if you had a lot of Dramamine on board to prevent seasickness."

U.S. car manufacturers produced vehicles that isolated the driver from his environment, that allowed the owner and passengers to forget about the harsh world while they relaxed in luxury. Spaciousness, size, and ease of use were givens. Power steering and brakes were designed so that a small woman could easily turn the wheel of a Cadillac with one finger; a light touch on the brakes was more than adequate to bring one of those behemoths to a halt. "God, these cars feel bad," Telnack thought. "You feel like you've got no control."

Designers wanted to make cars more European. They knew that as more foreign cars were imported, consumers were getting a chance to experience how vehicles could handle if they were designed well. Both Telnack and Veraldi wanted to engineer in an experience that allowed the driver to feel as if he was actively in control of the car. To do this meant easing up on the power steering while making it more responsive to hand movements, making the brakes a little more difficult to apply, increasing the thickness of the steering wheel, and decreasing the body roll.

These goals coincided with Lew Veraldi's philosophy. Having worked on Fiesta, Telnack knew what it was like to cooperate in a team approach. And he knew what it was like to design a car from scratch, from a "plain sheet of paper," as they liked to call it. With some of Fiesta's key players in place on the Taurus, the talents and skills and working methods that were honed on that small-car program could now be transferred to the States.

Veraldi was happy to be working with Telnack again. He needed executives on his team who would not be fighting one another for turf. On a personal level as well, the two men liked each other. They both liked to drive, and they appreciated drivers' cars.

An engineer by training, Veraldi liked to call Telnack an engineer's designer. "He always keeps practicality, usability in view when he designs," Veraldi said, "and I respect him for that. He never puts two lines together on paper just because they look good. He wants to know that they make structural sense as well."

Others on the team quickly found this out. In some of the earliest sketches of the Taurus, one engineer pointed out a problem with the design. "We won't be able to get enough air through that narrow opening you made in the front end," he told Telnack. "The car will overheat with your design."

"Fine," Telnack said. "Then we'll just redesign the front to make it work for you."

The response surprised the engineer. Faced with a similar situation, most designers refused to make any concessions to their concept. They threw the problem back to the engineer; the engineer had to make a cooling system that would work. Many projects have turned into ongoing battles between engineers and designers, as designers try to be as adventurous as possible and engineers as practical.

The engineer determines the vehicle's "hard points," those areas in the car where the engine has to be located, where the pedals have to be placed, the permissible height of a windshield. These are dictated by the size of the engine, radiator, transmission, and all the other parts used. The designer then creates a vehicle that both fits within those technical constraints and can be manufactured within the budget set by the product planners.

Many designers do not take to outsiders who question their work. Ray Ablondi, Ford's head of research, knew that when he took on the Taurus assignment. Because his goal was to conduct research differently than in the past, he wanted to work closely with the design department as they turned out new concepts, not to arrive on the scene after the fact. Fortunately, this was what Lew Veraldi was expecting him to do.

"You're handicapping yourself if you don't let me help you out," Ablondi told Telnack. "When I worked in the advertising division, if they didn't like an ad I did, it was no big deal, Jack. But if they don't like the car you design, there goes the farm." Ablondi proposed that research be allowed to test myriad concepts, not so that consumers would dictate to designers how a car should look, but so that the staff could get a sense of whether their ideas were connecting with the public, and to alter them if they were not. If they did this work early in the process, the cost of changing something would be negligible.

Telnack liked the idea, but he didn't expect a cosy relationship between design and research to develop any time soon. Designers feel that, in a sense, they are already involved in research. Cars are not conceived in a vacuum. A good designer researches changes and trends in the styling of all products, not just automobiles. They keep an eye on changes in fashion, women's shoes, and industrial products. A typical design executive skims scores of magazines every month, looking for new developments in the products displayed and even in the magazine formats themselves. They eschew fads, opting instead for classic designs. They try to understand the factors that make that style continually attractive and appealing to consumers.

The key question a designer asks is if a new concept immediately feels acceptable. If so, something is wrong. A fresh design has to scare the person who conceived it, because that car has to look fresh five years after it is originally drawn. "I want everybody to be a little uncomfortable with the car initially," Telnack said. "If they're not, it's the same old thing." Adds a former General Motors designer, "If the folks in the three-piece suits smile and say, 'Yeah, I'm comfortable with that,' then you're in trouble."

Americans had not lost the lead just in automotive design to the Japanese and Europeans, but in all product design. For years the way a commodity looked was of little importance to U.S. manufacturers; its functionality was all that mattered. While Germans were designing sleek automatic coffee makers, Americans were producing bulky units that had no integrity of form. While Japanese and Europeans were experimenting with new pastels and fluorescent colors for their products, Americans used plastic wood appliqué on toaster ovens and televisions and produced avocado green refrigerators.

Good design was not an element that interested most American manufacturers. Even those intimately involved in the process often failed to keep up with trends, unaware of their competition. It was evident in many companies.

"You constantly read about design, so you know what's happening in design," said Doug Wilson, a former Chrysler designer now at Nissan's California Design Center. "A lot of the people I worked for at Chrysler just didn't care. They'd been there a long time and they weren't aware of what was going on around them.

"When BMW really started to take hold in America, we were working on a new car for Chrysler. One of the test cars we brought in was a BMW 320i; it was the designers' favorite—they loved that car." The BMW was a strong styling statement. It had become the Yuppie auto of choice, an instantly identifiable object to millions of American middle-class consumers.

"The head of Chrysler design came over, looked at the BMW, and asked, 'What's that car?' The director of Chrysler design actually didn't know what a BMW was!" said Wilson.

This tale would have been amusing if its implications had not been so broad. As the U.S. auto industry entered its most competitive period, it could not hope to succeed as long as its top executives were ignorant and disdainful of its competition. Design in America was regarded more as an entertainment. Designers specialized in providing pretty objects to help corporate executives feel more comfortable in their surroundings, and illustrations to help people understand complex issues.

"It's like the entertainment industry," said Jerry Hirshberg, a former head designer at Buick who left Detroit to head up Nissan Design. "The people who are running the entertainment industry don't go to the movies. They don't have that grit, that intuition. America has to relearn some things it used to know viscerally. We were product people. The people who headed up industry were involved with the product and had a feel for it. Design is all about the feel for things. And you can't do that in a sterile, mechanical way."

Detroit's auto designers champed at the bit to do designs that turned them on, but they were stifled by executives who were afraid of taking a risk. As a result, many designers fled Detroit to work in studios run by foreign manufacturers. Even then they ran into opposition. When Jerry Hirshberg and his team designed the Nissan Pathfinder, a small truck with a multipurpose rear, some of his American executives asked why he had come up with such a strange-looking window. "Why don't you just do a traditional car?" he was asked.

"Because this turns me on," Hirshberg said.

"Who says what turns you on will sell?"

"Because that way we're taking a risk. Risk sells. The biggest risk we can take is to avoid one. Who knows what's going to happen in the future?" The executives allowed him to proceed.

In Detroit, top executives at all the manufacturers were known for constantly sticking their two cents into a project. GM chairman Roger Smith regularly flew into his design center, demanding to see all new designs in progress. Chrysler chairman Lee Iacocca made his preferences for squared-off, boxy designs and vinyl roofs plainly known to his design troops.[2]

Iacocca's penchant for the traditional had a stultifying effect on his staff. Designers have blamed him for making the K-car, a vehicle touted as saving the company during its darkest days, poorly styled and mechanically unreliable. In fact, Chrysler cars overall were design platypuses, pasted together with the help of the chairman. At design reviews he would enter the studio to look at the drawings on the wall. "It was very frustrating to take four nice designs into the final showing," former Chrysler designer Wilson recalled, "and then Iacocca would come in and say, 'Well, I like the front off that one, and the roof off that other one.' He would just kill cars. It was incredible."

The resultant vehicles had no integrity of design. They were a collection of concepts that greatly disappointed Wilson and other members of the staff. "Look at the K-car's sun visor. When you move your seat forward, it hits your head. But the engineers or the designers could argue for that position by saying, 'Well, it comes right in the middle of what everybody else is doing, it ought to be the best.' And that's how their cars are done."

Detroit's executives in general were constantly on designers' backs. They felt a need to view and review everything that was done in the studio. By contrast, the style of Japanese executives, including Nissan president Yutaka Kume, was to stay away from the design studio. Once he made his needs known and approved of a project's basic goals, it was left up to the designers and engineers to carry them out. Without constant interference in the process from the top, car-development times were shortened.[3]

The Ford design process began with sketches. At first the stylists drew small renderings of a new vehicle, submitting them to their design team members for comments and criticism. Once the basic parameters of the car were captured, life-size versions were sketched. These were then tacked to movable walls within the studio for examination and study.

Designers surrounded themselves with cutouts of other objects they admired, pictures they found in magazines, brochures, wherever they came across an illustration that represented a direction in which they wanted to expand. Photos of ski boots, cars, refrigerators, door handles, were all tacked up around their work site. Stylists studied the trends to understand the competition, to know what direction design was progressing for all products.

For the next few months the team sketched various renderings of a car they wanted to see. Several sketches were chosen, a full-size drawing was produced of the car, and they were hung up on large easels in the studio. The design elements were melded with the vehicle's hard points—the height of the roof, the length of the car, its wheelbase, its width—to understand how the vehicle would look drawn to scale.

A vehicle that looked good on paper could look terrible once produced. To guard against that, three-dimensional clay models were constructed. Besides, top executives often had trouble extrapolating the look of a car from a flat image, and the clay model helped them understand how the car would finally appear.

Lines, indentations, curves, grooves, reflect light. Design is concerned with studying how differing reflections of light change the perception of an object. Through these reflections various shadows are created. When the shadows are combined with the dimensions of a car body—its

height, width, wheelbase, the length of its trunk or hood—
a car can be made to appear powerful and sleek, cute and
nippy, heavy or light.

Two distinct styles of design had developed in Europe.
The Latin, typified by the French and Italian makes of
Peugeot, Renault, and Fiat, emphasized "nervosity," a
sense that the car was dynamic, appearing to be in motion
even when stationary. The German style, advanced by designers from that country as well as Scandinavia and the
U.K., produced automobiles that appeared robust and
solid.

The Latin philosophy failed to catch on in much of
the rest of the developed world. Although sales of Fiats,
Peugeots, and Renaults were strong,[4] all three companies
were heavily dependent on their domestic markets for success. German and Swedish manufacturers, on the other
hand, had been able to spread their sales more evenly
among a number of countries.

The world favored German-influenced design, and
Taurus followed the German school. The car was going to
be robust and solid. It would incorporate lines that
European-trained designers liked to call "swaging," a series of indentations along the car's sheet metal that would
flatten light. The various shadows created by this series of
crevices and canyons in the body's metal would create a
sense of heaviness, of psychological strength to the exterior.

Those indentations would not only help the car look
good. It would sound better as well. Designers know that
a lack of angled surfaces creates vibrations. A door
slammed on a smooth-surfaced car sounds tinny, because
it drums and reverberates, creating a hollow oilcan noise
when shut. Doors with angled surfaces absorb vibrations,
allowing the car to sound more substantial even when it is
not.

"Rule number one for the Taurus," Telnack said, "is
that the car has to have a good stance—in spades. It's got
to have the right tire and tread to sheet metal relationship.
That will imply stability. We've got to suggest the dynam-

ics of the car through the design of the car. Then it's up to the engineers to deliver the road handling that coincides with our design."

If the car was going to look robust, it had to drive that way as well. Veraldi and Telnack were concerned that even if the country accepted a new exterior design, they would still favor those awful boulevard rides, not the taut, precise ones that both felt were essential for the Taurus. Veraldi was sure that any dissonance between the car's looks and its handling characteristics would be a disaster. To prove his point, he devised a test.

He took two Opel Senators, made by General Motors in Germany, and put in the suspension from two Crown Victorias, a car that personified an American big-car ride. The Crown Victorias in turn received the tight, responsive suspensions of the Senators. Two hundred consumers in the Detroit area drove and evaluated the four cars. Nobody liked any of them, neither the Senators with the big-car, passive suspensions, nor the American Fords with the European rides.

The researchers didn't understand. They thought at least one car would be preferred over another. If Detroit residents were used to American-type cars, they should have at least liked the Senators equipped with the Ford suspensions. But they didn't.

"Californians are more avant-garde," Veraldi said. "Let's redo the test out there." They got the same results as in the Midwest. They realized that the quality of the ride had to match the look of the car. If it didn't, customers would dislike the car, either for its styling or its performance. Here was perfect ammunition to use against the board, Veraldi and Telnack realized. Form and function had to mesh.

The designers knew that a complex body shape was not easy to manufacture. Each new angle introduced into a body panel might require a separate pass through the stamping equipment. And each pass would require greater precision, thereby increasing the cost of that piece of the shell.

Through experience the best designers had gained a good sense of the costs for each particular process. Elaborate designs, however attractive, often needed to be modified to ensure that they did not push the car over budget.

Since the Taurus was classified as a clean-sheet-of-paper vehicle, everything about it could be unique. Designers had the basic requirements from the planning committee: the Taurus needed to look sophisticated, at the forefront of design. It had to have smooth, flowing lines unlike the traditional, boxy vehicles of the day. It would hold five passengers and be available both as a sedan and station wagon.

Telnack had a sense of how he wanted to begin. When he had been stationed in Europe, he had sketched various concepts that would be appropriate for this type of vehicle. To check his assumptions, he decided to develop two alternate versions of Taurus; one would be produced by his Detroit staff, the other by Ford's European Ghia studio in Turin.

Even these first early, 1981 designs looked nothing like Sigma, the project's progenitor. Produced just one year earlier, Sigma had been characterized by soft external lines, but its overall design was bland. Resembling an inverted parabola, the car's turtle shape bore a similarity to a Citroën CX or a Volkswagen Beetle. It failed to project a strength seen in German vehicles.

The 1981 drawings looked better to Telnack. The Ghia design was chosen as the project's starting point, but even those first renderings did not go far enough. This was not a problem, since the development of a design occurs gradually. Early sketches allowed the team to see elements which worked and could be incorporated into later versions, and those which didn't.

The Ghia sketch portrayed the rounded edges that Ford was looking for, but still continued the long, flat front end. The car wasn't right. It looked too conservative, Telnack felt. It needed a lot more work.

That didn't mean, however, that Telnack could go any further. He had been adventurous and then shot down for it too many times. As far as he was concerned, corporate staff gave nothing but lip service to their wish to see adventurous designs. He still had no reason to believe otherwise—especially on a project as expensive and mainstream as this one.

"The first models that we presented to management were a bit of a surprise to them," Telnack said. "They were surprised with the shapes. They just said they were very 'aero,' they didn't say 'European.' 'Let's not change this car,' I said. 'Let's look at it; if you're uncomfortable, okay. We'll come back in three months and see if you're still uncomfortable.' " Both Phil Caldwell and Don Petersen made regular sojourns to the design center, inspecting all models under development. On one occasion Caldwell asked to see the latest Taurus/Sable renderings. Telnack wondered what he would think, for he knew that Caldwell had historically been conservative in his approach to car design. After Caldwell had reviewed the plans, he sought out Telnack. The designs were not very radical, although they were already quite different from the Ford LTD/ Mercury Marquis vehicles they would replace. Caldwell looked Telnack straight in the eye, and asked, "Jack, are you reaching enough with this car? We're spending $3 billion dollars on this project. Are you going to make this worth our while?"

Once before, Telnack had been given some design freedom. When he had been working on proposed themes for the 1983 Thunderbird, Don Petersen hadn't been impressed. "The '83 Thunderbird was one of our first really strong aerodynamic-design efforts," Telnack said. "But early on in the program, we had some fairly boxy, knife-edge cars under development. We weren't very happy with those cars."

To Petersen they represented nothing that hadn't been tried before. "Are you really happy with this car, Jack?"

"No, I'm not," Telnack readily replied.

"Would you really want to drive a car that looked like this? Would you want one of these things in your driveway?" he asked Telnack.

"No, of course not."

"Well, what would you like to do?"

"And I said I'd like to show him," Telnack said. He took out a number of sketches that showed the direction the designers really wanted to move in.

"Do it," Pete said. "Follow your instincts."

For the first time Telnack had been given the liberty to smooth out the edges of a vehicle and increase its aerodynamic styling. However, developing an unusual design for a lower-volume vehicle like the Thunderbird, a car that traditionally appealed to a sportier buyer, was far different from an advanced shape for the Taurus, a car projected as the company's bread-and-butter family sedan.

The design was beginning to work because it was being created as a totality by men and women who could transcend Detroit's normal ways of creating a new vehicle. The payoff, they believed, would be a car that exuded an integrity of design unlike any other recent Ford vehicle.

"Thanks to Telnack's, Petersen's, and Caldwell's European perspective, they had a pipeline to an alternative way to look at cars," Jerry Hirshberg said. "And they had the balls to use that perspective. They should get the Nobel Prize for showing America what it needs to know about succeeding in business."

8

FORTY ENGINES, FORTY FAILURES

After thirteen years of Lawrence Tech, Lew Veraldi just couldn't seem to stay away from the night school that trained him to be an engineer. He showed up on almost a daily basis at six-thirty, on his way to work. The school's president, Richard Marburger, and he had become good friends over the years, and they both looked forward to their dawn chats. At the expected time Marburger would stop working on his computer and walk outside to see Veraldi's imminent arrival, usually in a competitor's car that he was evaluating for its strong points. If Marburger was a bit late, he often saw the short, stocky man surveying the school's parking lot, making an informal tally of the number of Fords compared to other brands that were parked there.

Their common professional interests drew the two together, and Lew continually confided in Marburger about his hopes for the project. Every conversation they had always turned to Ford and the Taurus.

"Dick, I'm on a mission," Veraldi told Marburger. "Caldwell's given me $3.2 billion to spend on Taurus. That's all the money we have left at the company. I feel like they've made me the guardian of the crown jewels. I have to do something brilliant. I can't let Ford down."

"Lew had great regard for the Ford family," Marburger said. "He was very close to those people, they'd treated him very well. His great regard for the whole company was unusual. I've seen devoted executives, but Ford was really a part of the fabric of his entire life."

Veraldi wanted every aspect of the Taurus project to excel. As he liked to say, he was the conductor, and all the rest of his team were the musicians. "He never thought he was the smartest guy around," his son, Bill, said. "He always told me that he had guys from Harvard and guys who went to law school working for him. He thought his job was to find out who did what well and get them to perform at their optimum. He always used to tell me, 'You have to put the right person in the right place to do a good job.'"

Veraldi carried the Taurus message to all parts of the operation, even to areas like engine development. In 1981, when work was starting on a new power plant, Veraldi sat down with Thomas Howard, the man that component engineering had picked to head up engine development, and told him about the project.

"Lew said he was trying to do a European-style car, a car that had the handling, styling, and ride characteristics of a European sedan. I was really impressed with that. I knew that we had to make the engine for that kind of car the best goddamned one in the world." This power plant, Howard told himself, was going to be lighter, more powerful, and cheaper than anything before in its class. Two years of preliminary studies had already been invested in the new power plant before Howard left his work in carburetor research and joined the Taurus group as manager of engine development and design. During that early period the size and characteristics of the engine had regularly changed with the overall car's shift in concept. Now that the vehicle's dimensions were becoming finalized, more intensive, adventurous explorations needed to begin.

Howard was soon caught up in the team concept. Everyone around him was toiling together. He and his engine teammates spent almost all their waking hours as a group. They traded memos with their manufacturing comrades—the division responsible for executing their engine designs—on a daily basis, and met with them weekly to keep track of progress.

The team approach was refreshing and, as far as Howard was concerned, made much more sense. He remembered the way he and his colleagues had worked several years before, during the development of an earlier V-6 engine. To improve efficiency, Ford management had decided to divide the group into fourteen separate divisions, based on the task to which each was assigned. Everyone was so isolated that each person practically made up a unit of one.

Howard had thought the idea asinine. He and a fellow worker from manufacturing refused to be a party to the silliness. "We're not doing it," Howard told management point-blank. "It doesn't make any sense. We're all together and we should work together, not apart." Management finally decided to back down.

Ideally, Ford could have saved itself the trouble of development by grabbing an existing engine off their shelf and throwing it into the new car, but there was nothing on the shelf to grab. The only other six-cylinder engine Ford possessed was a 3.8-liter version that had been designed for a rear-wheel-drive car. Placing the transmission near it, as was required in a front-wheel-drive model, would have caused the entire car to inappropriately shake and rattle. There was going to be too much vibrating machinery up front to prevent the rocking and rolling. Re-designing the engine to eliminate the shaking would have been expensive and forced an increase in the size of the motor. Ford's European subsidiary did have a less power-ful 2.8-liter engine available, but it was also too big and heavy for the Taurus.

Once the car increased in size, it required a six-cylinder engine. The performance goals set by the product-development people necessitated it. To satisfy the market, the Taurus had to go from zero to 60 miles per hour in 11.5 seconds, generate 130 horsepower, require oil changes only every 7,500 miles, be able to "limp home" even if its computer died, run five minutes after its cooling system failed before burning up, and survive 100,000 miles with-out major maintenance.

Howard knew that his division was as guilty as the rest of the company in not caring about how to transform indifferent consumers into satisfied customers. "We're just sitting back here telling people, 'Here's the car you get, guys,' " Howard said. "But the problem is, the dogs are not liking our dog food anymore."

The same market studies examining customers' atti-tudes toward Ford cars had revealed that consumers were not interested in what was under the hood. Engine design, unlike exterior design, was not glamorous. Few cared that a car had an overhead cam sixteen-valve engine, and even fewer understood what that meant. They accepted the fact that they had to change the oil, but that couldn't be too often. Unlike European drivers, Americans were not car tinkerers by and large. They wanted a vehicle that started in all weather without hesitation, got to work and back, and never saw a repair shop. The customer wanted per-formance, durability, and fuel economy. If those goals were met, then quality, by definition, would be achieved.

One of the first problems facing Howard was to get the engine to fit in the car. He decided to place the oppos-ing cylinders at a sixty-degree angle to each other rather than the often used ninety-degree configuration. The smaller angle allowed the engine to sit lower under the hood, thereby giving the designers more freedom to sculpt an aerodynamic front end.

To increase performance, the cylinder walls were micro-honed. Lightweight 5w-30 oil was used and parts of the crankshaft were polished to a mirror smoothness to reduce friction. Spark plugs were long-life, copper-core units. An EEC-IV computer would manage all elements of the engine/drive-train systems and provide the limp-home system: if a major engine component failed to work, the computer would still allow enough power to be generated to get the car to a dealer, albeit at reduced speeds.

Ford's parts and service division provided Howard with a list of one hundred fifty wants that would make for easier engine servicing. Many items, they said, such as the oil filter, spark plugs, and oil dipstick should be up front, readily available to the driver. The engine group decided to mark the areas most often accessed for service, such as the dipstick and oil-filler cap, with yellow paint for easy identification.

"When the engine went fore-and-aft [typical for rear-wheel-drive cars], you'd get a false reading if the dipstick was up front and the car was tilted," Tom Page said. "So the dipstick used to be down about the middle and you had to lean way over and reach between wires to get at it.

"An engine engineer never worried too much about where the dipstick was. He was designing the most efficient engine he could. It was sort of an afterthought about where the dipstick went. When you say to the engineer, 'Look, you have to put the dipstick in this location because that's where it's convenient for people,' then he says, 'My God, I don't know whether it'll fit there or not. I've got to really look at this thing.' To reposition it, he has to redesign that part of the engine and make a new casting."

Ford's board of directors loved the dipstick's coloring and positioning. It was one of those perfect little gimmicks that marketing could exploit to show that Ford cared about the consumers' desire for an easy-to-service car. During each corporate design review Tom Page let Veraldi know that he had checked that the position of the dipstick had not been quietly pushed back by the drive-train engineers to an inaccessible rear location, hoping no one would notice.

Howard tried to think of every possible engine variation that the Taurus might eventually require, and adapt the new engine to fit. The team came up with two different fuel-injected versions, another that was turbo-charged, and a third that used two spark plugs per cylinder for greater efficiency. A three-by-six version of the engine was designed, with three cylinders shutting down when heavy acceleration was not needed. It operated on the same principle as Cadillac's unreliable V8-6-4 engine, introduced in 1981 with disastrous results. Howard even made a PROCO variation, Ford's highly touted programmed-combustion technology that the company eventually abandoned as unfeasible. After the testing phase almost every contingency was abandoned, since the engine team had neither the time nor money to develop everything that came to mind. Only the electronic fuel-injection and turbocharged versions were kept for further evaluation.

After the completion of the initial design in the spring of 1982, Howard ordered the parts for the first forty phase-one test prototypes. Once produced, everything was sent over from Ford's casting division to the experimental-engine machine shop where they were ground to appropriate tolerances.

"Originally, there were to be two phases," Howard said. "In the first, we'd select our cylinder head port and combustion chamber design, and get all our durability information. Then we'd redesign for the second and final phase. Things didn't work that way. We ran into some problems. As soon as we bolted the engines together during the first phase, we cracked our cylinder blocks on every one of the forty prototypes.

"We really tried to lighten the block so that we could lighten the whole engine. But we made it too rigid and thin." Howard ordered the specifications eased off a bit and new prototypes manufactured. He was disappointed by the delay, but at least he had taken a shot.

Phase one-A research began immediately after the forty cracked prototypes were remanufactured. This new engine, Howard decided, would be tested more rigorously than any other Ford unit. The power plants were first run externally, mounted on a dynamometer for up to four months to check horsepower, torque, fuel economy, oil consumption, and head-gasket durability. Actual drivers would not test the experimental engines until Howard was sure that the units wouldn't break down.

Next, the engines were road tested for driveability and federal emissions standards. Since the Taurus did not yet exist, the engines were inserted into comparable cars. Howard found the perfect one: General Motors' Chevrolet Celebrity. As a front-wheel-drive midsize vehicle like the Taurus, this retrofit was fairly easy.

"In 1982, when we had just started to buy cars for certification, Al Guthrie said, 'Wait a minute. I'm not going to buy a lot of GM cars. You're talking a lot of cars here.' He said there was no way he was going to have a certification car go out to Ann Arbor with a GM car and a Ford engine. So we took the old intermediate midsize Marquis/LTD, cobbled them, and used them throughout the program." The cars with the Taurus engines were sent out to Ford's test track in Romeo, Michigan, as well as to Arizona, Denver, Florida, and Bimidji, Minnesota, for cold-weather testing. Researchers wanted to see how the engines scored in oil consumption, cold starts, and durability once on the track.

The engines ran for over 100,000 miles, twice the distance normally used for a Ford engine test. For the first time the company also installed the motor in a fleet of thirty trucks that were then driven around the country. After each one clocked 100,000 to 200,000 miles, the engines were removed and torn apart to search for wear. The autopsied units were then redesigned and remanufactured for a phase-two run, which took an additional year to complete.

Howard was pleased with the results. The design team's initial goal had been to reach 130 horsepower, but the unit that they ended up with actually delivered 10 horsepower more. The engine seemed reliable. And its easy-to-reach servicing points would hopefully be noticed by the consumer.

As the team looked at the engine, they realized it still had one major fault: it was ugly. Nobody on the engine team had ever before worried about the aesthetics of their engines, but with the Taurus philosophy governing their thinking, they realized it was an important consideration. Howard told Veraldi about his concern during one of their regular meetings. "I think I'd like to ask the North American design guys to help us make the engine look better," Howard told him. "That's a good idea," Veraldi agreed. "Go talk to them." Howard had never turned to design for help in the twenty years he had been at the company. It was the Team Taurus approach that made him realize that it made sense to do so. Design came up with a new look for the engine manifold that actually improved the flow of air to the engine.

Regardless of its attractiveness, it would be the engine's power, not its beauty, that would most impress a buyer. For the ordinary family driver, the 3.0-liter engine's acceleration was adequate. Automotive writers complained about it nevertheless, chiding the car as underpowered. A 3.8-liter V-6 with superior acceleration was eventually developed and offered as an option. To cut the sticker price, a smaller, four-cylinder, 2.5-liter engine became the standard power plant for the base model and for a sporty, MT5 manual transmission version that would be sold in limited numbers.

In terms of power and acceleration, the four-cylinder was terrible. "It's primarily for fleet operators," Howard said, designed for rental-car companies and corporations desiring to minimize their transportation costs. "It's cheaper, it was developed for plain economic reasons. The engine is very marginal. It's not powerful enough for the car." Ford assumed that 20 percent of Tauruses would be sold with the 2.5-liter engine, but by 1989 the figure was actually only 5 percent.[1] By making the four-cylinder the standard engine on the base Taurus, Ford could attract additional customers by advertising a lower base sticker price than virtually anyone would pay once they equipped the car with the essential six-cylinder unit.

While the 3.0-liter unit was reliable, easy to service and sufficiently strong, technologically, it offered little that was new. Unlike some Japanese engines, it did not have two spark plugs or four valves per cylinder. Engine design, in fact, was one area where Ford would not be able to claim the high ground. But as far as some company officials felt, it really didn't matter. "We've elected over the years not to be a leader in engine technology," Howard said. "Not that we don't have the expertise or couldn't handle it, but the American buyer really doesn't care. The Taurus buyer wanted performance, he wanted durability, and he wanted value for his money. The fact that there might have been an overhead cam four-valve, the guy really didn't care. He wasn't that kind of buyer." The decision by Ford, for whatever reasons, to not lead in the area of new engine design meant that the company was, by its abdication, leaving the door open for one of its domestic or foreign competitors to step in and set the consumer's standard for the next decade. Still, Veraldi liked the new family of engines that Howard's team had produced. They exceeded the performance and durability requirements that John Risk's planners had established, and their development and manufacturing costs came in on budget. Fulfilling these less ambitious goals would help give the Taurus a shot at success. And for Veraldi, at this stage in the company's history, that was all that mattered.

9

HORSE'S HAIR
AND FAKE WOOD

By mid-1981, Ford economists concluded that the specter of skyrocketing gasoline prices had eased. Lou Ross and his colleagues realized that three dollars for a gallon of fuel, a price that many had predicted after 1978's OPEC oil embargo, was now likely to be half that rate. As a result, consumers were beginning to reconsider the purchase of cars larger than subcompacts. Ross and the product planners had to reevaluate the size of their new vehicles to make sure that they were not going to be too small for the American consumer by the time that they were launched.

After discussions between Ross, Veraldi, and Risk, they decided that the Taurus could be enlarged without hurting its acceptance. Veraldi wanted a bigger car because tests had already shown that using the original criteria for the car's dimensions, Telnack's group couldn't design a vehicle that had both adequate passenger room and a large enough trunk and engine compartment. Risk and Veraldi enlarged the original wheel base from 102 inches to 106 inches, increasing the car's overall length by the same four inches. The size of the Sable, Mercury's sister to the Taurus, would get an additional two inches. Both cars were now considered six- rather than five-passenger vehicles. As an added benefit, the larger size of the Taurus allowed its platform to be used for the planned Lincoln Continental replacement.

The Taurus would be priced in the middle range of the family market. When launched, the top-of-the-line model would retail for $14,000, including air-conditioning, stereo radio/cassette, power seats, windows, locks, and mirrors. A fully-equipped model, with leather seats, would cost $17,000.

The decision to make the Sable bigger than the Taurus was based on the needs of the marketers. Since Mercury appealed to more upscale buyers, and was priced higher, the company wanted to differentiate the two cars as much as possible. The added length allowed the company to make a bigger trunk for the car. And, the bigger the car, the more value customers would give to it.

Ray Everts, head of the exterior design team, was annoyed that Sable got those two extra inches; they wanted them for the Taurus as well. The smaller the car, the more difficult it was to shape. "Please, Jack, get us those two inches," Everts pleaded with Telnack.

"I totally agree with you," Telnack said. "The Taurus would look better then. But you've got to forget it. We can't have them. They made a marketing decision, that's all. Marketing needs this to separate the two models."

"But we need them for the car. Go and fight for them, Jack. The Taurus won't look right without the two inches."

"It will have to look right," Telnack countered. "Because we have no choice. Look, we agreed at the beginning of this project that Sable would be differentiated from

Taurus. Those were the rules. Now we have to live with them."

To make the cars as aerodynamic as possible, the designers had to figure out how to minimize wind resistance. The smooth shape itself was essential to that effort. In addition, the side windows were fitted flush against the door panels. Recessing the windows, as was normally done, created turbulence. Ford had petitioned the National Highway Traffic and Safety Administration[1] to change its rules regarding headlight design, and the NHTSA agreed. Instead of forcing manufacturers to use standard-sized round or rectangular sealed beam lights, the car companies were allowed to create just about any shape lens that still met the federal agency's lighting standards. The Taurus's headlight lenses were made flush to conform to the shape of the front of the vehicle; hence, air flowed up and over them. Door handles were also sculpted flush into the door to reduce air drag. The underside of the handle was covered with a smooth surface to prevent damage to fingernails. The distance between the tire and fender was minimized; by reducing the space, less air could get in the gap and slow the car down.

Wraparound bumpers were constructed to avoid damage for crashes up to five miles per hour. The bumper line met a rub strip that continued around the base of the vehicle, providing a continuity of form. Under the front of the bumper, designers fashioned an "air dam," a molding that reduced turbulence below the car.

Doors were "shingled," their tops curving into and overlapping the roof. The drip rails, channels that carry rainwater off the car, were hidden inside the overlap for a cleaner appearance. The doors were designed with an internal lip all along the rear vertical edge. With the door panel lying over, rather than next to, the frame, the chance of the door being jammed into the body during an accident was reduced. This shingling technique also allowed engineers to ensure that a greater number of cars coming off the line had doors aligned properly to the body, improving fit and finish. Misaligned body panels were not only costly, they slowed down the production process and produced disgruntled customers.

As the design progressed, Telnack remembered Caldwell's earlier instruction that the Taurus had to reach to be successful. "Caldwell was a very conservative manager, very traditional in his tastes," Telnack said. "I thought it was uncharacteristic for him even to pose a question like that. I wasn't sure if he was serious or not. We found out he was damn serious, he really wanted us to make a statement so that we did have some strong identity on the road and our cars did pull away from the rest of the herd. And then Petersen was pushing us all the time, too, so when we had the two top guys in the company really interested in making that kind of a statement, we knew we were serious. We knew the corporate culture had shifted."

Over two years' time the shape of the Taurus became more refined. From its rather conservative beginning, the car was enlarged and lost its angular look. Its rounded style gradually became more pronounced as designers fiddled with elements such as the height of the trunk, the angle of the windshield, and the shape of the doors.

The car was close to what Telnack wanted but not quite. To make it even more aerodynamic, he wanted to increase the angle of the windshield while lowering the cowl, the intersection of the hood with the windshield. Then he could also lower the hood and the fenders. The move would help the car aerodynamically and give the front of the car a much sleeker, tougher look. It was a terrific idea, he thought. He brought the sketches to Lew Veraldi.

"We can't do it, Jack," Veraldi said. "Mechanically it's just not possible."

A more angled windshield, Veraldi pointed out, would introduce unacceptable reflections in the driver's eyes. And that was just the beginning. If the hood was lowered, then the engine had to be let down, too, Veraldi said. That meant that the mounts for the shock absorbers would also have to be lowered. And that's where they'd get into trouble.

"If we move those shock towers, Jack, we're going to lose our ride quality. We won't have that smooth ride that we're aiming for."

"But it'll make the car look much better," Telnack argued. "Let's compromise on the ride. It's worth it."

"No, Jack, we can't do it," Veraldi said, pounding on his desk. "The cowl's as low as it can go."

Reluctantly, Telnack accepted the decision. Veraldi was the head of the project, not Telnack. The design was not perfect, but Telnack still liked what he and his people had done.

The final shape of the exterior was a shocking departure from Ford's other midsize sedans. Unlike the boxy look of its predecessor, the LTD, the Taurus's body panels were smooth, low, and rounded. The teardrop-shaped car was of a piece, like a mass of clay that had been sculpted by the wind. No bits of chrome stuck out like gargoyles. Door handles were recessed in, not protruding from, the body. The bumpers flowed around the vehicle. Side-view mirrors were not simple appliances, but were tapered and swept back. Headlights did not break up the integrity of the design but were incorporated into the sheet metal. Its downwardly sloped hood and wide stance gave the impression of power. "This Ford repudiates everything LTD ever stood for. This new family hauler is easily the gutsiest car of our time," *Car and Driver* would write before the Taurus's launch.[2]

Key to the potential success of Taurus was the creation of an interior that mirrored the style and theme of its body. Separate teams had always styled the inside and outside of Fords, and traditionally they worked apart. Neither group had the advantage of knowing what the other was doing. The result all too often was a hodgepodge, a vehicle whose exterior styling had nothing to do with its interior. Mimi Vandermolen was thrilled to learn that for once she did not have to work that way.

Heading up the Taurus's interior-design team, Vandermolen was in many ways an outsider. She was one of the few women in design. She had been educated in Canada, not at Pasadena's Art Center College of Design, or Detroit's Center for Creative Studies, the well-known American automotive design schools. And she was born in Europe.

As a child, Vandermolen had no interest in automobile design, even though she had a passion for automobiles. Her father, an engineer, encouraged her interest in machinery, buying her model cars instead of dolls. Even in high school, Vandermolen had no idea what she would do.

"I always liked art, watercolors, drawing, but what can you do with that?" Vandermolen asked. "I didn't really know. In the early fifties and sixties, they didn't get into career counseling, especially for women. You had a choice of three jobs—clerk, teacher, or nurse, none of which intrigued me at all.

"A close friend of my father's designed stoves and fridges. One day he dragged me down to the Ontario College of Art in Toronto. 'Fantastic,' I said. 'That's where I'd like to be.' In my second year I moved into product design. A car is just a big product with a lot of little products inside of it.

"In my last year of college, I was having a horrible time finding a job. I was fourth in my class out of twenty-four, and when I went around for interviews they were very courteous and looked at my portfolio, but the question would always come back: 'Can you type?' I was very discouraged.

"I had a professor who had been working at Ford in England. He said, 'Why don't you go down to Detroit and apply for a job? I know some people at Ford.' A friend and I went in a little beat-up VW, thinking this was stupid.

"I was hired by Ford's Philco division. I worked on

snowblowers and TVs. I spent six months in Philco and from then on, it's been car studios ever since."

Vandermolen had worked on the Mustang, Cougar, Granada, and other vehicles, but she was not supposed to be involved with the Taurus. Only after the original interior designer suffered a heart attack did the head of the design department ask her to join.

For years Vandermolen had tolerated the fact that no one outside of the design center cared about her ideas. When she showed Ford executives her work, they would politely look and ask questions, but she knew their interest was disingenuous. As a result, the cars that Ford turned out in the 1970s were drab and boring on the inside as well. Designers felt no attachment to what often were unimaginative knockoffs of competitors' vehicles.

"We were copying, not leading," Vandermolen said. "There never seemed to be a good thought behind what we were doing. I'd put my sketches up on the wall. Executives would look at them. But they already had preconceived ideas of their own, and they weren't willing to try. They were probably afraid of trying something new."

The interference by top executives in the design process was not a syndrome limited to Ford or the automobile industry. In every field that had a creative component, be it automobile manufacturing, magazine publishing, or motion picture production, those executives not involved in the creative aspects of the project look for opportunities to take control of it.

Part of the problem was that designers were not used to defending their ideas. "Designers are people that speak through their hands," Vandermolen said. "They draw. They normally do not write things down. It's all up here on the wall. If you told me to design a T-Bird, in my mind I know what a T-Bird is and how it should look and be perceived by the customer. But when a group of product planners and marketing people look at my sketches, they say, 'That's nice, but explain it to us.' And we couldn't. The truth is that management thought we were kind of weird people over there in design, just sketching pretty pictures."

Veraldi's team approach intrigued Vandermolen. "The executives are not the ones who are going to come up with the ideas," he told her. "You and your people are. You're going to be working with this whole community: planners, body and chassis people, component people, marketing, parts vendors. And you, the people on the design boards, are the ones we want to hear from." "This sounds great!" Vandermolen thought. "What a breath of fresh air."

For the first time, however, their approaches would have to be supported by more than just a sketch. Vandermolen knew that if they were going to command any power, they would have to stop working unconsciously. Designers could not sketch a shape without any understanding of why they liked it, or how it related to the rest of the car. Once they had decided what goals they had to fulfill, the execution would be a relative snap. "You can make a movie about a bowl of fruit," Hollywood film director Paul Schrader used to say. "You just have to find what makes that fruit exciting." Vandermolen had to find the drama in her own bowl of fruit.

The design team understood the Taurus's basic requirements. Vandermolen and her staff watched the aerodynamic styling take shape in the exterior body studio. They all understood that this would be a family vehicle, not a sporty sedan. Now they had to put their wish list into words.

Traditionally, designers were not told what sort of people the product planners were aiming to attract with a new vehicle, what they hoped their income or educational level would be. "I don't think the people on the design boards ever got assumptions," Vandermolen said. "We'd just hear from someone, 'This is what we're gonna do.' Sometimes they'd even sketch it for you. And then, sooner or later, some executive would come along and say, 'I like that one and that one. Go off and do it.' Without any real thought behind it."

As a result, dashboards, among other items, were designed to suit the needs of the engineer and the manufacturer rather than the driver. Controls were located on the dash based on whether they were easy for the engineer to put there, not whether they were easy to operate. For Taurus this approach was no longer acceptable.

A cockpit-coordination committee was formed to ensure that the placement of all instruments made sense. All sorts of ideas were kicked around at these Taurus staff meetings. People who had never opened their mouths before suddenly began throwing out suggestions. Everyone spoke, from the designers to the men and women who spent each day carving clay models. Outside groups were solicited, including a car-rental company, a woman's committee, and older consumers. As a family car, it was important that a wide range of consumers find the controls acceptable.

"We had a general idea of whom the Taurus was meant to attract. The designers were now encouraged to take that information," Vandermolen said, "read it, think about it, take a look at our competitors, bring them into the studio if we wanted to. Tear them apart, almost. It's interesting to sit and sketch, but now we had to understand cost and waste. Now the designers could sit down and write, in their own words, what the Taurus was going to be like and whom they were reaching for.

"Before a designer ever put pencil to paper, we said, 'Don't do that yet. Let's take this information, and let's talk about how we are going to tell the rest of the world in words what the car is going to be.'"

Objectives for switches, doors, lights, controls, every aspect of the interior, were discussed. The clay-model makers pointed out that the knobs that controlled the windows and lights in previous cars were difficult to use. They wanted switches that were "friendly," easy to find at night and capable of being turned on without looking at them.

Women were very different from men in the way they used their vehicles. "Women have long fingernails," Vandermolen mused. "They wear a lot of rings, so they can't grab a door handle without breaking a nail. Women are not as strong. They wear skirts, so it's difficult to step up into a high car. Their high heels can scuff and tear up a carpet. If the car's controls are too low and out of sight, a woman with long fingernails can't feel them. She'll take her eyes off the road to find a control, and put herself in danger.

"Try opening an engine hood without getting grease on your hands. Most women have less money than men, so they can't afford cars with hood assists. So they have cheaper ones that require a rod to keep the hood open, but the hood is too heavy to lift comfortably. And women use cars differently. Men go to work in them, but for women they become school buses and food transporters.

"If I can solve all the problems inherent in operating a vehicle for a woman," Vandermolen told Veraldi, "that'll make it that much easier for a man to use." This was a new concept for many executives. They had never considered a woman's needs before. As Vandermolen continued to pressure them, they began to see her points and allowed her to proceed.

In addition, Vandermolen had to ensure that the switches blended in aesthetically with the rest of the interior. She started to sketch switches that were tactile, that were easily found and operated by touching them. She came up with the idea of providing a raised bump on one end of the switch and a depression on the other. That way the driver would be able to push the switch without looking at it.

One of the first problems was determining which side of the new tactile switch meant on or off, up or down, closed or open. It was not enough to decide that one side of the switch was to be raised and the other depressed. There had to be a logic to this process. Vandermolen tested the switch design with both men and women. Scores of people within the company were asked whether a bump logically meant on or off to them. It was decided that the raised side would always indicate on, up, or closed, the depressed side off, down, or open. Then ergonomic tests were conducted in which participants sat in passenger bucks and tried to manipulate the controls. Through such research designers learned that certain switches and door handles were placed too far forward to comfortably use and needed to be moved. In addition, the window switch needed to be angled appropriately so that the hand easily made contact with it. Too many cars had the window switches flat against the door, forcing the hand into an awkward position. And the depression could not be too deep. If it was, then a woman's long fingernail might break while trying to push the button.

Switches for the various controls were placed logically around the driver, within easy reach, operable without having to take one's eyes off the road. Slides to turn the heater on and off were abandoned in favor of large rotary knobs, similar to those found in Saabs. The knobs were easier to operate and their click stops gave the driver a sure sense that he or she had turned it to the desired position.

The speedometer's large needle allowed for a quick determination of incremental speed changes. The rear interior of the car was raised slightly to allow passengers to see over the front seats and avoid feeling claustrophobic. A Mercedes-like storage compartment was added on the shelf above the rear seats. Scores of drawings and discussions resulted in a glove box that was both large and that opened without hitting the passenger's knees. A separate compartment for the owner's manual was provided to help keep the box neater.

Ford's air conditioner had always been the obstacle to intelligent placement of the controls. With its transformation from a luxury to a necessity, the positioning of the air conditioner, with its many hoses and outlets, had always taken precedence over everything else on the control panel. As a result, other switches were placed where there was room, without sufficient regard for whether they belonged there. "Show me that grade-eight engineer who designs the air-conditioning duct," Ray Ablondi used to fume before the Taurus project started, "because he's the guy that for twenty years has unilaterally decided what the dashboard is going to look like."

From the beginning of the project, Vandermolen and the team decided that this time the instrument panel (the dashboard or IP) was not going to be designed by default. First of all, it would not be straight across. A flat, rectangular dashboard with instruments and warning lights stretched along its length was the traditional American styling standard. Virtually every car coming out of Detroit had a straight dash, regardless of whether it fit the exterior design or not. "I love the Oldsmobile Ciera on the outside," Vandermolen said. "But as soon as you open the door, you say, 'This car's for a ninety-year-old person.' The inside doesn't relate to the outside at all. I've heard of people who have gone out to buy one, opened the door, and said, 'I don't want that car.' "

The straight-across style had already been abandoned by the Europeans in favor of a cockpit approach: in many European cars the driver was surrounded by the instruments and gauges as if in an airplane. Vandermolen didn't go along with that look, either. A cockpit was appropriate for a sports car, in which the driver often traveled alone or at most with one other person. Also, in a sports car the driver wanted to feel in control of a powerful machine. But the Taurus was going to be a family car. The passengers needed to feel that they, too, had access to the instrument panel, that they were riding in a spacious, inviting car and not shut off from the experience. Its drivers would be normal people. If they wanted to think of themselves as Flash Gordon, they weren't going to act that out with the kids in the backseat.

Still, Vandermolen could not accept a linear dashboard, one that shouted "bland American car." A compromise had to be reached. After trial and error, she decided that the instrument panel would be angled toward the motorist, but still not wrapped tightly around the operator.

This way the driver psychologically felt in control, because everything that was needed to operate the car was within easy reach. At the same time front-seat passengers were not cut off from the driver. They'd even be able to check the speedometer to see if their spouse was driving too fast.

The first sketch of the binnacle, the panel that housed the various instruments, was curved but completely vertical. Like so many other American cars, a massive wall of instruments was put directly in front of the driver's face. This placement allowed for a good amount of space in the seat, but Vandermolen saw that sitting in front of a huge panel was intimidating and unpleasant. The team decided to alter the design. Instead of a completely vertical set of instruments, they slightly angled the binnacle downward. It was, Vandermolen thought, an elegant solution to a potentially annoying problem.

The sketches for the new instrument panel were placed up on the boards at the design center. A few days later, a top executive came onto the floor to check the newest plans. "What's that?" he asked when he saw the sketch.

"That's the new instrument panel for the Taurus," Vandermolen said.

"No, it isn't. This is a mistake. Instrument panels are vertical, they're not angled. I don't like it. Do another panel."

Design staff couldn't believe their ears. Vandermolen was stunned. "Everything has been going along so well, until this," she thought. "We'd all been meeting regularly. Everyone had discussed what was needed for the car's interior and exterior. Work had progressed following the set goals. And now some executive shows up and vetos the whole thing."

Vandermolen knew that the only reason the executive didn't like the design was because it was new. But how could she convince him to be more receptive? She returned to her office and looked at the calendar. Time was short. The next review was coming up and the designers had to be ready to present their new sketches to the planning board for approval. They had to figure out how they were going to redesign everything in time. Weekend work was now an obvious necessity. Even then design staff wondered if they'd get the job done.

Vandermolen and her colleagues debated the executive's order. Yet the more they discussed it, the more incensed they became. They were agreeing to change a major part of the look of the car. How could they do that? They knew what they wanted.

Fritz Mayhew, Vandermolen's boss, dropped by her office to see how the sketches were going. Vandermolen told Mayhew of the encounter and how they were now trying to reconcile the idea of redesigning the dash.

"Wait a minute," Fritz said. "Not so fast. Get those objectives out. Look at them again. You're doing what you were asked to do. Sketch another panel that looks more ordinary. Then put the two side by side. We're not going to go his way without fighting for what we believe."

Vandermolen and her team became energized by Mayhew's stance. They convened a meeting with the stubborn executive and showed him their original sketch for the dash and a more conservative one. She discussed the objectives for the interior, the need to make the dash attractive, to both surround but not isolate the driver, to place the switches in accessible locations. Although the dash was different, it met the goals that had been set by the team. His conception would not.

"Now, do you really want us to do what you've instructed us?"

"No," the executive said. "I was wrong. Do it your way."

The designers had saved the dash. Yet they came within a hairsbreadth of losing it. "Our program works," Vandermolen thought after the fight was over. "Its premise is so simple, it's pathetic."

A prime concern was that the interior match in theme the sculpted look of the body. Straight, angular panels anywhere—on the doors as well as on the dash—would be unacceptable. The doors had to mimic the smooth lines of the exterior. To accomplish that, the team sketched sixteen different door designs that seemed to flow into the instrument panel. Rather than attaching a map pocket onto a flat door like a painting on a wall, the pocket was sculpted into the panel. The purpose was to give the door a three-dimensional effect, to give it depth and make it look all of a piece with the dash.

Finally, there would be no fake wood in this car. Not a bit! Fake wood was going to be banished from the Taurus, Jack Telnack decided. It was one of the designers' bêtes noires. Fake wood, real wood, it was all the same. It was completely useless. If form truly followed function, what function gave birth to this awful stuff? Telnack gave the order to design an interior without it.

To a person, stylists hated fake wood. It was idiotic. It stemmed from an earlier day, when real polished wood was embedded throughout automobiles, on the dashes and door panels. When wood was removed from cars, cheesy Contact-like paper took its place. Station wagons sported great sheets of it on their exterior door panels, and virtually every car with pretensions of class pasted it somewhere on the interior.

Once the instrument panel was redesigned and useless decoration eliminated, the designers turned to what was traditionally one of American car manufacturers' greatest weaknesses: the car seat.

U.S. car owners took for granted that they would suffer back pain and be tossed around as they drove. The slab of upholstery in a bench seat offered neither back nor side support for drivers. Even American bucket seats were often ill-conceived. To alleviate pain, motorists regularly purchased devices to fill in the small of their backs. Plastic slipcovers became synonymous with a 1950s obsession to keep a car's poorly made interior from fading, ripping, and shredding.

Bucket seats had once been for British sports cars or American pretenders to the throne. As American cars downsized, buckets became standard, but they were as uncomfortable as the old bench. Initially, few provided much adjustment. Seat backs had limited ability to recline, and the sides were as unsupportive as a bus bench. Many seemed to curve in exactly the wrong direction if they were to help the critical lumbar area.

Ford lived up to its heritage, providing the same uncomfortable seat design for each succeeding generation of cars. The Taurus design team started all over. Like a child taking apart a watch to see how it ticks, the staff was going to dissect seats from around the world to understand what made them work. They knew that in this area they had much to learn from their competitors.

Designing a car seat is not like designing a sofa. In fact, it is the most difficult part of a car to get right. It needs to be comfortable over long periods, and it has to support a variety of different sizes, shapes, and weights. A driver sitting in a seat for hours still has to feel relatively fresh and relaxed. Also, the fabric has to last for years despite being exposed to extremes of temperature and sunlight. It cannot rip or stretch. The foam support has to be permanently resilient. And the entire package has to be produced within a vehicle's budget constraints.

Developing a comfortable seat was a difficult process for any manufacturer. Even pricier cars don't always succeed. The lauded Honda Accord, America's best-selling car in 1989 and 1990, has been the subject of frequent criticism for its uncomfortable seating. Dealers have even allowed purchasers to return their Accords after their backs went out while driving them. "I never have a nice thing to say about the Honda Accord," the cohost of a nationally broadcast auto show cautioned his listeners, "because my back always hurts whenever I sit in one."[3]

Car seats could not be individually molded for each owner. As the designers discussed the different types, they knew right off that a cushy easy chair, while good looking, was the worst type of seating for a car. Easy chairs are made for slouching, and slouching is a disaster for a driver, causing fatigue and decreased alertness. The team knew that increased driver support decreased fatigue, and fatigue has long been one of the biggest problems of driving.

The most supportive seats were found in race cars, but tests showed that after several hours of driving in this type of seat, the driver's leg often became numb. The problem was due to the extra padding put in the cushion. There was too much support, and the resultant pressure against the leg reduced circulation. Vandermolen liked the support available in custom car seats available in accessory shops, manufactured by such companies as Germany's Recaro. They were ideal at holding passengers tightly in place. But their drawback was that their high side and seat bolsters made them very difficult to use, especially for women. Vandermolen had ripped a few skirts along the seam trying to get in and out of one. The key for the Taurus was a compromise between support and maneuverability.

The final consideration was designing a seat that looked inviting, covered in attractive material. The attractiveness, Vandermolen decided, should come from the fabrics, not from pleats or fabric buttons, which trapped dirt and particles of food. Button- and pleat-free seats also meant a cleaner look and a savings in construction costs. The only way to understand which manufacturers had conquered the seating problem was to have the public drive cars for extended periods of time. After 10,000 miles of consumer test driving, the design team found that research groups preferred two car seats, the Ford Continental's and General Motors' Opel Senator. The Continental scored higher on some tests, but Vandermolen took those consumer comments in perspective. She knew that Germans preferred stiff-bodied seats, while Americans perceived plush seats as luxurious. The times the Ford scored higher was more likely due to cultural preferences than to the actual ride quality of the seat. The Senator's seat was made the target to beat. Vandermolen told her staff to take one and tear it apart.

At first they found no surprises. The autopsy revealed

that Opel seats were constructed of a metal frame, a set of bedlike springs, foam, and fabric, just like all auto seats. Then they noticed that the springs went all around the seat, but where more support was needed, the springs were thicker. Digging deeper, a team member felt something unfamiliar. He stuck his hand in and grabbed. Horsehair! The Germans were sticking horsehair in their seats, as if they were making Victorian furniture!

Foam was very supportive, but it always lost its resiliency. Horsehair prevented it from slackening with use. This was a good solution but prohibitively expensive for the Taurus.

Clay models reflecting the basic shape were carved, and then various prototypes were made based on these models. Nine identical Crown Victorias, Ford's largest-sized car, were equipped with seat mock-ups and sent out to be tested by the research group. Over 100,000 miles were put on the prototypes, making this Ford's most extensive seat-evaluation program. Survey results then indicated changes that needed to be made with the models.

To imitate horsehair, the Taurus engineers decided to use differing thicknesses of foam in areas subject to greater stress. A method was found to keep the weight of the frame low and thereby decrease overall body weight. Although the car was destined to be a six-passenger vehicle, the front seats were designed with contours for two. A third person was still able to sit in the middle, yet the appearance was more of buckets. Fabrics would be trilaminated, glued to the front and rear of the foam. This method would prevent the material from buckling over time and was the only solution that ensured that the fabric took the shape of the contoured seat. It took nine months to find an acceptable seat fabric, because the material had to be tested for wearability, resistance to scuffs, mold, heat, sunlight, chemicals, colorfastness, and shrinkage.

The entire process took over two and a half years. In addition to figuring out construction techniques and continually testing prototypical designs, dummies were lowered in and out of seats up to 100,000 times to ensure seat and fabric durability.

The designers felt that they had ended up with an interior far superior to any ever produced at Ford. Controls were logical. Switches made sense. The seats were sturdy and comfortable. It was as close to a driver's car as they'd ever seen in America.

In fact, the interior was a dramatic departure from American car design. Most of the normal push–pull switches were gone, replaced by rotary dials. Speedometer and tachometer, as in foreign vehicles, were half circles, not long horizontal scales. The optional digital instrument panel looked like a video game screen.

Despite the design team's effort, no one would mistake the interior for that of its ideal, a European sedan. The softly angled instrument panel, its curves in concert with the shape of the exterior, was still too large and imposing. Forced to design an IP that would work with both bench and bucket seats, the panel stretched too far across the width of the dash and too high into the driver's line of sight. The fold-down armrests folded down at too high a level and were uncomfortable to use. Once down, the armrests jiggled in position and as a result felt flimsy, even though they were not. The automatic transmission selector was on the steering column, rather than on the floor, as in European cars. A floor console was an option, but the gear selector lever used there was thin and anemic looking. It did not have the strong stance and robustness that Ablondi and Telnack had mandated.

Although the designers managed to place window and headlight switches in the right places, they were still hard to find at night. The team had designed an entire lighting group to illuminate all the electric door buttons, headlight switch, mirror adjustments, even a light near the door's interior handle, but they were all cut because of budget restraints.

"In the doors you're talking four dollars a side; it's wire harness connectors, bulbs," Vandermolen noted. "You have to put the harness through the engine compartment, so you need seals, wiring, connectors, another seal for rainwater, so the costs rise very quickly.

"The lighting was a disappointment to us, because we even put a model together with it all intact. But the Taurus was basically the first vehicle that we really felt we had total company support to put as many features in for the customers."

The designers were not getting everything they wanted. They never did. But for the first time, they were having a say in operations. They presented their needs and they had learned how to argue for them.

The change that had come over the design group was nothing short of astounding. They had learned a new language, the language of persuasion. "Can you believe it?" Ken Corey, one of the company's top product planners said after listening to a presentation by Vandermolen and her group. "Designers can actually think!"

The early exterior and interior designs scared many top Ford people. "What are we doing a shape like this for?" executives not directly involved with the project continually asked. "We must be crazy." They were familiar with the upcoming Lincoln Mark's aerodynamic curves, but this car was even more radical. The Taurus was projected as a high-volume, mainstream car. Had they put themselves out on a limb? No other company seemed to be following their styling lead in their future models.

"Don't be scared," Vandermolen told her superiors over and over. "We're on the right track. We're meeting our objectives. Of course this vehicle looks different. But give yourselves time to get used to the car."

At least her Team Taurus members supported and understood the project. And they were really working together. The way of life at Ford had altered.

"Now that we're in trouble, we're changing," Vandermolen said. "No longer will directions from the top down be acceptable. Now it's coming from the bottom up. They have to listen to us."

10

HAVE YOU DRIVEN A FORD . . . EVER?

By the summer of 1981, the design center crews in Detroit and Turin had come up with initial sketches of a possible Taurus. Everyone had agreed the car would be more modern and rounded than its predecessors. What no one knew was whether the public would give a damn.

The answer to that question became a personal quest for Ray Ablondi. In the early 1980s the director of research was leading the cry for change, extolling an era when the customer would truly come first. It was a message that not everyone wanted to hear.

He and Martin Goldfarb continually praised the virtues of a "customer-driven" company, and they had a receptive audience in Don Petersen. He was constantly quizzing Ablondi about what new techniques could be used to improve their products. The imprecise data that had traditionally come out of the research department frustrated Petersen. He hoped for the day when Ford could market cars that had proven themselves with the public even before they were launched.

"I'd have a private meeting with Petersen," Ablondi said, "and he'd say, 'Tell me what you're doing in the whole research area. What kind of techniques are you using? Why can't you come up with a way to predict the future?' And that was the ultimate. Everybody in the world wanted to be able to predict the future. And I'd say, 'Don, if I could do that, you'd be working for me.' He laughed and agreed that I was exactly right."

It was an impossible goal, Ablondi knew. But it was one to which research people aspired. If Ablondi could discover techniques that would predict the kinds of cars and features people would want to buy, not just one, but ten years hence, then he could greatly reduce the risk to the company of producing vehicles that nobody liked.

What seemed like an obvious corporate need had all too often been ignored. For example, the styling and marketing strategies of the 1957 Edsel, applauded within the company during development, had not been adequately tested with the public. As a result, the shape became a source of ridicule. What Ford stylists perceived to be Edsel's unique vertical grill was likened to a horse collar and a toilet seat. The car was promoted as an all-new design, ten years in the making. But that marketing concept also proved false. In truth, the only part new about it was its exterior body shell. The vehicle's mechanicals had been pinched from existing models. Quality was so poor that one Edsel used in a live television commercial during its introduction didn't even start.[1]

Despite the fact that the Edsel debacle had occurred over twenty years earlier, it still left a mark on the company's consciousness. Its name had become synonymous in American popular culture with disaster. And the car's failure had never left the minds of many Ford executives.

Even with all the new techniques for interpreting data that had emerged by the 1980s, research remained a dangerous business. A misinterpretation of an answer, an unnecessary amount of weight given to a response, a bending of the data to fit preconceptions—all could contribute to false assumptions about a car's potential success.

Taurus could not fall into this trap. Ford had to accurately assess the public's desires. The problem was that those people involved in managing a business often lost sight of their ultimate goal: to make a product that would sell.

Perhaps the members of Team Taurus would become too subjectively involved in their project, and their zeal to make a radically new automobile might blind them to some of Taurus's underlying faults. Ablondi wanted to ensure that a designer did not solve a problem in seat styling without knowing if the end result appealed to buyers. He wanted to guard against engineers creating a space-saving suspension without considering the new suspension's ride characteristics.

This myopic approach to business was not limited to the automobile industry. Even the American motion-picture trade, a commodity that depends on mass appeal for success, has become caught up in its internal problems. The successful completion of a film is often seen as an end in itself. Producers, directors, and editors become so intent on solving technical difficulties that they lose sight of the fact that the film may have major story-line and acting problems that cannot be solved in the cutting room.

Team Taurus was meant to correct this sort of short-sightedness. The approach was nothing less than a system of checks and balances in which workers with different agendas could challenge assumptions made by their colleagues in other areas.

Above all, the customer's opinion had to remain paramount. Focus groups were a must, but the team needed more. They needed to bring a consumer ombudsman into the decision-making process. For this reason, the team appointed one of its own as a surrogate consumer.

The job fell to Joel Pitcoff, a twenty-year market planning and statistical analysis veteran who loved to slug it out in the trenches. A tall, broad-shouldered, husky man with a deep, rumbling voice, Pitcoff was one of the few executives who dared to be different. He rejected Ford conservative dress, wearing a goatee, three-piece suits, and unusually colored shirts. Bob Rewey, Lincoln-Mercury's representative on Team Taurus, had long ago christened Pitcoff the "bulldog," not for his looks but for his tenacity. Pitcoff relished a chance to challenge the status quo, to puff on his pipe and thoughtfully expound on his marketing theories, to fight for his causes.

Pitcoff's office was reminiscent of a college professor's. The door to his prefabricated cubicle was decorated with cartoons that Pitcoff had cut from magazines. His desk was piled to overflowing with a mound of documents. Pitcoff loved to work. Continually sipping from a half-gallon container of Diet Pepsi ("It's 99¢. The 44-ounce size is 79¢. I'm a good businessman, so I get the bigger size"). Pitcoff could be found in his office six days per week, until seven or eight every night. He didn't mind the hours. After all, it wasn't such a long day. "I don't come in that early," he said. "I don't get here until nine in the morning."

Unlike some Ford people who changed job categories rapidly in their quest for corporate advancement, Pitcoff had done similar work for many years. His longevity was an asset for the Taurus project, he felt, because the rest of the team knew that he would be involved from beginning to end. "I understand the customer," Pitcoff told his colleagues. "I was a consumer advocate before Ralph Nader invented the term. What is a market planner if not a consumer advocate?" Pitcoff apparently did not see any conflict of interest in Ford's consumer advocate receiving his paycheck from the same company he was charged with critiquing.

Pitcoff attacked his job with gusto. An avid motorist,

he crawled all over the test cars, looking for things he wanted to change. He evaluated looks, driveability, interiors and exteriors. He went to all the focus groups, making suggestions to Goldfarb for avenues to explore. He attended the weekly design reviews, in which body engineers, designers, product planners, and marketing representatives examined clay models, and addressed specific product decisions that needed to be made.

As marketing-plans manager, Pitcoff had an ear to the outside. He spent his days analyzing data and research, working with dealers so he'd know the customer end of the business. His presence meant that engineers and designers, who had little contact with the public, could hear his perceptions about the vehicle. Over time they learned to trust Pitcoff. If he said there was a problem with the car, even if he couldn't always explain exactly why, he knew what he was talking about.

Pitcoff served as Taurus's voice of the customer. But his position was an adjunct, not a substitute, for actual consumer research. Contrary to former company practices, Ray Ablondi was intent on getting customer feedback. With it the designers and marketers could avoid mistakes early on that could become costly to fix later. To get the information he needed, Ablondi and his team devised a ten-stage market-research process. The reason was that since each element of a car was not developed at the same time, it did not need to be tested at the same time.

The first two phases of research had been completed before Taurus design work began. The research department was regularly conducting its annual surveys of owners of Fords and competitive makes, asking them to discuss the quality of their cars and their components. Over a year earlier, the company had asked Ford owners literally how they bought cars. They wanted to know owners' behavior while shopping—did they look under the hood, take a test drive, sit in the driver's seat, or bring their spouse along with them to the dealership? With this information the company learned what elements of a vehicle were initially important to consumers and therefore which ones to emphasize in design and advertising.

"I want to get to know our potential customers so well," Ablondi told Petersen, "that I'll be able to tell what kind of car they like by the size of their underwear."

Months after Lou Ross had taken over planning at Ford, he decided to put research operations under his overall command. Research became part of North American Automotive Operations (NAAO). Not only would it be an integral element of Team Taurus, but would also be intimately involved with the development of other new projects. "We were becoming a part of the NAAO team," Ablondi said. "We were not going to be the team peeking over NAAO's shoulder, doing a report card on them."

"Who let you in, Ray?" Ford stylist Gene Bordinat demanded to know, half in jest, as Ablondi showed up at the design center for the first time. "I thought I gave them instructions to lock you out."

As Ablondi's division became more integrated with product development, so too did the role of its chief outside researcher, Martin Goldfarb.

Goldfarb's company confined its automotive work to Ford. This relationship benefited both parties. After years of work, Goldfarb had secured an enviable position for himself: he now had a lock on the Ford research contracts. Competing research companies were relegated to ancillary contracts. The danger of giving so much business to Goldfarb was that he would become the corporate guru, but Ford decided to take that risk. His work, the company felt, was too good. The Goldfarb–Ford connection became very close and trusting; many things went unsaid between the two parties during research studies because the other partner knew automatically what needed to be done. The relationship "was almost like a marriage," said Henry Wolpert, a former Ford researcher. Goldfarb also knew how to turn around work quickly. Ford appreciated this, since many of his competitors took too long to complete studies.

Most of the time that Ford contracted research projects to other companies, they wound up regretting it. One luxury-car study prepared by a competitive firm pointed out that the name *Ford* actually tainted the good name of Lincoln. Ford didn't need reports that told them things they already knew. "We've known that stuff for years," one researcher pointed out when he read the report.

Stage three in Ablondi's process was the first time that consumers would be exposed to the nascent Taurus designs. Goldfarb's company rented large halls in New York and Los Angeles for these July 1981 focus groups. Over three hundred participants agreed, in exchange for twenty-five dollars, to give their opinions about what they wanted and needed in their present and future cars.

At a folding table at one end of the large rented room, a group of clerks handed out questionnaires attached to clipboards. The participants then studied black-and-white photographs hung on the hall's portable boards. Scores of photographs affixed to the movable walls showed front, side, and rear views of the preliminary Taurus designs, as well as the cars that the team was targeting as prime design competitors: the Audi 4000, Oldsmobile Cutlass, Mercedes 300SD, and the Opel Senator. To eliminate any unwanted prejudice for or against a particular make, the cars appeared unbadged.

This was done because researchers knew that public perception of quality and dependability of a car had less to do with the actual vehicle than with the fantasy that the public ascribed to it. Certain automobiles, such as Toyotas, become defined as reliable. Conversely, if a Mercedes were sold with a Ford badge on its hood rather than its famous three-pointed star, its perceived monetary value, comfort, and dependability would automatically diminish.

The first sketches of the Taurus had been transformed into life-size clay models and then photographed for this session. This early in the research process, using photographs made better economic sense than showing the life-size models themselves, since transporting clay models was expensive. By showing pictures, the designers could also use one clay for two different versions, sculpting one version on either side of a model and thereby reducing costs. In the old days each version had been constructed and tested separately. Designers ordered up eight to nine separate clays, at a cost of $200,000 each. Now only two or three were needed for the entire program.

This was an important focus group for Ford executives and designers. The Taurus was still in its early stages of development and would not receive final approval for several more months. Program executives had been claiming that the public would accept a radical aerodynamic design. For the first time they would find out if they were right.

The phrase *focus group* was coined by Dr. Irving White, a Los Angeles-based industrial psychologist, in the early 1960s. At the time White was one of a small group of industrial psychologists and consumer researchers who were developing modern marketing techniques for automobiles. In a focus group, the client's representatives watch a round-table interview from the rear of the room. If the group leader decides that the presence of the executives would dampen the spontaneity of the responses, they are placed behind a one-way mirror. In this way executives see and hear real people reacting to their products. The interviews often become theater for the observers, a voyeuristic experience where they can secretly witness consumers making uninhibited responses to their wares.

The focus group occupies a middle position between quantified, "hard" results—those obtained by asking interviewees to answer multiple-choice questions or to rank a particular product on a scale—and "soft," qualitative discussions in which participants simply state their likes and dislikes.

By watching these discussions take place, the client often believes that he has become some sort of instant ethnographer, capable of immediately understanding a consumer's psyche. But raw data actually tells nothing. To be meaningful, the interviewer must thoroughly analyze a round-table discussion, placing the responses in a historical and social context, understanding as much of what wasn't said as what was.

White was a successful independent automobile researcher. Consulting for a range of businesses, from car companies to banks to movie studios, he had built his one-man operation, Creative Research Associates, into one of the best firms of its type in the country. He had authored several seminal analyses for Ford that had clarified their efforts in the luxury segment of the marketplace. In one such study in 1977, White concluded that Lincoln Continental sales were plummeting because the car was perceived as too stodgy.

Cars go through cycles of symbolic meaning, White told the company in his report. What is classy one day—fins, hood ornaments, etc.—is considered trashy the next. Luxury does not mean fancy fabrics; it means safety, protection, comfort. Car buyers looking for luxury want to feel that they are protected from the turbulence of everyday life when they drive. To be defined as luxurious, White believes, a car needs to become an extension of one's own living room, a fortress in a dangerous society.

"The Lincoln Continental owner is an old man. He is somebody who wants to insulate himself, to ride high above the masses," White wrote. "He is seen as a tremendous snob." To increase sales of the Continental, White suggested, it should be featured alongside the more sporty and better-selling Mark I in all Lincoln ads. Sure enough, sales took off. The work proved to be so important to the car's success that Ford executives called the new campaign the "White commercials."

To these early Taurus focus groups came not just market researchers, but planners, designers, sales and finance heads, a smattering of every division involved in the project, all eager to hear what consumers had to say about Ford's direction. Everything was taped so that executives who were not present could also see the proceedings.

The participants were given as much time as needed to view the photographs. After they looked at them, they sat down with an interviewer from Goldfarb's company. "I'm an independent researcher," the host would typically say. "I do research for a lot of companies. I have no vested interest in any of the companies I do research for. That includes this car company.

"People hire me to talk to you to find out your feelings about different things. It makes no difference if you like things or dislike things. What is important is I find out how you really feel. Go ahead and say what you want to say. So, if there are no questions, let's start."

Ford management had no need to worry that the public wouldn't think these first Taurus designs—the ones done in Turin—were modern and aerodynamic. They were definitely seen as such. The problem was that people hated them. The Taurus designs received the lowest scores, far surpassed by Ford's traditionally styled LTD, the Olds Cutlass, and the Opel Senator.

"What is this thing, a stink bug?" one person asked while viewing the first Taurus pictures. "It's horrible looking."

"Where's the chrome grill? What kind of car is this?" said another.

"This thing looks just like an armadillo," said a third. "It's an anteater. I can't stand it."

The negative responses were too much for one designer attending the New York focus group. After holding in his feelings, he finally exploded. "That's it, I've had it! What the hell do these dummies know about good design?" he demanded. "I'm the designer. I know what's good. Nobody here is going to tell me what's good and what isn't!" He proceeded to storm out of the room, sick of these know-nothings.

Ablondi let him leave, realizing that the designer didn't understand the research process. The purpose of these focus groups was not to take a respondent's opinions at face value. Such initial thoughts needed to be used as a starting point for a discussion, in which the interviewer probed to find out what was and what wasn't liked about the car.

Goldfarb and his colleagues did not accept one-word answers. If a respondent exclaimed, "I hate Fords! I'll never drive them as long as I live!" he was then asked to elaborate.

"I hate them. I hate their cars. They're garbage."

"There must be something you like about them," Goldfarb asked.

"Well, the wheels are okay."

"Okay, you like the wheels. What else do you like?"

The purpose was not to convince the participant that his or her initial assessment of the company was wrong. Rather, Goldfarb wanted to provide an accepting environment in which he could move beyond gut reactions into product analysis.

The idea that the company has to listen to what customers wanted in a car and then give it to them was revolutionary to the company's designers and managers, but was not news to Ray Ablondi. He had come to understand that Ford researchers did not understand how to segment their potential customer base. Among other discoveries, he had learned they did not sufficiently understand regional differences that could make one car a smash success in the East but a failure in the West. In fact, the simple act of looking at a car differed from one part of the country to another. In the West, car owners were more interested in driving. For instance, California focus-group subjects were shown mock-ups of the upcoming Thunderbird, Ford's first attempt at creating an aerodynamic design. As participants studied the driver's area, they told Ablondi, "Keep your cotton-picking hands off my cockpit. Don't mess with the dashboard, don't screw it up." On the contrary, when they showed the car in Rochester, a blue-collar town in northern New York, one buyer barely glanced at this acclaimed driver's area. Instead, he immediately jumped into the back.

"What are you going back there for?" an interviewer asked.

"To see if it's big enough for my mother-in-law," the research subject said. "If it's not, she'll make our lives miserable."

Even when designers' initial lines were right, though, they were still operating in a void. If they liked a design, they were apt to carry cues from one car to another, without knowing whether another vehicle would appeal to the same type of buyer. For example, because the Thunderbird's dashboard received strong critical acclaim, cues from it were adapted to the Ford Tempo/Mercury Topaz. But Tempo/Topaz buyers were more conservative and older than T-Bird owners and did not like the dash.

During a later Dallas focus-group session, Ford LTD owners were asked to judge the attractiveness of various radios. Ford officials were proud of their latest designs, which combined ease of use with modernity and state-of-the-art equipment. Nonetheless, an older man approached Ablondi. "You know, when I used to buy a car," he said, "the radio had two buttons: volume and tuning. Now, that radio over there has twenty-two buttons. Who the hell would want a stupid thing like that?"

The responses left a deep impression on Ablondi. A shotgun approach to research was not going to work for the Taurus project. The car couldn't be designed or marketed properly if nobody knew who was going to buy it. With Ford's slipping market, the company vitally needed to increase its share of the midsize, family sector.

Although the Turin "stink bug" was disliked at the first Taurus focus group in 1981, the American rendering was even more reviled. "More prospects dislike the NAAO [North American Automotive Operations] theme," Ablondi reported to management. "Resistance to the Turin and NAAO drawings is generalized. Prospects see the themes as aerodynamic and advanced, but unattractive."

Lew Veraldi was devastated by the clinically rendered negative report. After hearing the results, he stormed back into his office and sulked. When his secretary, Terri Glowacki, brought him some paperwork, he shouted, "Look, get out of my office, Terri! You are the last person I want to talk to."

Glowacki had been on the receiving end of this kind of inappropriate outburst before, and she had learned to ignore it. Both she and John Risk began to wonder if his mood swings had less to do with his dissatisfaction over the research and more with sugar imbalance. A diabetic, Veraldi was often incapable of keeping to his restricted diet. He loved food too much. On the rare times that he'd leave his office for lunch, he always headed to his favorite Italian restaurant down the street.

A few minutes later, a more relaxed Lew emerged from his office and told Glowacki about the research results. Reflection had made him more rational. "I know that's how consumers feel today, but this car isn't going to be out for three years. In three years people will be sick of looking at the boxy cars that are around now."

Jack Telnack was more sanguine about the public's first reaction to the Taurus. "I wouldn't have voted for them either," he said. "The cars were not right. We showed them because you have to start somewhere. I wouldn't have researched them, because I wasn't happy with them. But we had the [ten-step] program laid out, and we had to research at different intervals.

"Before, that kind of response would have thrown us off base, and we'd say, 'Jeez, maybe we screwed up.' This time I had told [management] before the cars went to research that they were not hundred-percent cars. 'Hey, give me a chance to come up with an idea, okay? I mean, I've only had a couple of months on it. It's not a mistake. It's a design process.' "

Indeed, Telnack did calm down senior management. Not just the concepts but the man as well convinced them to let him keep on trying. A primary reason was that Telnack avoided the usual design/management conflict. "Ten or twenty years ago," Lou Ross noted, "anything you said to a designer like Gene Bordinat [the original designer for the Mini/max] was dismissed. I used to run heads with Bordinat all the time. Jack was easy to deal with. He'd listen, he'd accept criticism and respond to it positively. And he wasn't even the head designer."

"Jack was one of those persistent guys who found ways to sell management on what he was doing," said Tom Page, who had become a member of the Taurus executive styling committee. "And he was very clever at it. He seemed to have an unusual ability to read management's mind. When he knew he'd gone too far, he'd seem to sense that."

A cardinal question remained. Were the designs scoring lower than current models because they were modern and unknown, or were they just truly bad shapes? As soon as consumers were shown other designs from around the world that approximated Taurus in their contemporary styling, they'd have the answer. If ratings for the Taurus designs started to improve, then at least they'd be on the right track.

While some top company officials were wringing their hands over the new shape, Martin Goldfarb took the bad reactions to it in stride. He heard all the negative comments, but he didn't feel that Ford was off in a wrong direction. The focus group and design processes were evolutionary. Designing a car was a trial-and-error process.

Yes, people hated the first Taurus designs. But Goldfarb heard something else in those meetings. People hated the car, but they were also intrigued by it. Some cars that Goldfarb had tested over the years were flat-out disasters—they had no appeal. When that happened, Goldfarb had always told Ford nothing could be done to save the project.

The styling cues were present in the early Taurus, but they had to be properly exploited. If people thought the car looked like an armadillo, the rear end needed to be lowered. If the front looked too choppy, it had to be smoothed out. Taurus was meant to be a breakthrough car, but it couldn't look like an oddball.

A faction of executives felt that the poor scores were

due not to the car itself, but to the type of people that research had decided to interview. A potential Taurus buyer was going to be a progressive individual, these executives said. They were not the traditional midsize car buyers looking for a new vehicle. A cadre of marketing personnel argued that the Taurus customer base was not even going to be owners of midsize cars.

Historically, midsize cars had been nothing more than shrunken large-size cars. For instance, the Ford LTD had been purposely named to promote consumer recognition between it and the larger LTD Crown Victoria. The original Ford Fairlane had been a smaller version of the Galaxy 500. The strategy worked because most midsize car buyers had traditionally been owners who liked large cars but due to the fact that their children had left home, or their income dropped upon retirement did not need large cars. They liked the aspects of large cars, so they were attracted to their midsize clones.

This market sector had changed in recent years, however. A new generation of American buyers had come to admire the Japanese manufacturers' approach to handling, ride, and fuel economy, an approach very different from a normal American vehicle. As this new import-owner body aged, it began to want larger vehicles. They didn't like the ride characteristics of traditional American midsize sedans, and Japanese manufacturers did not offer any vehicle large enough. European sedans, such as Saabs and Volvos, appealed only to a small segment of the population that were willing to accept high prices and sparse dealer organizations.

Team members wanted to ensure that the Taurus would be positioned as the only practical alternative: an American car that could draw in those import buyers looking for a larger car, or American car owners who had had an experience with foreign cars but were looking for something bigger.

Research was not talking to those people, though, these team members argued. No wonder they were getting skewed results. All of these people were oriented toward traditional American styling. Research should isolate what the team thought of as the country's trendsetters. After all, adventurous consumers, not cautious ones, would buy a unique car.

While asking questions about cars, Goldfarb was also classifying the participants as "style progressives" or traditionalists. Through attitudinal surveys, style progressives showed that they were not afraid of change but in fact looked for it.

Ford wanted to talk to these people, because the Taurus was being positioned as a progressive vehicle, and would appeal initially to those most accepting of novelty. The other consumers would follow. To avoid winding up with only a tiny minority of the population, the term *progressive* was defined to include 50 percent of the nation. To be designated as such was not a question of age but of attitude. Different age groups could be interested in the same vehicle if they held the same outlook on life. Design progressives were people who were interested in new objects, new ways of looking at things, those willing to take more risks than others.

Progressive-minded drivers, for example, liked Taurus's curved dash. It looked European and sporty, considerably different from the traditional American straight-across instrument panel. But more conservative buyers didn't want that; they liked a "normal" instrument panel, which stretched the width of the vehicle.

While the Team Taurus members knew they were creating something unique and for progressives, a visit to the biannual 1981 Frankfurt auto show reassured them that the world's designers were working in concert. Audi displayed its soon-to-be-released 100 (sold as the Audi 5000 in the U.S.), and a number of other German manufacturers premiered prototypes of styling themes for the 1980s. Everyone seemed to be thinking along the same lines. The boxy look was giving way to aerodynamic styling, rounded edges, and a general sense of robustness. Indeed, Audi's and Ford's styling directions were so similar that when the Taurus was later launched, Ford would be accused of copying the design of the 5000.

After the July 1981 research sessions, the designers decided to lengthen the car yet again. In December 1981, after a redesign of the car, they were tested once more. Five different full-size fiberglass versions of the Taurus body were shipped to Chicago. Over four hundred participants again compared the shapes to unbranded versions of the Ford LTD, Cutlass Ciera, and Opel Senator. They also had a first look at the proposed interiors. These featured full-size passenger bucks, interior compartments with nonfunctional controls, meant to look like the real thing. But they were still mock-ups, handmade prototypes that didn't look quite like a production interior.

This time three of the five reworked models were judged higher than they had been in the first test, but they scored below their competitors. While they were still not liked, the new versions did continue to be perceived as aerodynamic.

The designers worked on two variations of the basic design. Called "LTD" and "Marquis," the latter featured a more aerodynamic front end, reminiscent of the ultimate production vehicle, while the LTD used a more traditional front, with four standard recessed rectangular headlamps rather than flush aerodynamic lights. A further variation of the Marquis, known as Marquis II, had its third c pillar (the vertical pillar between the rear and side windows) painted black, rather than the car's actual body color.

The next focus group was held in Santa Ana, a working- and middle-class suburb of Los Angeles, in March 1982. Respondents did not like the LTD version—with the regular-looking front end—at all, but they did like the Marquis version. Ablondi was relieved. This was a major step forward from the Taurus's initial poor showing.

To management Ablondi reported: "Among midsize and basic large buyers, the Taurus designs are competitive with the GM entries—Ciera and Celebrity—although still weaker than the Opel Senator and the 1983 LTD. It is clear that the market will accept advanced designs as long as the concept is right."

In July 1982, the car was configured as a six- rather than a five-passenger vehicle. With gas prices stabilized, the company could now afford to position its car as a traditional-sized, American family sedan. In October of that year, the car was redesigned again. At a focus group in Los Angeles, the new version, now looking essentially like the production Taurus, scored higher than the Chevrolet Celebrity, though not as high as the Datsun Maxima.

The car's design still had been bested by the Datsun, but its popularity had risen over the past two years. Remaining negativity, Ablondi knew, may very well have been due to the unfamiliarity of the shape. Testing and tinkering couldn't go on forever, though. At some point a leap of faith was required. Goldfarb tried to reassure the Ford people that by the time this version of the car was ready for the market, the market would be ready for the car.

In November, the product-planning subcommittee signed off on the design. A month later, the project came before the board of directors for final approval. The board had been following the design changes, and by now they were quite familiar with the car. It was agreed: this design was ready to be taken to market.

Suddenly, Don Petersen interjected. "I'm not so sure if this design is really radical enough. I'd like to see another rendering of the front of the car before we make any final decision."

Lou Ross was in shock. "I'm in love with this design," he thought. "Why should we change it now?" He was also worried that spending another three months on a redesign would unacceptably delay the project. "There was the clock running, we had to get on with it, and the design we had was an excellent choice. In addition, the North American automotive group felt that based on the research, we had a pretty good design.

"I decided I had to get the whole North American product committee together to discuss this. I got Phil Benton, the head of sales operations, myself, even the vehicle vice-presidents, the head of the Ford Division and the head of the Lincoln-Mercury Division. We got together and said, 'Nope, as a group we're going to make a hard stand on this. This design is where we want to stay. We don't want to go beyond that.'

"Pete came back and said, 'Okay, I guess that's the way we're going to go.' He seldom wanted to overturn a group decision. So he went with our decision, and he wasn't uncomfortable about it," Ross said. "I felt good about that. That was a turning point in the program. It was a tough enough project to do, and it was already reaching far enough." There would be no more second-guessing. The project was now a definite go.

Six of the ten research stages had been completed. In the coming months Goldfarb and the team would test various names as well as customer response to the car's pricing and marketplace positioning. As the vehicles literally came together over the next few years, new research groups were asked to evaluate seat materials, ride, handling, and the ease of use of instruments and switches.

Research studies revealed that consumers were not always pleased. When evaluating seat fabrics, the designers decided, as with much else on the Taurus, to start from scratch. A wide range of seat fabrics was considered, but they knew that Americans preferred muted, simple tones, compared to Europeans, who liked much more adventurous colors and prints. Bold green and orange pinstripes against a gray background, even bright plaids, regularly popped up on European autos. But those same cars received toned-down materials before they were shipped off to buyers in the States.

Mimi Vandermolen personally favored dramatic colors and patterns. Her supervisor, a British-born designer, came up with a whole variety of English tweeds, which he was convinced would be a big hit with the public. "He came up with all these bad fabrics," Ray Ablondi said. "But everyone was afraid to say anything because they thought he must know what he was talking about, because he was British and he was a designer. They tested very badly, and we eliminated them."

Ford's efforts at learning customer desires paid off in new design approaches, but the Japanese remained a step ahead. While Ford was trying to learn from the customer what they wanted, the Japanese were trying to figure that out themselves. The now ubiquitous cup holder was introduced into Japanese cars after a research team traveled the California freeways and noticed that many drivers drank coffee while on the road. The idea didn't come from a driver's suggestion, but from an executive's observation.

That type of research is much more difficult but often more fruitful. The Japanese electronics manufacturers have been successful because they have created markets where none existed before. No consumer wanted a videotape recorder, a telephone answering machine, or a Walkman before those items came to market. The need was created, and the demand followed.

Consumers are not good at suggesting what new amenities they would like, but tend to comment on what things they'd like changed. The reason is based on a simple principle of learning theory taught to beginning psychology students: it's much easier to recognize something than to try to recall it. As a result, multiple-choice tests are easier to complete than essay exams. And drivers can point out what they like or dislike about a cup holder, but can't as easily think about inventing one in the first place.

Ford research people were not familiar with this basic learning principle. Japanese car manufacturers sent researchers to the United States, where they were instructed to literally move in with American families to observe how they interacted with everyday objects. Ford, on the other hand, was content with asking consumers what they wanted. When they asked them if they wanted cup holders, the response was overwhelmingly no.

The Taurus wanted to build its reputation, though, on what Lew Veraldi liked to call these "tremendous trifles." As the Japanese were already learning, installing such creature comforts as coin and cup holders, passenger assist handles, a lighted vanity mirror in the sun visor added up to a perception that the company cared about its customers' comfort. If Ford got enough of them wrong, consumers would feel that Ford was unable to please them.

The statistical and qualitative analyses that Ford was perfecting in its research techniques also couldn't substitute for plain common sense. In one telling example, it had been decided that the station wagon version of the cars would have a split sixty–forty rear seat; 40 percent of the seat would fold down to accept long articles, while 60 percent of it would remain up to allow two passengers to sit in the back in relative comfort.

The team went back and forth trying to figure out on which side of the car the 60-percent portion should be placed. There seemed no logical reason to favor either side. The only solution, they decided, was to conduct another research study to see if there was any innate consumer preference.

"Hold it," an annoyed Joel Pitcoff piped up, "who's going to sit in this backseat when it's half folded down?"

"Children," one team member answered.

"And where is one kid going to be while the other kid is getting into the back?"

"Outside, waiting to get in."

"Right," Pitcoff continued. "Do you want that kid standing outside on the curb or in the street?"

"On the curb," was the meek reply.

"Right. So we put the sixty percent side of the seat nearest the curb. Anybody got any problems with that?" he demanded.

The room was silent. The solution just required a little thought.

Consumer research also showed that customers did not like the Taurus's steering characteristics. American cars had historically favored loose power steering, the kind that allowed a driver to turn the wheel with one pinky. With so many straight roads and freeways, driving in the U.S. often involved little more than climbing behind the wheel and pointing the car in a particular direction. Lew Veraldi had spent considerable time in Europe, where road conditions were vastly different. With few freeways and wide boulevards, Europeans needed a car that responded quickly to the need to pass an oncoming truck on a winding, mountainous road, or negotiate a traffic-filled roundabout in the middle of London.

Veraldi wanted tight steering on the Taurus, but as soon as he tested it with consumers, the results came back negative. Still, Veraldi didn't budge on his choice. He was convinced that tighter steering was the way to go with the Taurus, and nothing was going to make him change his mind.

"What's the status on the steering?" Don Petersen asked Veraldi during one of their meetings.

"I'm going with the tighter steering," Veraldi told him.

"But I thought your research pointed in the opposite direction," Petersen said.

"Look, I'm not going to listen to the consumer research. It's just a matter of people getting used to the steering. If I change it, the car won't be responsive. It'll destroy the aesthetics of the Taurus. I refuse to change my mind."

"All right, Lew," Petersen said. "Go with the tighter steering if you think it's right."

John Risk agreed with Lew's stance, but was embarrassed by his presentation. Risk didn't understand why Lew always had to come on like gangbusters when a civilized discussion would have accomplished the same thing.

Veraldi won the battle on steering, but he lost the battle on wood. Jack Telnack had decided that the interior would have none. But when consumers began to drive the car, they complained that the exterior looked dull. "Where is the wood and the chrome?" they wanted to know.

They didn't care if it was fake or real. Marty Goldfarb

had found out that customers couldn't tell the difference—
at least not for four or five years until it started peeling off.
Wood made them feel that if they were paying $13,000 for
a car, they were getting something for their money.

"The traditionalists liked wood," Veraldi said, "so we
put some on the instrument panel about eight months before production. The tightrope we were walking was: could
we bring families into the new Ford look and new Ford
dynamics without alienating all those people that still liked
traditional cars?"

As launch time approached, some top management
were plain scared. Lou Ross, for one, thought that the front
end of the car was too radical. Others wanted to tone down
the interior of the doors. "They thought we should drop
the doors and go with cheap doors like GM uses on a lot
of its cars," Vandermolen said. "GM has these cheap doors
which are really flat cardboard with some very thin poly-
foam formed over the board. The armrests and all the other
pieces are applied on. The door is squarer and flatter.
Management thought, 'This Taurus door is so new, are we
really doing the right thing?' They were very nervous."

Telnack, Vandermolen, and their team would not accept this eleventh-hour change, one that would have severely compromised the interior, making it nothing out of
the ordinary. Vandermolen and others talked at length to
the executives, trying to calm them down. "Give it a
chance. Don't get so nervous," Vandermolen cautioned.
"It'll work out. Trust us."

Design could learn from market research. Yet, they
could not become slaves of the data. Ultimately, they had
to trust their own instincts, a reaction that even now was
being systematically discouraged by top management.

11

SAVING FORD FOR ITS WORKERS

Ford's designers worked several minutes' drive from Glass House, the company's executive headquarters, but the problems that faced Phil Caldwell and his top lieutenants were always close to their thoughts. Telnack, Vandermolen, and their team were well aware that their work on the Taurus was taking place at a time when the company had little financial cushion. The massive layoffs at Ford—85,000 U.S. jobs were lost between 1978 and 1981—underscored the major restructuring that Phil Caldwell was conducting to keep the company afloat until Ford's new models began to appear.

The large number of dismissals that Caldwell felt necessary naturally embittered the hourly factory workers and their United Auto Workers union. Even in the best of times, company executives had failed to help integrate the UAW and its workers into the manufacturing process. Now that its losses were high, Ford officials somehow expected employees to rally to their side, but the conditions under which these people worked precluded that.

Assembly-line work was little short of slave drudgery. The workers were paid a good wage, but that didn't make up for the fact they were treated like children. Management had no interest in their opinions. The old union complaint, "We don't pay you to think," was unfortunately too true. The goal was to produce. What came out at the end of the line didn't matter, as long as it was built well enough to be driven out of the factory. Workers who offered suggestions to improve quality were told to shut up. Sign off on the part, sign off on the car, and don't worry about its problems.

The UAW had tried to make changes in Ford's feudal system. Along with General Motors and Chrysler, the company had pledged to improve its working atmosphere by involving its employees in the decision-making process. Even before a contract provision mandated it, a Quality of Worklife program had been started in the early seventies by General Motors. As a first step the company had hired some industrial psychologists in an attempt to understand better how to improve conditions. In their 1973 contracts the Big Three agreed to formalize the idea.

Don Ephlin was very familiar with the General Motors' employee program. As former head of the union's GM department and later assistant to Leonard Woodcock, the union's president, he worked at length to get it implemented. For the past seven years progress had been made at GM regarding management–employee relations, but nothing positive was happening at Ford.

Even in 1980, the company was giving the notion of employee involvement lip service at best. As administrative assistant, Ephlin had tried to make progress but got nowhere. The Ford executive in charge of employee relations, Sid McKenna, wasn't interested in changing the power structure. "He just won't budge," Ephlin thought after several meetings with him. "He's an autocrat, he doesn't care about employee relations. McKenna's in the traditional Ford mold: 'It's worked this way for forty years, we'll do it the same way again.' "

McKenna's stubbornness was no secret to other Ford executives. "McKenna treats Ephlin like a baby," observed Tom Page. "No wonder they're not making any progress."

Page himself had been hankering for years to change the lot of Ford workers, because he knew that by doing so he'd improve morale. His diversified products factories became test beds for a number of experiments in workplace democracy, most of which worked. Productivity increased, costs decreased, and jobs were saved.

Ephlin, a stocky, soft-spoken man with a ready smile, was appointed head of the union's Ford department in 1980, just months after his intransigent counterpart at the company was replaced. Ephlin was a longtime union man who had supported the UAW from his first days on the GM assembly line in Framingham, Massachusetts, in 1947, before there even was representation at the plant. He quickly became involved in union activities. Because of his experience in accounting, he took charge of the local's credit union, becoming president of the local in 1955. The job became so demanding that he had to quit his GM job the next year to work full-time for the union. Four years later, the UAW moved him to Detroit.

The attitude of many Ford managers was that workers looked out only for themselves, with no interest in improving either their colleagues' lives or the company's health. Senior management was not immune to that attitude. Even Tom Page, a strong advocate of worker participation in the decision-making process, held union workers in disdain. "Union people are incredibly selfish," Page said. "They forget about the unemployed. If there's some overtime available, they want to work it themselves. It's more money in their pocket and they don't want to share." In another growing problem area, when layoffs occurred, many thought that as long as it was a woman losing her job, it really didn't matter. "They're housewives and they don't mind," Page said. "It would be tougher if they were all men in the plant. Even if they lose their jobs, there's still a second income in the household, and the women could always use the time at home."

Those kinds of attitudes exasperated Ephlin. The idea that a top executive who made "unconscionable" annual bonuses, whose salary in the 1970s was often twenty times that of an assembly worker's (in the 1980s, this would climb to thirty and forty times as high) had the nerve to call a worker greedy for wanting to work overtime infuriated him.

"That's crap on all counts," Ephlin said. "The union has pressed for restrictions on overtime consistently when people are on layoff. Ford from the early 1980s never increased their capacity. Instead, they ran 120 percent of capacity, far more overtime than was justifiable. Of course an individual worker would like to get twelve hours' pay for eight hours on Saturday. But in principle the union proposed restrictions on overtime long before this crisis, and the company resisted."

On the related issue, he noted, "Women are not working because they want to. They're working because it's necessary to take care of families. Of course they minded being laid off. Many didn't qualify for benefits for long. We had lawsuits over some of the layoffs, claiming sexual discrimination, because in some plants where corporations didn't hire women for years, all the women had the lowest seniority. So when you eliminated the second shift you eliminated all the women. So we had some serious problems."

At a critical juncture for Ford, the company's hard line did not prevail. The appointment of Peter Pestillo as Sid McKenna's successor was an unusual choice, for he was recruited from B. F. Goodrich, a company outside the industry. This was a good sign, as far as Ephlin was concerned. "Somebody at Ford knew they had to make a change." Despite the enmity between the UAW and the company, these two believed that they could work together.

Pestillo had an uncanny knack, certainly unusual in a corporate executive, of understanding the needs of both workers and management. This quality surprised Ephlin, but it drew the two close together. When a senior Ford executive shortly thereafter made disparaging remarks to the press about the inability of their employees to perform quality work, Pestillo came to the rescue. He understood that such comments spoiled the atmosphere that the company was trying to develop, and set workers against management. He spoke to his colleagues to ensure that such statements were not made again.

Pestillo's conciliatory attitude was shared by those at the top. Ford was in trouble, and the company needed the union leader's support. As soon as Ephlin took up his new post, Don Petersen and Phil Caldwell were anxious to see him. They wanted economic relief, and they wanted Ephlin to understand how jeopardized his workers' jobs really were.

"My God, Donald," Caldwell exclaimed to Ephlin, "don't your people understand the terrible problem we're facing?"

"No, they don't, Phil. How could the average worker know anything about the business? You never told them anything over all these years. When Ford was highly successful, you didn't share information. When you suddenly say you're losing money, you don't have a great deal of credibility out there."

Caldwell pleaded, "You have to make them understand how bad things are at this company."

Layoffs were a new phenomenon for the UAW. In the past, because permanent layoffs had been virtually nonexistent, the union had never bothered to fight for protection against them. The United States was at the top of the list of major industrialized countries that did not protect its workers from plant closings. Workers could be let go without warning and without recompense, no matter how long they had worked at a company.

In 1980, Ephlin was already watching the hemorrhaging of his workers' jobs, and a consequent decrease in the strength of his union. Ford was losing billions and laying off thousands. Work was being "outsourced," transferred to other countries where labor was cheaper and quality better. Even for the new Escort, the Batavia, Ohio, transmission assembly plant, opened that year, produced only half the expected number of units. The rest of the anticipated business went to Mazda in Hiroshima. Between 1979 and 1986, the union would lose more than half of its Ford workers, dropping from 200,000 to 95,000.

Ephlin agreed with management's notion that if the company was going to produce a new midsized family car unlike one ever seen before, it had to be of high quality. But quality wasn't the workers' problem to solve. "The level of quality one achieves is primarily a management decision," Ephlin said. "The workers can help solve problems if they want to. But even if the worker makes junk, management makes the decision whether to ship that junk out or to fix it. And if they say to a worker, 'This is the job we want you to do,' and the parts don't fit, there's nothing a worker can do about it. As of now, when a worker says, 'We ought to fix this,' management says, 'Mind your own business.' "

Quality was not going to change overnight after a management pep talk. The same workers had been on the assembly line for years; they were not suddenly going to alter their work styles even if they knew that the company was doing poorly. They had little control over their workplace. In an assembly plant, the machinery was already laid out in a particular order decided on by engineers, not them.[1]

During recent contract renewals, Ford negotiators often had claimed that the assembly-line workers' higher labor costs were the sole reason why American manufacturers could not compete with Japanese cars. In particular, Ephlin was tired of hearing about a proclaimed $1,700 financial advantage per car that Ford claimed the Japanese had. One day he confronted Phil Caldwell about it.

"Phil, I'm fed up with hearing about this Landed Cost Differential nonsense. It's garbage. Why should we believe you? Give us the numbers to prove it."

Ephlin suggested that Ford and the union study the issue to learn why the differential existed. The union would pay for the consultant to do the confidential research if Ford agreed to open up its books and convinced Mazda to do the same. "All right," agreed Caldwell, "we'll do it."

Unbeknownst to Caldwell, Ephlin had already briefed Ira Magaziner, a well-known industry consultant, about his idea. Magaziner had agreed to conduct the study, and after extensive research he found that there was a cost differential. But it wasn't caused solely by paying American workers more. A host of factors contributed to the differential, including executive pay scales and plant overhead, as well as employee incompetence. The study gave Ephlin ammunition with which to answer his critics who charged that U.S. workers were lazy slobs who were only concerned with making money.

Ephlin had proposed the research not just to get comparative data, however, but to change fundamentally the balance of power between Ford and the UAW. "The traditional role of the union was to handle the bargaining process, grievances, negotiate crisis bargaining on a plant-by-plant basis," Ephlin said. "A purely negative, reactive role. Management does something, the union reacts. Every three years you go into bargaining and you bargain. During this period we changed the role from purely negative to positive."

Ephlin understood the straits that Ford faced. But getting his workers to sympathize with the company was a daunting prospect. Union leadership began its campaign, as Ephlin and others spoke to union councils across the country. The task was difficult. "How could the mighty

Ford Motor Company be losing money?" workers wanted to know. They refused to believe it. To many of them, it sounded like another corporate snow job. Ford was paying the price for their years of deception.

Ephlin preached continuously to Tom Page that the workers had to be trusted if the company expected to improve the quality of its product. Ephlin wanted the workers to have the right to voice an opinion on every aspect of their jobs. After all, who knew better than the one doing the work?

This idea angered many of the old-time senior production-line managers. Many of them had started out as hourly assembly-line workers themselves. They had been smarter and more ambitious than their colleagues, and as a result, they had risen to a salaried position. Even though many were just one notch higher than their former cohorts on the line, they had become management. They had spent years bossing workers around. Now the men who had fought so hard to get to the top were going to be told that they had to relinquish power to the very guys who had never made it.

Ephlin spent long hours talking to his union about the company's problems, reassuring them that Ford was ready to discuss the improvement of working conditions. At the same time, Tom Page was working with his various plants to institute more direct control by his workers. The schemes that Page was considering had already been in operation in Japan, and he was eager to start some here. He approached Ephlin with a suggestion: the two of them go to Japan to learn firsthand how the Japanese involve their workers in the manufacturing process. "I'm ready to introduce changes in our plants. I'm not trying to buck you, Don. I'm trying to get your help," Page said.

Despite their differences in philosophy, Page liked working with Ephlin. He greatly respected the union leader, calling him "the most intelligent union man I have ever met. He understood what was happening in the whole auto industry." Page added, "He didn't just go around bashing the Japanese. Ephlin knew that we had problems and he was working very constructively to solve them, in contrast to many of the union people who kept saying, 'Why don't you go to Washington and just shut off imports?' Ephlin was a learner. He went to Japan and looked at their factories, and understood full well the implications of our not becoming competitive in this country."

Ephlin made several trips to Japan over the next few years. He went not because he was so enamored with the Japanese way of working, but because the Ford executives seemed to be. "Everybody's telling us about the Japanese," he said. "How marvelous everything is over there. Management people come back and they tell you, 'Boy, the workers over there are great. They work, they never go to the bathroom, they work twice as hard as you,' and all this stuff." This Ephlin had to see for himself.

In 1981 Ford's Peter Pestillo and Ephlin took a trip together. They were joined by their staffs and six union leaders from various plants, including transmission, engine, assembly, tool and die, and the company's steel mill. The Japanese were willing to let them tour their plants, for they had not forgotten that after the war, the same favor had been bestowed upon them by the American automobile industry. When a Japanese assembly plant was visited, the assembly plant union leader toured the facility and made careful notes. The same procedure was followed with each plant they toured. Upon their return, each team member was responsible for giving a report to senior union people so they could learn how to improve their own procedures.

The Japanese workers were indeed dedicated to quality, Ephlin found. Japan was excelling, he thought, because they had no choice. If they were going to build an automotive industry, they couldn't rely on their own country for profits. "The unions there had a pact of sorts with management," Ephlin concluded. "To thrive in a competitive world, they had to export. And if you're going to export you've got to beat the other guy, so you have to have high quality. It's a national cause, really. Unlike in America, where our main thing is to blame the other guy."

The UAW's 1979 Ford contract would expire ten months hence in September 1982. Ephlin was concerned that as domestic automobile sales weakened, more and more factory jobs were going to be lost. Ford officials were badgering the UAW, complaining that without a change in the contract with workers, they would go under. Ephlin thought that might be true. In any case, his first goal was to stop the loss of jobs. "I approached our international executive board and said, 'Let's open the agreement early.' That idea was rejected, for political reasons. The board didn't think that we could successfully get our people to support such an effort. If we did it at Ford, we had to do it at GM at the same time. Also, there was a danger to doing this. Ford wanted relief, and you're giving away something you've already got."

Soon General Motors came to the union and proposed their own early contract modifications. GM, which needed not only to reduce its costs but to increase its sales as well, proposed such an interesting and novel plan that the union decided to start negotiations with them.

The company's idea was to ask workers to cut their salaries. It, in turn, would also cut costs in other ways. The resultant decrease in expenditures would allow GM to lower the price of their cars. The price reductions would spur increased sales, and then everyone would profit. It was a great plan, and if negotiations succeeded, Ford would virtually be forced to accept the same deal.

The two sides were unable to agree on other issues, however, and negotiations stalled, much to Ford's relief. Whereas cutting wages in exchange for cutting prices made sense for GM, it could have spelled disaster for Ford. Ephlin noted, "GM is much more highly integrated. If we reduced wages one dollar per hour, GM would get much higher savings than Ford. But whatever GM did in the marketplace, Ford would have been obligated to follow, because GM was always the price leader."

After the impasse with GM, some UAW officials wondered if anything could be hammered out with Ford. Ephlin wasn't giving up hope. He convinced UAW president Doug Fraser that they at least had to try. Fraser supported his efforts before the union board, and they in turn agreed to let him negotiate with Ford.

Discussions began in February 1982. This was nothing like a typical negotiating session. Neither side came to the bargaining table with a list of demands to increase their power or profits. Both parties were hurting. Several factories had already closed, including the Flat Rock, Michigan, foundry which twelve years prior had been touted as the most modern in the world. Ephlin was prepared to make concessions that in the short term would hurt even more.

The subsequent negotiations were the shortest in memory. "This was unlike any other bargaining I've ever been in. Our world was falling apart, and we had to do what we could to save it," Ephlin said. "In 1980 and 1981, a lot of people in America in high places were ready to write off the auto industry. 'Who needs it?' Well, I happen to think we needed it, and I think what we wanted to do at Ford and GM [in cutting costs and increasing job security], with little or no help from the government, would be a real achievement."

In a normal contract discussion, hoards of people converged on Ford World Headquarters, the traditional negotiating site. Don Ephlin alone would bring his twenty staff people, including technical experts and actuaries. Representatives of the twelve locals would also turn up for the bargaining. The meeting room would be filled to overflowing. For this session, the room was virtually empty. Just four people took part in these extraordinary talks: Ephlin and UAW president Doug Fraser, Ford's Peter Pestillo and his assistant.

The normal sixty-day deadline to conclude negotiations was thrown out. "If we're going to do something, let's do it," Ephlin told Pestillo. "If we can't, the hell with it. We'll see you in September."

Discussions were helped by the personal rapport between Ephlin and Pestillo. "Pete Pestillo is a very unorthodox kind of labor-relations person," Ephlin said. "And he was billed by the press when he came here as an egotistical, ambitious hot dog. I found him to be a very fine guy to work with. He had a very good feel for hourly workers and the politics of the industry. He had a great ability to influence the Ford hierarchy. When he and I were working toward an end, he would make sure that the top brass at Ford understood what we were doing. And he didn't make speeches or do things that would hamper the process. We approached things together to solve problems. The press used to make fun of us. They called us 'The Pete and Don Show,' because we did so many interviews together."

Negotiations went quickly but not always smoothly. In just three weeks they were nearing a conclusion. At the last minute a Ford executive present at the meetings balked. "We need more relief than you're giving us," he said. Pestillo arranged for the executive to sit down privately with Don Ephlin. When the executive reiterated that he wanted more union concessions, Ephlin scolded him.

"Doug Fraser and I have to be the ones who decide how much this union can give. We're the ones who have to bring this contract before the executive council for approval, not you. First of all, there's a limit to what can be done. Second, it behooves you to decide whether you want to go before the world and say Ford lost and continue that image of being losers. Or do you want to hold your head up and say 'Together the union and Ford have achieved something great. And we're going to go forward together'? You decide, because you've got everything you're going to get from us."

In the end, the Ford executive capitulated. The new deal contained significant concessions on the part of the union, all in an attempt to save its members' jobs. The

UAW agreed to help Ford save money by cutting back on employee costs, and Ephlin tried to do it in the least painful way. The payment of some cost-of-living increases that were due to take place automatically during the life of the contract were delayed. But the major concession was a retrenchment on paid holidays, a chip the UAW had gained six years earlier. Under the arrangement, workers were to receive nine holidays in 1982, in addition to the regular vacation periods. The days were taken in rotation, with Ford bringing in another worker to take that person's place. For each employee Ford was paying seventy-two hours worth of wages that were not being worked. The entire program was cut.

In return, Ford agreed not to close any more plants during the life of the new contract. Outsourcing of components would be limited. Ford could still contract elsewhere for parts, but they would first see if a Ford plant could provide the same item at a competitive price. Also, any laid-off long-term worker would be guaranteed lifetime benefits, a provision that would cost Ford dearly if too many people were let go. And to limit the salary decreases under the new contract, Ford agreed to institute profit sharing among its hourly employees.[2]

One of the most far-reaching programs was Ford's agreement to introduce a training fund, to be jointly administered by the company and the union. Ford contributed five cents per hour per worker to retrain laid-off workers for other jobs. The program evolved into a major component of what came to be known as Employee Involvement. "We train people when there are layoffs, but we also train employees who are continuing to work, to improve their skill levels, to allow them to even change careers. Some of the earlier training programs would take long-term unemployed and train them for some high-level jobs, but you couldn't get there from here."

"You need computer programmers," Ephlin told Caldwell. "We have people with degrees working in the plant that with very little effort can become programmers.

You move those people up, and you open up jobs on the bottom." "All right," Caldwell said, "we'll fund the EI program."

The negotiations went relatively smoothly, but the process was dimpled by dissension within the union. Not everyone at the UAW agreed with Ephlin's tactics of giving up gains that had been sought for so long. Ephlin saw them as obstructionists who never wanted to give management any concessions. They regarded the deal that he had structured not in terms of the present hard times but in terms of what they would have normally expected to gain. "You can't apply the good-times formula to today and then complain we lost a million dollars," he said. "That's faulty thinking. We never had it to lose."

"The trouble with you, Ephlin, is that you worry more about the Ford Motor Company than you do your own union!" one irate worker shouted at him.

"Look, I don't own one share of Ford stock," Ephlin countered. "If they went bankrupt tomorrow, it wouldn't hurt me one bit. The only problem is, if that happens, you guys are going to get laid off, and I don't know where the hell else to find a hundred thousand good-paying jobs. Do you?"

Ephlin's argument became his battle cry. In later years when involved in negotiations with GM, Ephlin enjoyed saying, "My job is to save the General Motors Corporation for the General Motors workers."

The twelve-man local union committee agreed to accept the new deal. According to UAW rules, Ephlin then had to take the pact before the Ford Council, the union group that oversaw all relations with the company. "Our meeting was held in Chicago. We tried to keep the details of the agreement secret, so we could be the first to tell them, but as usual it leaked out in the press. As we arrived at the hall, there were union people outside from the U.S. and Canada, giving out handbills, telling people to vote no, not to make any concessions."[3] As the meeting began with its typical formalities, Ephlin sat on the podium, not knowing what to expect. After the opening business ended, his assistant introduced him. "I got a standing ovation before I said a word," Ephlin recalled. "It was one of the warmest greetings I had ever experienced in my life."

The representatives listened attentively to his report of the negotiations, and when he had finished, two-thirds of the union rank and file accepted the new deal, a strong vote of confidence considering that they were agreeing to decrease their salaries. Ephlin was relieved. He had always been convinced that his strategy represented the best that the workers could expect. The new pact would save jobs, and the cutbacks would help Ford get itself back on its feet.

The new agreement set the stage for greater cooperation between management and labor. Ephlin stepped up his trips across the country, touring plants, sometimes in the company of Pete Pestillo, other times with Phil Caldwell. The trips were morale boosters meant to show workers that they were being appreciated, that the company and the union were behind them.

It was an unusual tactic for Caldwell, and one that he normally would have avoided. He did not mix well in situations that required shooting the breeze. But Caldwell rose to the occasion, even donning union baseball caps and jackets as he posed in group photographs with the guys and gals.

"When I look back on the agreement," Ephlin said, "I have no regrets. I had a lot of anxiety and concern because Ford was deteriorating, and coming to grips with it quickly enough was the problem. I'm very proud of what I accomplished. But you're never satisfied that you've done enough. I did what I felt was important not for my political career, but for the people whose lives I represented." Labor had sown the seeds. Now management had to show that it knew how to reap the rewards.

12

LEAVE NO STONE UNTURNED

Top Ford management, including Phil Caldwell and Don Petersen, signed off on the final design of the Taurus in November 1982. Now it was time to consider how this car was going to be sold. Soon after the new year, Jack Telnack hosted a gathering of J. Walter Thompson's top Detroit management at Ford's top-secret design center. For JWT general manager Joe Schulte, the meeting was unlike any he had ever experienced.

Schulte oversaw the team responsible for all of Ford's automotive advertising. To help create those ads and a consistent look for the company, Ford executives regularly shared their advance product plans with him, showing photographs and technical descriptions of upcoming vehicles. Thus, Schulte had known about the Taurus for the past year, but until this day he had never been offered a good look at it.

Once past the design center's electric security door and the softly lit executive offices, the five ad men walked down the long corridors to one of the design spaces. The interior of the building opened up into a structure reminiscent of an oversized high school, a cold industrial space flushed with fluorescent light. Its corridors were wide and high, wide enough to easily park several future models and competitive vehicles across its linoleum floor.

As Schulte entered, he found himself in a giant arena, shrunken by the presence of prefabricated offices and free-standing panels. Arrayed before him were twenty-foot drawings of Tauruses sketched at various stages of the car's development.

Jack Telnack hosted. Usually these vehicle-introduction meetings were simple affairs. The ad agency people would be shown "clays" of the upcoming car, and questions would be answered. Today's meeting, however, was an unprecedented show, an elaborate presentation of the history of the Taurus. Telnack took the five JWT guests through the entire evolution of the car, discussing each huge sketch, explaining how the final form had come to be. It was on a par with the fanfare reserved for Ford corporate executives evaluating the worth of a new program.

On an adjoining panel the designers had mounted several pictures of competing vehicles, to illustrate styling cues that had been adapted for the Taurus. As Schulte looked at the photo of the upcoming Audi 5000, a car that bore an unmistakable resemblance to the new Ford, he sensed some of the designers resented the fact that a European manufacturer was thinking along the same cutting edge. Yet they were also proud of their accomplishment, Schulte could see. The photographs of Audi and the other competitors were not road maps to follow, but signs that they had been going in the right direction all along.

In one corner of the room were full-sized painted clay

models of the approved Taurus and Sable designs. Interior bucks—complete mock-ups of the driver's and passengers' compartments—were nearby. Schulte was very impressed. "Jack, you've really got something here," he told Telnack. "This is wonderful."

Virtually every JWT executive involved in the project thought the car was a hit. Kinder Essington, the agency's creative director on the Ford account, first saw the car a few months later at a focus group in Fort Worth. Essington, who would write most of the copy for the car's introductory print campaign, regularly attended focus groups. He felt it was invaluable to get a sense of what consumers found interesting, attractive, and important about the cars that JWT was going to promote. This day, waiting in the huge auditorium for a group to start, Essington wandered around the floor, looking at the identically painted gray cars lined up for consumer inspection. Suddenly his eyes focused on one unusual vehicle. He was shocked. "Holy cow! Look at that!" he exclaimed, eyeing the Taurus. He related later that he "damned near dropped dead, it was so pretty."

This had been the opinion of JWT representatives from the very beginning, even when they had first seen black-and-white photographs of the proposed Taurus. William Jeanes, JWT's senior vice-president on the Ford account, had loved the car the moment he saw it. He was positive that the car was going to be a winner. "This car is light-years ahead of anything anyone in the U.S. or Europe is doing," Jeanes told Telnack. "Don't worry about how Ma and Pa Kettle in Peoria will accept this. They'll get into it. It may look radical now, but by the time it comes to market, it'll fit right in, it won't look like a Buck Rogers dream anymore. Please, guys, just don't screw this up."

"Look, William, don't worry," Telnack said. "If I didn't want the car to look this way, I wouldn't have designed it this way. This is exactly how the Taurus will look when it's manufactured. We're not changing a thing."

The ad men were relieved to hear it. Although the

agency always put their all into a campaign, they were glad to know that they truly had a product that they could get behind, personally as well as professionally. They cared because they all loved automobiles. They loved talking about them almost as much as driving them. The soft-spoken, low-key Schulte spent hours discussing the differences between versions of cars sold in the U.S. and those sold overseas, the merits of various marques, the ups and downs of the industry. Midget racing was one of his loves; he kept an immaculately restored machine in his garage that he proudly showed off to guests. For his part, William Jeanes would leave the agency in 1984 to become editor of *Car and Driver*, one of the top three car magazines in the U.S.

By the time the November 1982 gathering was finished, Schulte realized that the Taurus was going to be an exceptional car, and an important car for Ford. Now he and his team had to come up with an exceptional advertising campaign. Schulte was prepared to bring in people from JWT offices around the world if that's what it took to make the difference.

The agency had very specific goals for its campaign. Initially, few would know the name *Taurus*, so JWT had to find a way to make it mean more than the bull in the zodiac. Taurus had to come to symbolize an important all-new family car. By the launch time, Ford's public relations office would have concluded its own extensive campaign, one that would expose the car to a wide segment of the public through preview articles in automotive and general interest publications. But there was no guarantee that a reporter would write favorably about the Taurus, or mention what Ford felt was necessary to stimulate sales. That's why JWT's commercials and print ads were so important. While advance publicity would prime the pump, JWT had to properly position the car to help motivate people to get inside a showroom and actually drive the vehicle.

Sable advertising was handled by Young and Rubicam, Lincoln-Mercury's advertising agency. Throughout the developmental process Ford's head of sales and marketing would keep an eye on both shops' campaigns to make sure that they had unique thrusts. The advertising for the Taurus and Sable was unlikely to clash in any case. From the beginning the cars had been designed to appeal to slightly different markets. The Sable was seen as somewhat more adventurous in design. The car was made longer to distinguish it from the Taurus, and the rearmost *C* pillar was blacked out to give the car a glassier look. The idea was that it should attract a more upscale audience.

J. Walter Thompson had another, equally important advertising goal. Its ads had to help put the magic back into the Ford name. "Ford" had to stand for something besides "fix or repair daily." The public had to perceive the car as the *Ford* Taurus, not the Taurus, and that overall perception needed to be positive. The positive image generated by the success of the car would then transfer to other vehicles as consumers began to associate Ford with quality.

The public would be ready for such a perceptual change, Schulte felt, because the claim would soon have some substance. Ford had begun rising from its darkest days of poor quality and tremendous losses. Sales were turning around. The Escort had been launched in 1980 and was a best-seller both in the U.S. and Europe. Schulte also knew that the redesigned, "aero" Lincoln Mark VII would be introduced in 1984 and then the compact Tempo/Topaz twins.

A common symbol was needed, Schulte felt. He had always loved the blue Ford corporate oval that spelled out the company name in flowing script. The logo had appeared at the top of the radiator of its classic models and was still affixed to the trunk lids of European vehicles. But it had been absent for years in the U.S. because the company had not wanted to sully its solid performers with the bad image of its parent. Now it was time for a change.

Schulte and another JWT colleague lobbied extensively for the return of the logo on American models. It reappeared first on the Escort and then spread to other cars.

Schulte also lobbied for the creation of a new product slogan, one that would hopefully have a long life. In the 1970s and '80s, corporate automotive advertising lines changed almost as often as car designs. As soon as the public became accustomed to one theme, a manufacturer's ad agency dreamed up a new one. In the early 1970s it was "When America needs a better idea, Ford puts it on wheels." Toward the end of the decade, it had become "Ford has a better idea."

Actually, "Better Idea" first appeared in the 1960s, used as a corporate-wide slogan. Replete with the obligatory light bulb, print ads and TV commercials of the times extolled those ideas, such as a two-sided key for easier entry and a dual-opening tailgate in its station wagons. By the end of the 1970s, the Ford car division resurrected the slogan for itself. Then, after 1980's successful Escort launch, the tag "Look out world, here comes Ford" became the next new theme. The agency knew at the time that it didn't have much of substance to promote for the next few years, so it selected this effervescent, upbeat, but vacuous phrase as an appropriate cover for a lack of new products.

The imminent introduction of the 1983 Thunderbird, Ford's first aerodynamic car, spurred the development of the next ad line. The company needed a new one because it wanted to talk about its new products, ones that were breaking away from its past styles.

Several copywriters at JWT were put to work to come up with appropriate lines. As usual, they brainstormed, jotting down hundreds of ideas, some good and some terrible, as they popped into their heads. Bill Lane, the agency's executive creative director, perused the lists and spotted "Have You Driven a Ford Lately?"

"That's it," he said as he pulled it from the list. The line drew immediate accolades from everyone on the Ford account. William Jeanes, for one, was crazy about it. He loved the fact that it implied that Ford was changing. He felt that it also evoked a confidence in the product. It virtually challenged the consumer to go out to the dealership and see what Ford was so excited about. The line clearly implied that consumers who tried them before and hated them should try them again, because Fords were better today. On the positive side, the slogan also acknowledged that many people had driven Fords. The name was ubiquitous in American life in a way that no other single make could equal.

The new theme was sent to JWT headquarters in New York for top-level approval, since Ford was one of the firm's biggest accounts. The endorsement came without a hitch.

The theme was now ready to be presented to Ford Division. Because the agency wanted to ensure that the company was as excited about the line as they were, they had to do everything they could to put it in as attractive a surrounding as possible. JWT would do its own internal promotion ad to sell the advertising.

A music house was brought in to provide the theme with an appropriate jingle. Sample storyboards and advertisements were created to illustrate the use of the line with Ford's entire campaign for the coming year. Focus groups were assembled by the agency to test the efficacy of the concept.

The theme was first revealed to Ford Division executives at a World Headquarters meeting. The introduction was handled by Bill Lane, widely regarded within the agency as a masterful presenter. As William Jeanes said, Lane "could have sold Ford on an ad line that said nothing more than 'This is a good car.' "

As Lane began speaking to the assembled audience, music began to play softly in the background. As he continued, the tune started to swell until "Have You Driven a Ford?. . . Lately!" reached a crescendo.

A number of Ford executives applauded; they thought

it was a terrific approach. As discussion of the concept continued, Martin Goldfarb rose to speak. "If it was for me to recommend," he said, "I'd recommend we don't go with this theme."

Goldfarb was supported by Ray Ablondi. They both argued that the tone of the ad was inappropriate. The theme was apologetic, and people would interpret it as Ford asking consumers for forgiveness for its past mistakes. The thrust of the line brought up more negatives than positives, they said.

Doug McClure, Ford Division's advertising manager, had apparently been expecting dissension, because he came well prepared to support the line. William Jeanes was fuming; he tried to hold it in, but he knew he was getting angry. "Whenever I get infuriated, my ears turn red, and I felt them warming up then," he said. They and others rose to defend the line, arguing that every focus group had liked it. Yes, negatives were heard, agency people agreed, but the positives outweighed them by far.

The Ford research people were overruled, and the theme won approval. Jeanes was proud of himself. He was glad that he defended the theme. It positioned the company perfectly, he thought.

Several years after the theme's introduction, the company took a look at all its advertising. To assist, J. Walter Thompson had prepared an analysis of the competition's campaigns. As usual, other companies had been changing themes left and right. But "Have You Driven a Ford . . . Lately?" was still running. Perhaps it was time for a change, Ford's vice-president of sales, Phil Benton, suggested.

"Do you recommend that we stay with this line?" he asked William Jeanes.

"Absolutely," Jeanes said. "It's a great line. Don't get rid of it until we can prove that people are tired of it. And they're not. Don't change it just because every other car company is changing theirs. If you do, it'll be a terrible tragedy." Ford decided to keep it. The theme proved so popular that it was used not just for another year but throughout the decade and into the 1990s.

Suggesting names for new vehicles was another part of JWT's service. *Taurus* had never been meant as any more than a working code for the product. Thinking up car marques was always fun, and JWT staffers were eager to contribute. When asked, the agency pulled out a list of names, some stockpiled, others recently gathered through brainstorming sessions.

By 1982, three years before launch, Ford's in-house research department was already investigating the public's response to possible names. The tests constituted stage seven of the ten-step research process. At three different locations around the country, focus groups were asked to judge a selection of words for their attractiveness, imagery, and suitability. Some of the names under investigation included:

Aerostar	Logic
Ancona	Lucerne
Destiny	Lumina
Entry	Optima
Fanta	Orion
Forte	Probe PR-11
Frise	Spectra
Genesis	Telstar
Innotek	Tiara
Integra	Ultra

"Based on the names researched today," JWT wrote in a memo to Ford, "the agency recommends Integra as the most desirable alternative. Orion is our second choice and Optima our third."

Ford had its own extensive lists of suggestions and at a naming meeting convened at Detroit's Renaissance Center, the participants spent several hours tossing possibilities back and forth. As one name after another was offered and then rejected, the meeting began to take on the seriousness of purpose of a college fraternity party.

"I have the perfect name!" William Jeanes shouted to the bunch. "Let's call the car Howard. I've always liked the name. It evokes a real sense of honesty. It's got a certain Jimmy Stewart quality to it, don't you think?"

"No, no," said Doug McClure, "I've got a better one. Let's call the car the Edsel. Our slogan will be 'Edsel: This time we really mean it!' "

Nobody could agree on a new name. And nothing tested higher than the car's working name. So ultimately it remained Taurus. The Integra name would be taken by Honda's Acura division, Lumina by Chevrolet, and Orion by a midsize Ford sold in Europe.

The ultimate challenge to an advertiser is to construct a campaign that "breaks through the clutter," the slew of advertising constantly competing for consumers' attention. Although an agency may spend months researching and producing what it considers a brilliant piece of promotion, it is all meaningless if a magazine reader doesn't give it a second of attention as he flips through the pages.

The process unnerved many corporations, whose executives pushed their agencies to devise outrageous ads to attract attention. Outlandishness doesn't sell products, though, Schulte knew. Nor, on the other hand, does predictability, even though that is the approach that is least likely to anger a client.

The Ford Escort was the world's best-selling car, but creating an ad that screamed "Escort—the world's best-selling automobile" would not have worked. Buyers didn't care about car companies tooting their own horns. They needed to arrive at an understanding of what being the best-selling car in the world actually meant. It was a concept that had as much meaning to the average consumer as the size of a billion dollars.

JWT created an ad that showed a picture of the Escort in front of the name of every car—including those not available in the U.S.—that it outsold. There were hundreds of models mentioned in the ad, from the Fiat Ritmo to the Oldsmobile Cutlass to the Wartburg. The piece was hard to look at without becoming engaged. It invited readers to play a game, to read all the models up and down the columns, to figure out which ones were recognizable. By the time every name had been examined, the consumer was going to be overwhelmed by the quantity and understand the concept of being the best-selling car in the world.

Before any Taurus ads were devised, the agency needed to figure out what concepts they could exploit. Ford regularly provided JWT with preliminary product information to help them in their planning, but the scope and nature of the Taurus project encouraged Ford officials to go overboard. Account executives were provided with voluminous amounts of material about the car's engineering and design features, its intended demographics, its best-in-class approach.

The only way to determine which aspects of the car's overall design to highlight in its kickoff campaign was to test various concepts in focus groups. The features that interested the designers and product planners could be irrelevant to the consumer. The fact that the car had five-mile-per-hour bumpers or rub strips along the doors did not mean that those features, or safety in general, was going to get consumers' attention.

In addition, the public's interest in various concepts was not static. As consumer taste and societal needs came into vogue or lost favor, advertising thrust had to change as well. When Ford first placed seat belts in its 1950s models, the public couldn't have cared less. In the early 1980s, it would have been foolish to emphasize the speed and size of a car's engine when customers were looking for high fuel economy.

JWT took many of the aspects particular to the Taurus and used them to create concept boards, cards that tested ad concepts but were not ads themselves. They were gleaned from a variety of sources, such as the material that Ford had given them and research studies that indicated what people wanted in a new vehicle. Then a photograph of the car was attached to a large card, with specific features of the car written underneath that the agency thought might be of interest to consumers. Under the heading were several paragraphs further explaining the feature.

Producing useful concept boards is difficult. A copywriter wants to write the best copy that she can. A layout artist is not happy producing sloppy work. As a result, concept boards are continually turning into actual advertisements.

To guard against the tendency to make a concept board look too good, the photographs were reproduced in black and white. The agency wanted to ensure that the members of the focus group did not perceive the board as a rendering of a proposed advertisement. If they did, they might confuse a concept with an ad slogan, explanatory paragraphs with actual advertising copy.

The participants in these concept focus groups had never seen the Taurus before. Arrayed in front of them were huge color pictures of it along with other Ford cars, for comparison of its size and other attributes. This way they would have some knowledge of the car whose aspects they were about to judge.

Concept clinics were held throughout the country, in Boston, Atlanta, Chicago, Kansas City, Los Angeles, San Francisco, virtually anywhere but Detroit, where it was next to impossible to recruit people who did not know something about new cars or who worked for car companies.

A wide range of concepts was tested, including the value of aerodynamics, "All-New Car for the '80s," "Beats the Imports," "Finest American Car Ever Built," "World Class," and "Efficiency."

Martin Goldfarb and his associates conducted the focus sessions, while members of the agency watched behind one-way glass, not wanting participants to feel inhibited. One particular hopeful of the agency people was the company's "Best-in-Class" program. Lew Veraldi had given them a special two-hour presentation of the Best-in-Class approach for the Taurus, and they thought it was a great idea to promote in a campaign.

Each concept card carried three or four paragraphs explaining why that theme was significant. For instance, the aerodynamic card explained what aerodynamics was, why it was important, how Taurus's coefficient of drag compared to that of sports cars without losing spaciousness or comfort. The participants then discussed whether the ideas that they just read would favorably dispose them toward a particular car. As usual, Goldfarb kept the meetings on course; if someone criticized a particular line, saying it was badly worded, he would return the discussion to the idea behind the line.

The vehicle was so new and different that it engendered a great deal of confusion and dissatisfaction among consumers. "The car was an absolute shock to the public," Kinder Essington said. "People who saw it said, 'What the hell is that?' People were driving around in Fairmonts, and many of them thought, 'That thing came from the moon. It's too small and I wouldn't like it at all.' "

The responses unnerved Ford executives. They were so worried about the acceptance of the car that they now feared taking a stand on the use of a particular concept for its advertising. If they approved one that later didn't work, they thought they might thoroughly damage the launch.

In their nervousness Ford's advertising executives told the agency to continue to test. And test and test again. Ford brass had to be completely convinced that they were not making a mistake. JWT executives followed the directive, until they had presented well over a hundred different themes to focus groups. The process was an exhausting, trying time for some agency executives, who must have wondered if they'd ever find a concept that Ford would accept.

Aerodynamics did not check out well. Consumers liked the fact that an aerodynamic car was quieter, but they didn't seem impressed enough to make it a cornerstone of a campaign. In the 1980s every car company was shouting "aerodynamic." Unless the car was the most aerodynamic, there was little point even dwelling on it.

"European in design" did not work, because it wasn't very believable. People certainly did want European cars; Joe Schulte thought that it wouldn't be surprising to find that two out of three Americans had a fantasy of owning some European model. But the Taurus was made in America and everyone knew that. It had a prominent Ford badge on its hood.

The biggest disappointment to the J. Walter Thompson team was its inability to get consumers interested in the Best-in-Class concept. The notion was so powerful and important to the design and production of the Taurus that agency executives expected it to test well. Schulte and his colleagues devised concept cards that would communicate the importance of Best in Class, but nothing took hold.

Schulte was dismayed at the impasse. The problem was that the definition of the Best-in-Class concept could not be simply explained in an advertisement. Over four hundred items made up the list, culled from cars throughout the world. Ford decided that the Taurus was best-in-class in 75 percent of those categories. But a concept card that stated "The Taurus bested the world's cars in 75 percent of its categories" would only draw attention to the items that didn't top the list.

People did like what Lew Veraldi called "tremendous trifles," such as a dual sun visor, power window switches angled toward the driver, a cup holder, minor but thoughtful items whose collective value was greater than the sum of their parts. The hoped-for implication was that if Ford paid so much attention to those items, they must have put out even more energy for the components that really counted.

After examining the responses and consulting with Goldfarb, the agency concluded that one concept above all others stuck in people's minds: the Taurus existed because Ford listened to the customer. The car was, in essence, designed by the consumer. They had said they wanted a four-door family sedan or a station wagon that didn't look like a tank, wasn't dull, and didn't typecast them as plain Jane and stodgy. Focus-group responses told them that customers didn't like ads that shouted a car's greatness from the rooftops. People clearly understood that this was a thoughtful automobile.

In the end, the agency decided that the true message behind all of this was simple: the Taurus was the answer to the American Dream. That would never become a headline in an ad—the agency wasn't deranged—but Joe Schulte and his colleagues were sure that's what people were ultimately trying to tell them. People perceived the car as distinctive in appearance, even a bit avant-garde. It was also practical, taking their needs into account. The vehicle stood out in a category usually known for its relentless sterility. What's more, the car pleased people who experienced it. The Taurus wasn't dull, therefore its owner was automatically not dull. People could feel proud to own this vehicle, and yet it was still affordable.

Five months after the concept testing phase began, the agency was ready to start the initial preparation of actual ads. Proposed ideas ranged from lighthearted musical ditties to competitive ads showing the car driving on European roads to surrealistic science fiction, with Tauruses materializing out of blank screens. Then prototype commercials were produced from a shortened list, a sixty- and thirty-second version of each. The field was narrowed down to three contenders that were presented to Ford executives and tested before focus groups. One showed the Taurus actually in operation. A second spot was stark, the camera used almost like a snorkel, as it probed various attributes of the car. The third presented the car in a folksy setting and used a narrator that projected a down-home, friendly style. Both the car and the camera were stationary during the entire thirty-second spot. "Good old-fashioned breakthrough," drawled the narrator as he discussed the attributes of the Taurus.

Good Old-Fashioned Breakthrough was the favorite of many of the agency executives. Not only was it as different as the car, but it was a brilliant way of linking its modern, European look with mainstream homey feelings. This car is American in its traditional elements, and it's American in its inventive novelty.

Ford wasn't interested in novelty. They rejected all three concepts. Since time was drawing short, the agency quickly put together a simplistic concept: a family, their dog, and a Taurus lined up in front of a simple green hedge. A line thought up as an afterthought at JWT's music house, "Taurus. For us," became the campaign's theme song. It was a disappointing end for the agency to such an extensive search for a campaign. But when the ads and the music were tested before consumer groups, they received a strongly favorable reaction, so the company was pleased. Ford ordered print and television versions of the "Taurus. For Us" spots.

To supplement the photograph of the Taurus, the family, and the hedge, six-page newspaper ads showed detailed views of the interior and exterior. Short paragraphs clustered around the picture explained the car's unique features. The consumer finally had a reason to consider the question that rounded out the end of each page: "Have You Driven a Ford . . . Lately?"

After all the effort by the agency, this spread became the most adventurous aspect of the entire operation.

The new Taurus would hopefully impress the public with its technological and creative breakthroughs. But in the world of advertising, both Ford and the consumers it was wooing wanted only to play it safe.

13

THE RULE OF THE IRON FIST

Regardless of how conventional one may have thought of its execution, the Taurus's six-page advertisement, with its long list of the car's features, created a strong image of a unique, high-technology car that was created by listening to the customers' needs and desires. In the competitive automotive world of the 1980s, the car's execution had to live up to that advance billing. To accomplish that, the construction of the Taurus had to be of the highest quality. And that could happen only if the assembly-line workers felt that they had a greater stake in their work than just collecting a paycheck.

The United Auto Workers had made concessions on wages, and in return Ford had agreed to institute Employee Involvement programs to bring the workers into the plants' decision-making process. EI was another version of Veraldi's team approach. Ephlin knew that if management agreed to listen to its workers, it would find out that they could make important contributions.

The changes were needed because for many years the principal tools of the trade for many Ford workers had been a hammer and rubber mallet, not the pneumatic drill or torque wrench. Body assembly was frequently lackluster, engineering errors caused difficulties in fit, and Ford's outside suppliers often delivered pieces so inferior that the worker crudely had to stretch and bang the part into shape before the vehicle could be shipped off to market. Good "fit and finish" was supposed to be the goal. In reality, the cars that went out the door often weren't finished and the parts didn't fit.

Bob Jacobson was used to shaking his head as the bodies traveled down the line. Jacobson, a Chicago Assembly Plant inspector one step in status above the assembly line, knew that the cars were not ready to be shipped because they had been poorly assembled. On some vehicles, gaps were so large that Jacobson could practically put his hand between the door and the fender. On others, the bodies rattled and squeaked. Judging by the way some windows fit into their frames, any worker with a little experience knew that these cars were going to leak water and wind.

The quick-fix pulling and twisting tactic didn't always work. A bad fit at one point meant that the next section, and then the section after that, was off its mark; the problem escalated as one ill-fitting piece affected the next. An improperly seated window frame prevented the glass from being air- or watertight. A badly fitting door made the hood impossible to align. Sometimes the pieces were too poorly made to join properly at all. Squeaks, leaks, and rattles resulted from a poorly manufactured part. If a problem was found and a worker failed to fix it properly, the car was regularly sent on its way regardless. Worst of all, many defects were never caught because vehicles were merely spot-checked.

At one point during the 1970s, Jacobson, unhappy with the quality at the plant, decided to document the situation so that there would be no question about the problems. He began to keep a log, recording all the units with major uncorrected defects. Jacobson's actions were an open secret, and his interest in quality did not sit well with some of his superiors. He soon received a visit from someone in quality control.

"I want you to buy these cars, Jacobson," the supervisor told him.

"But they've got defects," Jacobson said.

"Don't argue with me. I said pass them, don't reject them. There's nothing wrong with those vehicles and you know it."

Because Jacobson knew just the opposite was true, he was infuriated by the directive. Quality control had caved in to the needs of the plant manager to get out more cars. The idea of knuckling under was unacceptable. Jacobson couldn't willfully approve a car that he knew had problems. If he refused, however, he put his job in jeopardy. He came up with an idea: he'd sign off on the defective units but not with his own name. He'd put the quality control supervisor's signature on the paperwork.

His actions prompted another visit from his boss. "Listen, Jacobson, I told you to buy those cars. When I tell you to buy something, you buy it. You put your own name down on that sign-off sheet, not mine. If you don't do what I tell you," he said, "I'll break your arm and get you demoted!"

Jacobson could report the supervisor, but that wouldn't serve any purpose. He knew the plant higher-ups wouldn't support him. If he blew the whistle, he feared he'd be out of a job. He could do only one thing: he started to sign off on the defective work. To protect himself, he kept a running log of all the problem cars. If nothing else, he could at least show he was acting against his best judgment.

Chicago Assembly Plant workers knew full well that

this was often standard operating procedure. For men and women like Jake Chavers and Marilyn Aiken, it was "the rule of the iron fist." As far as the plant supervisors were concerned, there were two ways to do things: the workers' way and the right way. Aiken knew her opinion didn't matter. "Even if we have a good idea, all they say is 'I'm the supervisor, you're just a peon,' " Aiken grumbled. What mattered was that supervisors were obeyed.

The plant was inhospitable for all people, but was especially trying for women. Although the number of females on the employment rolls was high, the factory did little to accommodate them. Aiken was recruited to do relief work in one of the pits, sunken areas in which workers stood and worked on car chassis that passed overhead. Once in the pit Aiken found that she could barely reach the underbodies of the cars as they went by. Though of normal height for a woman, she had to stand on tiptoes to get any work done.

"Can't you lower the cars, or raise the pit so I can reach the bodies?" Aiken asked a supervisor.

"No way," she was told. "There's nothing wrong with those pits. They're made for an average man."

"I'm not an average man, I'm an average woman," she protested. Her complaints went unanswered. "Either find another job at the plant," she was told, "or accept this one." Fortunately, she was able to be reassigned.

The 1979 contract with the UAW offered Ford a chance to make changes. The institutionalization of a program that would involve employees meant that, in theory, life on the shop floor would be different.

Plant management needed the cooperation of its workers in order to improve the quality of its cars, and in the early 1980s it began to make overtures to them. Plant manager Joe Bobnar, Ford EI coordinator Jay Stanwich, and the UAW encouraged employees to set up EI groups that could suggest how to improve the production process. Bob Jacobson was one of the first recruited by the company to participate. At first he wasn't interested. He wanted to do a good job, but he was a union man, not a company stooge.

"You're doing this Employee Involvement business to spy on the workers," he flatly told management. It was a common belief: Ford management wanted selected workers to take over shop-floor decisions so that they could squeal on others. What's more, by making workers feel like they had some control over the process, the feeling went, the company could loosen their ties to the UAW while increasing their allegiance to the bosses who put them in power.

Plant executives insisted it wasn't true. A new day was dawning, they told him. If he volunteered to be part of it, he'd be sent to school and trained in the latest production techniques so he could impart that information to other workers.

"I'll try it out," Jacobson warily agreed, unconvinced of the company's sincerity. "But if I ever think that this whole program is to break the union, I'm out of here."

No matter what he said, though, his UAW colleagues were angry at his decision to help. He was attacked by his workmates, accused of cozying up to management. A fellow worker Jacobson had known for years was incensed at his decision. The two were old friends, often frequenting the same bar after work. The fact that they had been close made matters worse.

"You goddamn son of a bitch," the worker cried out to Jacobson when he spotted him across the bar after their shift. "You're working for the company. You ain't no union man." He dared Jacobson to step outside to settle the matter, but Jacobson refused. His friend had had too much to drink, he decided, but still, the taunt stung. Jacobson wanted to give the program a chance, and he didn't like being denounced for his decision.

By 1981, Jacobson and Jake Chavers, among others, were making monthly trips to Detroit. At first Chavers didn't take the task too seriously. "When they came to me and asked if I wanted to go to Detroit," he said, "I thought it would be fun. When I got there, they had instructors from seven-thirty in the morning to four-thirty in the afternoon. By the third day I had to change my attitude totally."

Chavers became a fierce defender of EI. He benefited from it, gained power from it, and now believed in it wholeheartedly. Nonetheless, he remained quick to defend his fellow workers against management. When a supervisor came to the EI office to complain about the performance of a worker, Chavers cut him short. "Don't come up here finger pointing. Come here because you want to solve a problem. That's what EI's about. That we'll help you with."

The EI program got off to a rocky start. The early training programs were forty-hour ordeals that bored its participants, and soon the trainers were forced to cut them down to sixteen. In addition, when plant management wanted to recruit more workers for the program, they asked Chavers, among others, for his help in selection, but he refused. "That'll look like I'm playing favorites," he told them. "Let each group on the floor pick its own participants. Then it'll be a voluntary program." As a consequence, workers on each assembly specialty, such as doors, electrical, and engine, had meetings and picked their own leaders.

The employees' first attempts to alter conditions met with strong resistance. Workers felt that their lower-level managers routinely ignored them. The concept of a worker having a good idea seemed incomprehensible to some.

It took plant manager Joseph Bobnar to alter the divisive atmosphere. Bobnar had begun his career with Ford as an accounting department clerk. Since 1948 he had worked in six assembly plants around the country, most recently as plant manager of Ford's truck operations in Norfolk.

Bobnar liked overseeing the building of vehicles. "I like cars, anything that's a challenge," he said. "Sometimes

I feel inadequate, because I was raised during the war, when building cars just took muscle. Now we have robots, computers, you feel you're not quite prepped to handle this." However, the success of the Taurus and Sable, Bobnar understood, depended on him and his work force rising to the occasion.

The new cars would be built in two plants, Atlanta and Chicago. Atlanta was to be the lead plant and would start production first. The delay gave the Chicago workers an advantage, since they could learn from Atlanta's mistakes. Training to learn how to assemble the Taurus and Sable at Chicago began in mid-1984, a year before the first car was due to roll off its line. Five hundred of the plant's skilled workers, 20 percent of its work force, including toolmakers and electricians, spent a week in the Atlanta plant, learning from the Georgian workers' attempts to manufacture the car. Upon returning to Chicago, they imparted the techniques to the nonskilled laborers.

When Bobnar first saw the Taurus, during a design center preview, he loved it. His first concern, though, was "Can we build this thing?" The car was extraordinarily different from anything built before at Chicago. Bobnar carefully perused the car, noting immediately that careful attention would have to be paid to the carriage-roof doors to achieve a proper fit. Plus, the engine powered the front wheels rather than the rear; therefore, the power plant would have to be inserted into the body from below rather than from above as with rear-wheel-drive vehicles. The dashboards of the Taurus and Sable were different, and each would have a variety of available instrument clusters. Assembly workers would have to keep a keen eye on exactly which vehicle and model they were building. Assembling any new car required the learning of new techniques, but the Taurus/Sable required the assimilation of a good deal more.

"I wondered if we could build it. The all-new styling, the carriage-roof doors, all those things bothered me. This car was front-wheel drive, and I had no experience with it. We would be using new roof-welding techniques. We knew we'd be getting sophisticated automation, but how that would work out was also an unknown."

Before the Taurus and Sable were built, the plant's equipment would be completely changed. Sophisticated automation would be coming, most of it out of the realm of the workers' present experience. The plant had had twenty robots in place for several years, but they were now dated. Plans called for a complete retrofitting of the robotics. One hundred and fifty new German and Japanese units would be installed to take over the line's more drudging jobs, including welding and windshield installation.

Employee Involvement was a passion of Bobnar's. He felt that it was essential to implement if car-build quality was going to improve. "As a plant manager, I set the tone for quality. My job is a coaching job, to make my manager and the guy on the line understand what quality is. That's the biggest problem you have: getting people to understand what quality is. People don't realize that one little problem on the line then becomes a customer problem. Instead they just accept it. I'm a great believer that quality is the result of an attitude, and it becomes a habit. People who hate coming to work every morning, you'll see that in their work. And whatever level you sustain, that's the level you're going to get, because that level falls into a pattern."

Bobnar wanted the EI program to move beyond its humble beginnings—a means for workers to improve their working conditions—and make it into a true force for dramatic change. Early in his tenure he approached a maintenance crew who repaired plant equipment. "If you've got problems with the equipment," he told them, "then go to the operator for advice on how to fix it. They're the experts who can tell you what's wrong with the machine." The statement impressed Marilyn Aiken; Bobnar clearly understood that workers would be happy to share their expertise if someone would only ask.

Fifty EI groups were formed at Chicago, eventually involving over three hundred fifty workers. People met based on their tasks; groups were formed to discuss the assembly of brake systems, chassis, electrical systems, interior trim. Workers gathered during company time for one hour per week. It cost the plant an additional $450,000 per year in salaries, but it was an expense that had to be made if quality was ever going to improve.

At first, workers discussed how to improve their immediate working environment. Simple changes were made: large parabolic mirrors were mounted at the ends of some aisles to avoid colliding with forklift trucks zooming down blind corridors. Later, discussion moved on to how to improve the construction of the car built at the plant. During the development of the Taurus, mock-ups of the cars were brought into the factories so employees could suggest ways to simplify assembly.

The value of their input was immediately apparent. One team suggested that the number of panels used to construct the sides and doors be reduced from the nine in the LTD/Marquis models to two in Taurus/Sable. The reduction would decrease variability and assembly time. Another worker pointed out that a bolt on the hood assembly was unnecessary, and it was designed out of the car. One welding gun would be used in place of the three that had always done the job before, thereby saving time and space. Instead of using different-size screws, necessitating a change in torquing heads, a worker argued for the use of just one size. Using the same head reduced production time and decreased the number of parts on the car.

Even before the start of production on Taurus/Sable, when Chicago was still manufacturing the Ford LTD and Mercury Marquis, workers learned the importance of their new power. The plant had required special drill bits to make holes in the doors of the LTD/Marquis. Drill bits were being ordered by the boxful because they were breaking as fast as they arrived. The bits were expensive, and the EI group didn't understand why workers couldn't seem to make them last.

The group decided to call the Walton Hills stamping

plant and ask them to come to Chicago and discuss the problem. When the stamping plant people were told what was wrong, they were confused.

"Why are you drilling holes in the doors?" they asked.

"Because we need those holes in the doors," they were told.

"Of course you do. But the other LTD plant that we supply gets its doors with the holes already stamped into the metal by us. They're not breaking any drill bits because they're not using any."

"Then why aren't you supplying us with the same doors that you give them?" the C.A.P. workers asked incredulously.

"Because you never asked for them," the stamping plant people replied.

The two plants had specified different doors, and the stamping plant obligingly filled the orders. A lack of communication and the unwillingness of anyone at Walton Hills to show some initiative created a problem that never needed to exist.

In later years, as Taurus production progressed, several dramatic suggestions were implemented. Management was stymied by a problem inherent in the car's design. Every Taurus station wagon had its rear door deformed after passing through the paint ovens. Every door coming off the line had to be reshaped by hand, a costly and time-consuming procedure. The only solution was to reengineer the door, but that promised to be an expensive proposition: the redesign alone would cost two dollars per piece, not including the costs to retool.

Not until the beginning of 1989, more than three years after production first began, was the solution found. A worker devised an inexpensive tool that was attached to the car before it entered the ovens and prevented the door from being stretched during drying.

The value of workers' suggestions was proven time and again. Getting the Taurus's cruise controls to work correctly was a double problem. First, a worker had to adjust it upon installation. Then 35 percent of them needed re-adjustment before the car could be shipped. Bobnar was frustrated by this waste of labor time.

One worker suggested that a new, nonadjustable type of speed-control valve be used. Not only would the failure rate drop, he pointed out, but time would be saved as workers would know that every unit was perfectly tuned. The 65-percent first-time acceptance rose to 100 percent. Customers no longer complained of faulty or failing cruise controls. Pete Pestillo calculated that a typical adopted suggestion saved the company at least $300,000.[1]

Although Ford and the UAW exhorted workers to im-prove quality and get involved in changing the production process, Employee Involvement failed to become a mass movement at the Chicago Assembly Plant. By 1990 just 14 percent of the work force was involved in the program. Some employees still did not trust the process, and they didn't want to engage in activities that plant management was promoting. Others simply felt they had more impor-tant things to do with their time than stay after work.

The low level of EI participation was not crucial, claimed those most actively involved. The workers in the program became the factory's natural leaders. "Every worker here is affected by the Employee Involvement pro-gram," Jake Chavers said. "They sense the new attitude whether they participate or not." Chavers was damned if he was going to let somebody else slack off while he did his work. He figured that EI gave Ford the best hope for suc-ceeding with the Taurus and Sable, and the best hope he had for keeping his paycheck. This feeling he did not hes-itate communicating to his colleagues.

"If you're working in front of me and you're con-stantly messing up, I'm not going to support you," Chavers told other workers. "I'm going to tell the boss to get rid of you. You know why? Because my loyalty is not to you. My loyalty is to me. My loyalty is to my job."

14

THINK QUALITY

Despite the changes brought onto the shop floor by Employee Involvement, only so much could be done to alter the basic experience of factory life. Ford's Chicago Assembly Plant was a grim place. It was situated in a swampy, weed-choked industrial area of south Chicago near the Indiana border. Workers entered the plant by riding up an escalator to a huge, grimy walkway tunnel. In an early Employee Involvement scheme workers painted the tunnel a rainbow of colors, but other parts of the plant remained unattractive. The plant's small reception room, the first way station for visiting businessmen, held a collection of mismatched 1960s industrial furniture covered in garish hues.

The overwhelming sensation at the Chicago Assembly

Plant, though, was noise. Banks of welding robots, scores of smoke-belching forklifts racing up the aisles, the hundreds of new-car bodies shuffling forward on tracks to the paint room, all contributed to a deafening roar. Some workers tried to block the sound out by wearing Walkmen, but most were oblivious to it. Shouting to their fellow workers was part of the job.

Not only that, in the heart of summer the heat at C.A.P. was stifling. Air-conditioning the place was next to impossible. Two hundred tractor trailers and thirty rail cars rolled in and out of the plant every day. The plant itself was immense. Opened in 1924, the gargantuan factory had been expanded twelve times, eventually comprising 2.3 million square feet, equal in size to over twelve hundred homes. "Memorize the number on the pillar you're standing next to," Bob Jacobson told new assembly-line workers joining the crew of 2,500. "If you don't, you'll never find your spot again."

On November 7, 1985, the plant was shut. The entire facility was gutted; bulldozers knocked down all existing apparatus until nothing was left standing except the factory's outer shell. In two months the factory was transformed as new equipment was installed to prepare for the production of the 1986 Ford Taurus and Mercury Sable. In addition to the computerized paint rooms and new assembly lines, the plant became significantly more automated. To standardize production and decrease errors caused by worker fatigue, the fifteen American-made welding robots used prior to Taurus production were replaced by 128 new German units.

The new increased reliance on automation was only the latest in a long string of assembly techniques that had changed since the days of the Model T. Cars were no longer put together with each component attached in turn as the vehicle moved down a never stopping track. Rather, Taurus/Sable was produced using the modular assembly method. Particular componentry, such as the engine, in-

strument panel, seats, and doors were worked up in separate areas of the plant, joined to the body only after the
car had been painted.

This new manufacturing system was touted as an example of the radical changes that were coming to Ford.
Don Petersen thought it was "the most significant development since Henry Ford introduced the assembly line."[1]
With modular assembly, the entire line did not have to
shut down if a shortage of certain parts suddenly developed. Excess subassemblies could be stored in corners of
the plant as a contingency, used whenever a shortage of
those parts developed.

To eliminate storage space, only small quantities of
many items would be kept on hand. The plant would practice a limited version of the "just in time" delivery process
pioneered by the Japanese industry. In truth, Bobnar had
little choice but to institute the system, since the plant was
300,000 square feet short of the space they needed to keep
their parts. An Indiana warehouse would store excess components, and ninety trucks loaded with goods would be
making daily trips on a just-in-time basis. As a result, plant
inventory was reduced from $20 million to $8 million. The
plant consumed material quickly; if a total breakdown in
the delivery system ever occurred, Chicago would run out
of parts in twenty-four to thirty-six hours.

The unpainted body panels, as well as completed parts
for the interior of the car, arrived via truck and rail, having been punched out at one of Ford's stamping plants.
Some items, such as taillight assemblies, arrived already
completed. Others, such as the instrument panel, gauges,
and wiring came partially assembled. Since there were a
large number of different options on the car, the workers
had to customize the electrical system to fit.

Doors and quarter panels were stored overhead for
later welding and assembly, saving over 120,000 square
feet of space. Before automation, workers had picked up
each heavy panel by hand and manually hoisted it up to

the racks. Now they were placed on hooks that carried the pieces to the ceiling for storage and future welding.

The Taurus production process began with the unloading of body panels from railroad cars. Each panel had a tab that fit into a corresponding slot on an adjoining piece, much the way cutout clothes are fastened to a paper doll. Workers grabbed the various panels, inserted the tabs, and lined the newly constructed silver-colored skeleton on one of two conveyors, ready to begin its trip through assembly.

The raw body shells, held together by no more than the folded-over tabs, were enveloped by a body buck, a huge mold that briefly closed around the nascent vehicle like a clam, gently squeezing the panels into place for the welding robots. Without the buck, the shells would be contorted and welds would hit all the wrong places. Until the unit underwent welding, the extremely flimsy frames could easily collapse with a quick kick to a quarter panel.

Sparks flew twenty feet into the air as one rickety chassis after another moved into position under the robot. The arm of each orange machine automatically swung into position, creating a weld every few inches along the connecting points of the body panels, fusing the pieces of the body together. At a preset moment the machines halted their monotonous procedure and swung their arms away from the cars to a special cleaning attachment. Each welding tip was then automatically filed down in the tip-dressing container. If the tip was not periodically cleaned, the apparatus did not transmit enough heat, and welds did not hold.

When the robots first appeared on the line, they were a blessing. Previously men had had to hold heavy, bulky manual welding devices all day long. Even with a counterweight attached, the gun remained an elephantine device. A muscular worker might do well with the task at the beginning of his shift, but by the end of the day, welding mistakes were all too common.

Robots were not free from making errors, only theirs were more disastrous than human ones. Machines performed perfectly as long as all external conditions were right. If the body buck did not shape the fragile shell correctly, though, the chassis arrived at the robot's station out of alignment. All the welds were then laid down in the wrong places, creating a useless body.

The body sections not only had to be welded together properly, they also had to arrive at the plant in perfect shape. However, many of the rear quarter panels, the sheet metal covering the rear wheels, were entering the plant already buckled. As a body shop worker, Jake Chavers was supposed to certify that those panels were free of defects. Fortunately, the new emphasis on Employee Involvement gave Chavers the freedom to talk about their poor quality.

During an EI meeting with sheet-metal vendors, Chavers stated his dismay over the shape of the materials. The time to cure the problem was now, early in the program, before the Taurus gained a bad reputation. Plant manager Bobnar walked into the meeting in time to hear Chavers' complaint, and after the meeting Bobnar called him into his office.

"Jake, why don't you go to the stamping plant and find out why they can't get this right?" Bobnar suggested. Chavers was incredulous. After years of working the line, nobody had ever asked him to do such a thing. Workers were not asked to travel and make decisions.

Three days later, Chavers was at the stamping plant, following the progress of the quarter panels from the time the raw sheet metal came off the rollers through every point of the process. "At the fourth stage I saw the buckle appear. Too much pressure." The machinery was pushing too hard on the metal, and the extra pressure was causing it to crease.

"These guys at the stamping plant saw it happening. But the guy on the line doesn't know it's a problem. He doesn't know what the buckle is going to make the car look like." Once Chavers saw why it was happening, however, he was able to sit down with the stamping plant workers and management and get it corrected.

After production began, Ford's own Chicago Heights stamping plant was turning out Taurus hoods that arrived at the factory with large depressions in the sheet metal. "They had big humps," Chavers said, "like someone put their hand on an oilcan. The worst thing is that when you try to fix it, it might look good on the bare metal assembly line, but once it gets painted, the reflections look like you can go skiing off them."

When the EI team checked with the factory, they were told that the hoods were leaving the plant in perfect condition. The Taurus plant managers decided they couldn't use those parts. They shut the plant down and sent everyone home until the cause of the fault was found.

Workers at both plants monitored the hoods from the moment they left the stamping plant to the time they arrived at assembly. They discovered that during transit the hoods were bumping around in the trucks, creasing every unit. The problem was easily solved by adding one more strap to the tie-down before the truck departed.

Chavers was pleased to see that the problems were being solved instead of glossed over. "Before, you would have continued to run the assembly line, and the body shop would have had to fix those hoods. Now those hoods were scrapped."

After the fastened bodies emerged from welding by the robots, they moved into a prewash and then traveled a quarter mile to receive an acid bath that helped with paint adhesion.

The silver car shells snaked around the plant, past a sign exhorting all passersby to "Think Quality." The bodies rose twenty feet in the air and then descended behind a glass wall into an enormous tank of deep gray liquid, called the E-coat. To the rear of each submerging shell was attached a wire, giving the body an electric charge that allowed the murky electrostatic bathwater to fuse onto the metal. The liquid soaked into every crevice of the still hollow shell and protected the body from corrosion. The E-coat liquid, du Pont's Automotive Finish Cathatic Electrocoat Primer, had been first applied in 1977. Its use allowed Ford to offer extended corrosion warranties. Prior to that time, auto bodies had received nothing but the acid bath, with much less satisfactory results. Occasionally the electrically charged wire failed to attach itself to several bodies, creating useless "white elephants," frames that emerged from the bath not gray but cream-colored from the failure of the E-coat to adhere. The bodies then had to be junked.

The painting process is a delicate task. Simple errors cause noticeable defects in the car's finish. A worker's belt buckle can easily mar the finish or a stray hairpin knock a chip of paint from the freshly coated surface. Before painting, cars at Chicago were machine-coated with brown primer and then touched up by hand. Workers kept their distance from the primed bodies, since the oil from a simple fingerprint would prevent the paint from adhering to the surface.

Every vehicle was made to certain specifications, depending on the dealer's order. A work sheet that identified the car's color and other options traveled with each chassis. The bodies moved into the paint booth, where mechanical guns blew compressed air across the surface to rid it of dust. Workers manually wiped the panels with a tack rag to remove any untouched particles, then programmed a computer to spray the appropriate color as indicated on the work sheet.

Before the process was automated in the 1970s, painting cars had been a hellish job. Workers had stood inside the paint booth and manually sprayed the body with large compressor guns. Some areas would inevitably be missed, while some spots received too much. With the advent of computerization, workers no longer needed to enter the booth during painting. As the car passed through the paint room, one of three triple-nozzled guns automatically rose and fell to cover all surfaces uniformly. In addition, the paint room had no solid floor. Instead, one walked across a large metal mesh grid, beneath which swirled a pool of foot-deep, pigment-infused water. Excess paint floated through the mesh into the water, from which it was later extracted.

The paint arrived via tubes from a room humming with the sound of over fifty large drums of pigment being continuously mixed. Each car received four coats of paint: two of base, a flat pigment that contained the color; and two of clear coat, a veneer that gave a car its shine. After the paint was applied, the body baked for thirty to forty minutes, emerging from the barnlike ovens warm to the touch. Finally these shells were beginning to look like automobiles.

The paint-inspection area was the brightest spot in the plant. The coated bodies, straight from the ovens, paraded past banks of five-foot-tall vertical fluorescent lights. Inspectors examined the vehicle shells to make sure that the car was painted the proper color and to look for surface nicks and imperfections in the finish. This was the most dangerous time for the newly created vehicles, for their freshly baked paint remained susceptible to damage. Yellow signs posted throughout the area alerted the inspection crew:

THE UNWANTED OPTION:

The customer needs your help to eliminate chips and scratches:

1. Is my pouch worn or too full?
2. Are there any unwanted chips or scratches or any exposed metal on my power tools or connectors?
3. Do I have any loose keys on my belt?
4. Do I have anything sharp in my pockets?
5. Is my belt buckle covered?
6. Do I have any jewelry that can touch the painted surface?

7. What can I contribute to stopping chips and scratches?
   Use the above as a checklist so we can eliminate "the
   unwanted option."

In addition to nicks and scratches, workers occasionally found foreign matter that entered the pigment prior
to its application. It was up to an inspector to track down
its source before the contaminated paint affected too many
other bodies.

One inspector, Lloyd Detright, stared intently through
the microscope at the miniscule fiber attached to the slide.
An assembly-line worker had found it on one of the freshly
painted shells and brought it to the paint-inspection area.
Detright was an old hand at the work, and he thought he
had pinpointed the cause of the problem. It had to be a
piece from someone's glove, he figured. He knew what shift
and what station the car had come from; tracking down
the culprit with the loose glove would be relatively simple.

Lloyd was pleased that only two fibers had been found
this morning. The problem was isolated and easily contained. Plant management had given him strict orders: he
was to find and track every paint problem, and to stop
those responsible for causing them. Even with the care
taken to keep the paint pure, problems did crop up. Vigi-
lance was necessary to ensure that the paint was pristine,
its batches consistent in hue, free from dirt and grime. A
misplaced hat could ruin the entire lot.

Lloyd especially cherished his freedom to blow the
whistle on suppliers of inferior and contaminated paint.
Previously he had had to ask permission from the supervisor to call a paint company to task; now he was expected
to act on his own.

C.A.P.'s paint-inspection area resembled a high school
chemistry lab. A microscope, a small oven, scales, and several piles containing hundreds of paint chips occupied the
stained tabletops. It was not common knowledge that an
enormous range of body colors were available to customers
at a premium charge. In a few months the factory floor

was going to be dotted by a couple of specially ordered purple or taxicab-yellow Tauruses, usually destined to become business vehicles, among the scores of stock maroon, blue, and gray cars waiting to be driven out of the plant. Every color, standard or not, had to be carefully mixed to maintain consistency and accuracy. Charts tracking paint uniformity hung at various places in the room, proof that the daily quality-control checks were turning up satisfactory batches.

Four separate indices were monitored in his daily paint analysis: viscosity, sag level, resistivity, and batch consistency. Paint problems were often detected, and Lloyd was rejecting batches from both of his suppliers on a regular basis. He wasn't interested in their excuses; if du Pont, the regular supplier of the base coat, couldn't come up with a satisfactory product, he was prepared to get it from BASF, provider of the clear coat.

The financial repercussions of this loss of business were dire enough to motivate both Taurus paint suppliers to keep their own permanent employees at the plant at all times. Ford often seemed better at detecting problems than the suppliers. BASF and du Pont regularly agreed with paint inspection that batches they had shipped to the plant were unacceptable and replaced them.

The result was batches of pigment with few defects. Ford's own inspectors rarely found more than one or two foreign fibers in the paint each day but, under the new thrust for quality, that was too many. "The company won't let anything pass," Detright said. "They told me they want to have the number one car, and that I shouldn't accept any defect."

While the bodies were painted, the interior components of the car—seats, dashboard, side doors—were assembled at separate stations throughout the plant. The basic instrument-panel shells were attached to a small overhead conveyor. Like sides of beef, each panel worked its way down the belt as workers attached various components.

By reading the work sheet attached to each panel, a worker determined which switches and gauges to install. Add-ons varied based on whether a base, luxury, sporty, or model exported to Japan or Europe was being assembled. To increase efficiency, the Taurus used fifty different possible appliqués, the covers for various switches, half the number used on previous models. After assemblage the completed instrument panel moved down the conveyor to rendezvous with its painted exterior shell.

Meanwhile, the painted bodies moved into position to receive their internal components. In the first step after painting, the doors were separated from the body and placed on overhead conveyors that traveled in synch with the vehicle. This solved the difficult problem of working on a car's interior. If the doors remained attached during assembly, workers constantly had to open them as they crawled onto the floor to install a component, and then shut them to walk around the vehicle.

As the bodies approached the next station, one worker would throw a windshield-wiper assembly into the passing body, grab a door handle with its distinct key code from a box, and with a pneumatic drill, tighten the lock into the left side of the door. Another person simultaneously performed the exact same task on the other side of the car. The wiper remained hanging loosely out the chassis, since the next person would position it properly.

Teams of people followed with an electrical loom, a gaggle of wires that connected the instrument panel to the engine, power windows, seats, ventilation controls, compressor, battery, and every other component that required energy. Depending on the model, the assembler selected one of twelve looms. Workers crawled into the body, still devoid of seats and carpets, pushing and shoving the intricate grouping of cables through the engine compartment before they ran out of time. When they finished, they jumped out of the chassis and hurried back to the next body to start the process again. Once the instrument panel was installed in the painted body, the car began to take on the look of the Taurus, and the evocative smell of a new vehicle became apparent for the first time.

The necessary hustling was not unique to loom installation. Whether workers were positioning carpets or the window mechanism, a limited amount of time was available. If a snag occurred in the process, a worker was able to pull a cord to shut down the line or call over a utility-upgrade man. Before EI, that would have been impossible. A worker stopping a line because he spotted a defect was unheard of. All a worker could do was let the defective car go by and hope that the next person in line would spot the problem and correct it.

The utility-upgrade worker was the plant's troubleshooter, roving from one location to the next to help a particular group complete a job on time. In a common example, a utility worker would rush over to a misfitting window, grab a rubber mallet, and tap, push, and shove the glass into its gasket. Each utility person typically worked with a team of seven people, covering for one worker or another as they took their allotted relief time. Each six minutes of work entitled an hourly employee to one minute of relief: a total of thirty minutes in the morning and eighteen in the afternoon in addition to the thirty-minute lunch break.

The elimination of plant inspectors, a tactic pioneered by Tom Page in his diversified-products plants, had spread to Chicago. Workers were given the power not only to reject inferior parts, but to call in suppliers for face-to-face talks. This proved important in one continually troublesome area. Electrical subsystems continually ran worst in reliability, and of all of Ford's plants, Chicago regularly produced cars with the least reliable electricals. At the start of Taurus production, only 70 percent of the vehicles coming off the line had fault-free electrics, compared to 90 percent from other systems in the car.

For a while Bobnar was unaware of the day-to-day trials that the workers were facing with their inferior supplies, and only learned about the problem once he read the production reports. The poor workmanship had serious sales ramifications, and Bobnar wanted it corrected. Consumers might not bother to take their car back for a warranty claim if they heard a squeak or noticed a bit of loose door trim, but no one would accept a malfunctioning power window or automatic door lock. Once back in the dealership, the unhappy customer would point out all the other minor problems that needed fixing. Warranty costs would rise, Ford's rating on the New Car Quality Survey would drop, and potential customers would lose faith in the car.

Since he was several steps removed from the action and felt limited in what he could do, he contacted the people who could develop a remedy, the workers directly involved with electrical systems. An electrical EI group was formed, and the participants scrutinized every applicable part for flaws. They discovered that inferior items were being manufactured by several of Ford's suppliers. The EI group got on the phone with one of them.

"We want you to come down to the plant so you can see the quality problems we're having with your material."

"All right, we'll send someone down," said the company.

"No, we don't want 'someone.' We want to see the head of the company down here," the EI representative insisted.

The president of the division of this large multinational corporation actually agreed to show up. Bobnar watched the developments with interest. He knew that if he had made the same request, the head would have found some excuse not to come. "The hourly people got a better response because they knew exactly what the hell was going on," Bobnar said. "When you're dealing with the plant manager, you're dealing secondhand."

The president met with the EI group and agreed to take the necessary steps to improve the quality of his parts. The company had little choice if it wanted to maintain its Taurus contract. Between 1986 and 1989, the number of

Tauruses coming off the line with electrical system defects decreased from 30 percent to 10 percent.

The assembly process was now close to completion. Once the electrical componentry was in place, the engine was "decked," inserted into the body from below the chassis. Hydraulic lifts raised the engine up into the car, and workers on either side of the front end secured it to the frame mounts.

After the doors were reattached to their bodies, the leader of one of the plant's variability-reduction programs inspected the cars. The variability-reduction concept was part of a larger program, Statistical Process Control, which charted defects throughout the plant. By carefully monitoring construction errors, it was theorized, their causes could be tracked down and corrected.

A year before construction of the Taurus began, customer complaints about fit and finish on other models had been relayed back to the plant. Problem areas were monitored on graph paper that hung on several folding panels set up near the line, and Employee Involvement groups met to figure out how to improve construction reliability. Variability-reduction team members used the paper to chart the problem areas, noting improvements or setbacks achieved in items such as door-opening effort or erratic spacing between doors and the adjacent quarter panels. The plan was for the team to stay at it until variability had dropped to predefined goals, and then move on to other assembly glitches in the plant.

A worker jumped into the car, started the engine, and drove to a second paint area, where workers manually applied pinstripes to the sides of the exterior. The vehicle was then placed on rapidly revolving cylinders, allowing a technician to align the front and rear wheels. As the final act, the car's headlights were aimed: a rectangular box was attached to the three glass bumps that protrude from the front of all American lights. A worker turned the lamps' aiming screws until a water bubble at the top of the hanging box, similar to a carpenter's level, was centered.

On January 20, 1986, seven years after Ford officials first proposed the manufacture of a new midsize car, five years after initial sketches, three years after the board of directors approved the design, and sixteen hours after unpainted metallic body panels were pulled off a railroad car and initially placed on a conveyor belt, the first Ford Taurus rolled off the Chicago assembly line.

The initial vehicle that was driven out the door and onto a car transporter would be followed by more than one other new Taurus or Sable every minute. Once it was at full speed, the Chicago Assembly Plant was capable of turning out 65.5 units per hour, 1,048 cars each day, more than 250,000 every year. The numbers were not just achievable; they were essential if the project was to come in on budget.

With the quality that they were building into the car, workers felt, there would be little problem selling the units necessary to become a success. It was an exciting moment for Jake Chavers and other workers who got behind the Employee Involvement efforts. The constant pressure exerted by Ford management in Detroit to improve build quality had changed worker morale. Chavers was flush with enthusiasm for his job. "This is the best-quality car I've built in the twenty-one years I've been working here," he said. There was the predictable employee boosterism. "Quality is the attitude of the workers now. Management's attitude is changing. Yeah, it's gradual, but all these meetings we've been having are paying off."

Chicago was proud of its achievements. Management hung banners and electronic signs throughout the plant, urging the workers on to even greater heights of excellence. Things were going so well that on August 25, 1988, management planned to shut down the assembly lines for the first time, to hold an unprecedented factory-wide meeting. During paid company time, union officials and management would spend four hours together telling employees about the gains in quality that had been made.

Statistics would be presented that showed improvements made throughout the decade of the 1980s. Via videotape, Ray Ablondi would discuss the annual Competitive New Vehicle Quality Study. The president of the Chicago UAW local would address the workers, and a national union official would elaborate the methods to achieve Best in Class throughout the corporation. Joe Bobnar would tell employees that Ford's CNVQ rating, an annual in-house study, indicated that defects per one thousand Tauruses and Sables decreased by 28 percent between 1986 and 1988.

As word of the extraordinary meeting spread, not all workers bought the reason for its existence. Some were convinced it was nothing but an excuse to gather everyone in the plant to tell them the real news en masse. And that news, they believed, was going to be very different from what everyone had been led to expect. Despite its important role in the production of the Taurus, Ford management in Detroit, the rumors went, had actually decided that there was no place in its corporate manufacturing strategy for the Chicago Assembly Plant. The factory, for some reason, would be out of production in 1990, permanently closed by 1992.[3]

The plant closing rumors were untrue. Veraldi had planned that the first Taurus would roll off the Atlanta assembly line, but with the car volumes predicted for Taurus/Sable, he needed Chicago up and running as well. That's exactly why so much money had been invested in new equipment.

At the tent meeting, Bobnar took the podium to immediately quell the plant shutdown stories. Despite all the time and money spent in the development of a radically new vehicle, as well as the production techniques and employee involvement programs needed to create it, he knew that the car's success could still be quickly destroyed by a disenchanted work force believing patently false alarms.

15

GOING HOLLYWOOD

In 1983, while members of Veraldi's team were still formalizing the manufacturing plans for Taurus/Sable, another group had started to create the proper public environment for the car's introduction. With the company's recent mammoth 1980 losses, Veraldi could not afford a public relations fiasco. More than with any other vehicle to date, the upcoming 1986 launch had to be perfectly controlled.

It would be the task of the public affairs department to ensure that by the time of the introduction, the names Taurus and Sable were on everyone's lips. Public affairs needed to create national anticipation for the vehicle, and that could only be done by convincing the press that Taurus was exciting news. While advertising created print layouts and television commercials to communicate directly with the populace, public affairs had to rouse an automotive press used to receiving glowing reports about every new car launch. Only by stimulating the press could they hope to get what was nothing less than free advertising, a host of extensive and hopefully positive articles about the car.

The goal of corporate public relations was not to disseminate news, but to carefully manage it. Ford had become an expert in the field. It had gained a reputation among journalists and book writers as an open, accessible company. It readily made its top executives available for interviews, and its public relations staff worked hard to provide reams of printed material.

Ford's public affairs department picked Chuck Gumushian to manage the Taurus launch. Gumushian loved cars and he loved Ford. While the top public affairs executives had large offices on the top floors of the World Headquarters, Gumushian worked in the trenches, bent over a metal desk in a small prefabricated metal cubicle, squeezed in between a computer and a filing cabinet. Still, Gumushian was a company man. "Even my children kid me about my attachment to the company," he said.

Gumushian had spent his first five years at Ford as a technical writer in the engine department. He was peeved that engine engineering never got its due, and in an attempt to right that wrong, he wrote technical articles about the staff and their work for industry publications. Unbeknownst to him, Gumushian was already performing public relations.

His work did not go unnoticed. When a slot in engineering p.r. opened, Gumushian applied for the job. From engineering public relations he moved into product public relations. It was the ideal position for him. "I'm a product guy," Gumushian thought. "I'd be all wrong in corporate p.r., dealing with noncar issues. I want to promote product. That's why I can relate so well to the engineering people."

Gumushian's ability to understand engineers was an important asset for Lew Veraldi. His empathy with engineering helped cement their relationship. Contrary to most executives' mere tolerance of their public relations staffs, Veraldi understood the necessity of a strong p.r. effort. "You have an open door on this project," he told Gumushian. "Go anywhere, ask anyone anything you want. And come to me if you're not getting what you need."

David Scott, Ford's head of public affairs, had asked Gumushian to get involved in the Taurus project because he knew cars. "We've heard this name *Taurus* kicked around," Gumushian's manager, Bill Peacock, told him in 1983. "We know it's a car, but none of us know what the hell it is. We need someone with a technical background like you to find out about it and prepare the launch."

Gumushian was eager for the job, but he was also surprised that it was being presented to him so early on. Traditionally, public relations became involved with a vehicle a few months before its official introduction. If a car premiered in the fall, p.r. first gathered together in June "long lead" magazine writers, people who had to submit their articles two to three months before publication. That was the first time that journalists and public relations staffers alike would usually see a new car. But now, Scott was sending Gumushian out on assignment in August 1983, more than two years before the Taurus launch.

"Why do you want me to get into this so early?" Gumushian asked Scott.

"We've heard that this is supposed to be a brand-new type of vehicle," Scott said. "We have to find out if it's going to fly. If it's not, we have to figure out how to make it fly. And you have to find out, Chuck, is the consuming public ready for this type of thing? Have we reached out too far? Have we not gone far enough? You have to determine that. By the time this car is launched, I want your campaign to have generated fifty percent public awareness."

This was an unprecedented goal. Car manufacturers

counted themselves lucky if 20 to 25 percent of the public entered a dealership specifically to see a certain car. "This had never been done before—never," Gumushian said. "I accepted it as another challenge, but I had no idea how we were going to achieve the objective."

Public affairs expected more than just a launch plan from Gumushian. Gumushian's initial job was to gather intelligence. Scott wanted a full report on the car, what it was about and who was involved in it.

Gumushian's first glimpse of the Taurus convinced him that Ford had a winner on their hands. "When I first saw the models," he said, "I thought, 'This is dynamite. In no way is Ford Motor Company gonna build this car. This must be a concept car.' "

Gumushian became one of the full-time members of the Taurus team. He was pulled out of his first floor office and given a private room on the third floor, where he would not be interrupted. He spent the next six months researching the Taurus project. "I read every piece of literature available on the program, advanced reports, advanced proposals. Everything I read was classified and confidential. Lew Veraldi told his people, 'Give him anything he needs.' Veraldi knew my task wasn't going to be easy.

"The reading led me to get interested in people I should talk with. And I did a lot of interviewing, in Chicago, in Atlanta, because I started going out and talking to people at the plant level that were going to build this car. Lew Veraldi told me from the outset: whenever I had a question about anything on this project to come in and see him."

In January 1984, Gumushian distributed his summary of the Taurus project to thirty-five public affairs staffers. Conscious of Scott's directive that the car generate 50 percent public awareness, Gumushian began to develop a launch strategy. By the middle of February, it was ready for presentation.

Given that the car was scheduled for a fall 1985

launch, presenting the vehicle to the press that summer would be a mistake. Its introduction could easily be overlooked among the announcements of the competitors' upcoming models. Ford needed to make a much bigger splash than that.

While Gumushian was planning his Taurus launch strategy, Ray Ablondi and Martin Goldfarb returned to Marin County, the home of some of Ford's sharpest critics. The first of Ford's aerodynamic cars, the Thunderbird, was now in the marketplace, the Tempo and Topaz had just come out, and the Taurus and Sable could finally be shown. Just the year before, the company had reentered the black after four years of heavy losses. Ford officials wondered if this time the response to their vehicles would be any better.

Goldfarb gathered many of the same people who had trashed the company two and a half years earlier. He wanted to conduct a follow-up focus-group session to learn if in the interim their negative perceptions of the Ford Motor Company had changed. After they viewed the cars, the participants once again sat around a table.

"I was really surprised you'd invite us back," one woman said. "Last time we really raked you over the coals."

"My perception of Ford over the last couple of years has increased dramatically," another said. "Ford's a much more contemporary company than it used to be."

"Of all the American manufacturers," said one man, "Ford is definitely ahead, and I would seriously consider buying a Ford in the future. The Taurus has, I hate to admit it, a better body-style design than the Audi 5000."

Ford's regained profitability, its cars, and its image campaign had greatly elevated the company's stature in the eyes of the focus-group participants. "I want to identify with something that's successful," one man pointed out. "Something that makes money. Something that's of today."

Caldwell, Petersen, and Ablondi were elated by the

responses. Clearly they were on the right track. Consumers now perceived Ford as a forward-looking company that was beginning to give customers what they wanted. When the Taurus was released in two years, it looked like the market would be ready for it.

Meanwhile, Gumushian solidified his plans for the car's official press launch. His idea was to beat all the other manufacturers to the punch by previewing the vehicles at a January 1985 press conference, an unheard-of nine months before they went on sale. The press conference would have to create as much hoopla as the cars themselves, and that couldn't be done by gathering the press in Detroit's Ford Auditorium. The glamour of the launch would best be set in Los Angeles, the home of the film industry, fantasy, and the unofficial capital of America's hackneyed "love affair" with cars.

Picking a special location to preview a car was not a new idea. Press conferences were held wherever a manufacturer thought its vehicles would get the best play, whether in an auditorium or on a ski slope. When Fiat launched its subcompact Uno, the company unveiled it in Florida. Cars and journalists were shipped over from Europe for the occasion, even though the Uno would never be sold in the United States.

Gumushian, Scott, and other public affairs staffers came up with the idea of a full-day Taurus/Sable affair in L.A. During the morning, reporters would gather at MGM studio's sound stage 85 for a press conference and introduction of the car. In the evening, a star-studded party and a reintroduction of the cars would be held on the same stage, the site of the filming of scenes from *Gone With the Wind*. What better way to ensure coverage of a business story than by promising the presence of movie stars?

Ford's ad agencies, Young and Rubicam and J. Walter Thompson, approved of the early-introduction concept. The consensus was that with cars as different-looking as these two, the extra promotional time would help the market get used to the new shape. JWT staffers pushed for even further exposure, recommending that after the January press introduction the car be exposed to the public at February's Chicago auto show. Nobody was worried about potential LTD buyers who might decide not to buy until the new Taurus came out. The higher age LTD buyers probably wouldn't be interested in the more modern-looking Taurus anyway, everyone felt. Even if they were, they would not be among the cars' initial purchasers.

The event was almost a year away, but the logistics needed to put it together were enormous. The evening event was planned as an extravaganza, so Ford decided to hire the best producer they could find. Rogers and Cowan, Ford's Los Angeles–based public relations firm, suggested Robert F. Jani.

Jani had made a name for himself as a producer of live commercial pagentry. His more spectacular affairs included the Bicentennial fireworks exhibition in New York Harbor and the opening ceremonies for the 1984 Los Angeles Olympic Games. By the time he got the call from Rogers and Cowan, he was already at work on planning the Reagan presidential inauguration ceremonies in Washington, D.C. Jani had always shied away from industrial projects, as he felt he never knew what he could accomplish with them. But the scope of Ford's goals and the importance of the Taurus to the company excited Jani, and he decided to take the job.

The Taurus and Sable sedans and wagons would be revealed to the public, as opposed to the press, for the first time during the evening festivities. The problem was that except for clay and fiberglass models, the cars did not yet exist. This gala introduction was going to take place in January 1985, nine months before the first cars would be produced at Ford's Atlanta plant, and close to a year before they'd be manufactured in Chicago. Showing mere clay and fiberglass models, however, would be inappropriate. No matter how good they were, in the final analysis they just did not look like true production units. Gumushian was determined that the cars on display in Los Angeles be exact representations of the cars that would roll off the assembly line nine months later.

Selling Veraldi on the idea was not difficult, even though building prototypes was an expensive and complex process. Veraldi estimated that making hand-built cars that actually worked would cost an additional $6 million, but he decided to go ahead anyway.

He was swayed by his recollection of an almost disastrous introduction of the Lincoln Mark VII, another car which he had supervised a few years earlier. At the time of the press preview at Detroit's Renaissance Center, the vehicle had not yet entered production, so a hand-assembled unit had to be shown. The car was a hodge-podge of parts and door panels swiped from other models. Ford even had to throw sandbags into various parts of the body to get it to sit level. The car's interior was all wrong, and to hide the errors, mistakes were painted over with an airbrush. Veraldi prayed that nothing would fall off before the press saw the car.

When the curtains opened, the Mark looked great, shiny and new, perched on its rotating turntable. Veraldi made sure that the platform was encircled with rope and kept strictly off limits to the journalists. He was not going to take the chance that an enthusiastic reporter would grab a handle and inadvertently pull a door off its hinges. That would do wonders for Ford's claims of quality.

The Atlanta plant would not start Taurus production until several months after the January press conference. Production models would be made with parts cast from dies, but many dies did not yet exist. Consequently, the cars that would be displayed at the Los Angeles preview had to be produced from scratch and assembled by hand.

In addition to the automobiles, Gumushian wanted to bring cutaway engines and transmissions, as well as working models of both front and rear suspensions. Large panel displays would complete the package, designed to promote Ford's emphasis on ergonomics, interior components, and seating design.

While preparations were under way, Gumushian turned to a more familiar tactic. For several years writers had known that a replacement for Ford's midsize car was due. Now, several months before the press introduction, it was time to kindle journalists' interest through selective leaks. This was a variation on a long-practiced theme. Auto manufacturers regularly drove new cars too close to their test track's fence in the hope that a spy for a car magazine would take a "scoop" picture. Prototype vehicles were tested on highways and in other public areas likely to attract professional photographers and auto fans eager for an exclusive shot.

In November 1985, Gumushian began to invite a few journalists over to the design center for exclusive previews of fiberglass mock-ups of the Taurus and Sable. They had to pledge not to write anything about what they saw until after the January event, but they were certain to talk about what they did see with their colleagues, and that would help build interest in the cars.

Four prototypes were to be built, a sedan and station wagon for both Taurus and Sable. Assembly by UAW factory workers was a tedious and exacting process, for many of the parts had to be shaped by hand and then reshaped to fit. Gumushian met with the workers every day to discuss production problems, helping to overcome a shortage of parts, for instance, or figuring out how to get a panel to fit.

Gumushian fretted over this project like a new parent. Not only was the press seeing these prototypes for the first time, but all the top brass, including Phil Caldwell, Don Petersen, Lew Veraldi, and Jack Telnack, would be there as well. The vehicles had to be perfect. Nobody could be embarrassed by them.

"This was not an easy task," Gumushian said, "let me tell you. And everybody worked over the Christmas holidays because it was so exciting. I can't begin to describe the air—there was such excitement around the company.

"These guys would do anything for you. And you're

working with UAW people, they're not easy to work with. But these guys got so wrapped up in this program that they worked night and day to get those cars ready for the California introduction."

Gumushian had not exhausted his repertoire, however. "I want Team Taurus to stand out," Veraldi told him. "What suggestion do you have to make that happen?"

"How about a jacket?" Gumushian answered.

"Good idea, go make one."

"I did Taurus hats, Taurus pins, Taurus satin jackets, Taurus key fobs. It was all part of Employee Involvement. The people who have these things cherish them because it means they were part of the team. It gets everybody pumped up. What is it, a few bucks? In the final analysis, everything paid off."

On Monday, January 21, 1985, Gumushian set up his command post at the Century Plaza in Los Angeles. Executives and the media would soon be flying in from all over and stationed at the hotel, and Gumushian was supervising the influx. The three Ford tractor trailers that Gumushian had requisitioned to haul everything west from Detroit soon arrived. The cutaway engines and transmissions, the dynamic suspension models, the ergonomic displays were all so elaborate that they filled up their own truck. They were unloaded at the Century Plaza hotel to be set up, and the other two drove to MGM in neighboring Culver City.

Work continued throughout the week. Gumushian had his construction crew flown out from Detroit to assemble the exhibits, and they continued working on the models, buffing and rebuffing them, until the last few minutes before the press conference began.

For those involved in Taurus, a feverish anticipation had set in, as happens often after a long period of intense, focused creative effort.

"We decided five years ago that we needed to try harder to learn what our customers wanted, and not worry how that made us different from the competition," Don

Petersen proclaimed to the hundreds of reporters from all over the world who gathered the morning of January 29. "These cars prove that beauty and utility can live very happily together."

Los Angeles was more than a press conference for Phil Caldwell, who celebrated his sixty-fifth birthday that same month. In a few days the man who had believed in Lew Veraldi's capabilities to lead the Taurus team, who had loyally backed Jack Telnack in his quest to extend the nature of American car design, would retire from Ford, replaced as chairman by Don Petersen.

Caldwell, Petersen, and Telnack took turns addressing one of the largest crowds ever to attend an auto industry press conference. After all, this was just an introduction of a new car; it wasn't an announcement of the sale of the company.

"The Tempo and Topaz were only the first wave of future products," Phil Caldwell said. "Here is our next wave. With the Taurus and Sable, we're seeking to redefine what a family car of the future should be."

These were lofty statements, opinions that once would have been considered ill-advised and risky within an organization that normally rewarded complacency and imitation. If one could believe these men, these words had ostensibly become the company's credo.

Like all press conferences, the day was filled with hyperbole:

"The past year gave us the biggest market share we've had in five years," Caldwell pointed out.

"Nobody expects a station wagon to handle like a sports car, but Taurus and Sable do."

"The Taurus and Sable have had the most extensive training program for service personnel ever."

"We expect to build 410,000 Tauruses and Sables the first year of production, and 550,000 after that."

As the speeches ended, the curtains were pulled back. The moment they saw the cars, 450 normally staid reporters broke into spontaneous applause. It was a shocking response from an industry gathering. Unlike the Mark VII launch of a few years back, these vehicles were not roped off. Everyone was invited up to the stage to examine the cars as much as they liked.

The morning conference was but the prelude to the evening event. In addition to industry executives and dealers, Rogers and Cowan invited a group of Hollywood personalities to attend the affair. These weren't big stars, but the kind seen on *Hollywood Squares*: Jack Carter, Buddy Hackett, June Lockhart, George Maharis, Danny Thomas, Richard Thomas, and Esther Williams.

With Hollywood in attendance, Robert Jani and his son, Jeff, were motivated to create an environment that would rival the grandest movie premiere. The problem was that the center of attraction was just a car, an inanimate object. The Janis had to create excitement before its unveiling so that the audience wouldn't be bored. "If we can heighten that anticipation and keep building all the way along," Jeff Jani said, "then once the car is revealed, all that people can do is to ooh and ah, because we'll have already presold them."

The Janis decided to capitalize on the film *2010*, which was then playing throughout the country, by designing a futuristic space-age theme to define the presentation. First, MGM's huge stage 85 was divided into reception and dining areas. They draped black curtains across the top to lower the eighty-nine-foot-high ceiling, and across a stage that had been constructed to divide off the dining room from a smaller reception area.

As guests arrived and were greeted by car valets, they entered the smaller area—which had been decorated with movie props to look like the landing bridge of a spaceship—for drinks. When it was time for dinner, the curtains parted to reveal a magnificent dinner area. Centerpieces resembling satellites hung over each table, suspended from the ceiling. A fleet of forty slide projectors illuminated the black curtains with star fields and photographs obtained from NASA libraries. Before the program began, the centerpieces rose in unison out of the way of the diners. "That surprise act alone almost got a standing ovation from the guests," Jeff Jani said.

As the evening progressed, movie screens were brought down along the walls as specially made films projected images that gave the sensation of flying through space. "None of this had anything to do with the Taurus," Jani said. "It had to do with building a presentation leading up to the car. The synthesized music and film built up emotions through the dramatic effect of the environment we created."

Jani knew that he was succeeding when Donald Petersen rose to speak. Part of Jani's plan was to structure the musical and visual effects so that by the time Petersen came to the podium, all attention would be riveted on him. Rather than read his prepared speech, Petersen threw away his index cards and spoke to the audience extemporaneously. Everyone seemed to be getting carried away by the excitement of the event.

As the music and lighting increased in intensity, the cars, which were hidden behind black curtains on the stage, began to glow. As their eerie outlines emerged, the multimedia effects began to rise to a climax. The pitch-black room was bathed in synthesized music, covered in swirling star patterns and theatrical effects. The room appeared to be moving as high-speed space films raced across the walls. At the peak of energy, the curtains were pulled back to reveal the dramatically illuminated, glowing cars. "The audience gasped," said Jani. "The cars looked great."

Among the overwhelmed onlookers, though, one was distinctly unimpressed. David Davis, an influential automotive-magazine writer, then editor of *Car and Driver*, looked around the conference room. He didn't see any of his colleagues bowled over by the presentation either. But then, Davis knew that this do wasn't really for him or his buddies in the buff-book business, but for television and newspaper reporters. Davis was more interested in getting in the cars and driving them unhindered on the roads, away from company test tracks and the watchful eyes of public relations foot soldiers. At this point he merely was pleased that the p.r. staff had succeeded in churning out tons of printed information, and that all of it seemed accurate.

Over the next few months, Davis noticed that the Taurus splash had made its mark. Although negative stories about Ford continued to appear, they were juxtaposed by positive stories about the Taurus, some appearing in the same day's issue just pages away. There, Davis believed, was the evidence of the genius of Ford's public relations effort. The overall thrust of the media's approach toward Ford began to change, becoming positive and concerned. Davis's perception was that most General Motors stories began with the phrase, "The beleaguered General Motors . . ." while articles about Ford positioned the company as striding from success to success.

For every Ford person involved in the launch, the audience's applause was a stirring emotional release after five years of work.

"This is the most exciting day in my career at the Ford Motor Company!" a beaming Jack Telnack told a television interviewer after the press conference. "These will be the finest cars built anywhere in the Ford universe. This project is full of heroes, and I could name a hundred of them now."

Even in the flush of his personal triumph, the team spirit had not left Telnack's consciousness. He knew full well that not one person, but a group working in a new way for Ford, had been responsible for bringing this car to fruition.

Compared to Telnack, Chuck Gumushian had been involved in Taurus for only a short time, just two years. But he, too, had been swept up in the camaraderie, the strength of commitment that came from a shared goal. Yes, this was only a car. But for Gumushian, like everyone else on Team Taurus, this was a unique experience in his long career at Ford.

"I get emotional. But when I recall standing in front of that stage at MGM in Hollywood, looking at those cars for the first time, I couldn't control myself. A car never brought tears to my eyes like this one did. I don't know. Is that a weakness?"

16

THE TAURUS AND SABLE SHOW

"Well done," was David Scott's response to Gumushian after the MGM event. "Now, what are you going to do for the next ten months?"

The early public introduction made that consideration easier. Now that its wraps were off, the car could be shown to anyone. Plans had already been laid for June—a long lead press introduction was set for the magazine writers. Public affairs needed to think of something to fill the gap until then.

Gumushian realized that there was a large audience of Ford supporters among the people who made parts for the car. Why not get them involved as Taurus boosters?

In fact, workers at Taurus's supplier companies, the firms that made glass, switches, insulation, grommets, and a thousand other items, were as much a part of the project as Ford people. But they never got to see the car until it was already in the showroom. And even then they often could only guess what role they played in producing the vehicle.

The suppliers needed their own version of an Employee Involvement program, Gumushian figured. What better way to encourage the workers to do a good job than by showing them the finished goods? It would be easy. He already had the prototype cars and the trucks to transport them in. "We're always talking Team," Gumushian thought. "If these people really are part of the team, then let's act like it." He proposed to public affairs that the cars hit the road in Taurus and Sable's own version of a dog and pony show.

For $95,000, Gumushian said, he could make a two-month-long tractor-trailer caravan that would visit a number of small towns and help get the workers excited about their own handiwork. The idea proved just mildly interesting to some Ford staffers. They were concerned as to whether or not it made any financial sense.

"Is this a cost-effective idea, Chuck?" Scott wanted to know.

"I don't know, Dave. I have nothing to go on. This will be our first time trying this."

The idea made sense, Gumushian argued, because the visits would generate a lot of free publicity. Many of the Ford suppliers were based in small cities and towns around America, and were the areas' major employers. Not much usually happened in these places. The local television and radio stations, he figured, were always looking for stories. Two tractor trailers rolling into town, painted up with the Ford Taurus and Mercury Sable logos, would be one of the biggest events in years.

"Every supplier is a potential salesman for us," Gumushian continued. "We go out there with our cars that he has inputted into, he'll buy one. Or he'll tell his friends about it."

Still, Gumushian could not convince the others. "We don't know. We're not crazy about this," some of the Ford parts executives said. "You want to go out there and spend our project's money, but you can't justify the expense."

"How the hell can I justify the expense if I've never done it before?" Gumushian demanded to know. It was just that kind of small thinking that had put the company in the position it was in today.

Instead he asked Veraldi to intercede. Veraldi liked the caravan idea because it fit in with the philosophy that he had first applied in the 1970s for the Ford Fiesta. "Give the guy with some equity in the business a stake," Veraldi used to say. "If you just give him or her a chance to put their oar in the water, the job's gonna work better."

"If you think it's a good idea, Chuck, just do it. I'll support you. I'll get you the money out of my own budget."

Gumushian wrote to every Taurus parts supplier. They all loved the idea, and he soon had a filled tour schedule. Each stop turned into a major event. "Invite the mayor and other local dignitaries. Coordinate the show with the local dealers, whatever. It's your town," Gumushian told local suppliers, "you bring who you want."

The beauty of the whole idea was that on a per-stop basis, the caravan cost practically nothing. Gas for the two trucks, the drivers' salaries, a thousand dollars per diem and that was it. Food, drinks, balloons, everything else was supplied by the local company.

Gumushian joined the crew for the first stop. He journeyed to Huntsville, Alabama, to show off the cars to the employees of Inglehart Industries, suppliers of the Taurus/Sable's catalytic converters. "They were overwhelmed at what we were doing," he said. "Nobody had ever done anything like this for them before." Suppliers began writing Gumushian and Veraldi, thanking them for coming to their plant. One was so impressed with the presentation that he told Gumushian he was ready to order a car.

Auto-assembly plant workers at least saw the finished

product. Automobile-parts manufacturing, on the other hand, was a specialized business. It was often impossible to imagine how in the world a small, oddly shaped piece of rubber or plastic an employee churned out would ever fit on a car.

One of the Sable's distinguishing characteristics was that its rear window was separated from its side glass not by a metal pillar as on the Taurus, but by a black rubber seal. That seal was made in a mold, and before it was sent off to the assembly plant, a worker had to trim protruding bits of rubber, called flash marks. If they weren't, the rear window looked sloppy.

When the Taurus/Sable caravan stopped at the Oklahoma plant that made those seals, Veraldi approached one of the flash-mark cutters.

"Ma'am, do you realize how important your job is to the car we're making?"

"No, not at all," she answered.

"Well then, please come with me. I want you to see something."

Veraldi brought her over to the Sable display that had been set up in the factory. He showed her exactly where her rubber seal went and why the car would look bad if she didn't do a good job.

A few days later, Veraldi received a letter from that woman. She thanked him for explaining, for the first time, how her work was important to the quality of the cars being produced. She finally felt that her work was part of a bigger whole.

The Trico windshield-wiper-blade company, a longtime Ford supplier, was thrilled to have the caravan stop at its plant. The cars were placed in the middle of the factory, and during lunch hour workers were invited to inspect the result of their labors.

"A few days later, Trico wrote to Lew Veraldi," Gumushian remembered. "They said, 'Lou, in the seventy-five years we've been in business, no one—not one company—has thought enough about us to bring their cars out before and show it to our employees.' That's the kind of feedback we got from these people. It was gratifying to me because it was my idea. I had to fight for it, but now it's becoming institutionalized."

By the time the program was completed, 110 cities and towns had been visited by the Taurus and Sable caravan. Gumushian compiled a "play report" at the end of the tour, documenting all the free newspaper, radio, and television coverage that the caravan had generated. He calculated that at normal advertising rates, the $95,000 investment had produced $3 million worth of publicity.

In February 1985, at the same time that the Taurus and Sable caravans were traveling around the country, Veraldi decided to do one last market test in Boca Raton. Having usable prototypes that exactly resembled a production car was a first for Ford. Usually the only available model had been put together from various pieces, with mismatched doors and interiors.

When one female participant was asked to open the hood, she got her hands covered in grease. "Why don't you put a piece of yellow plastic over the latch?" she asked. "That's a good idea. Find out how much it'll cost," Veraldi said to an assistant. The thirty-cent plastic cover, an item that would normally have had to wait until after the first model year was over to be incorporated, was added to the car before launch. It was these design "trifles" that Veraldi considered as vigorously as more major elements of the car, for he felt that each detail subtly contributed to and defined the overall package.

As a result of his concern, Veraldi was adamant that the car be launched only with a highly styled front end that featured the Ford logo in a "floating" oval design. The stylists had also designed a more traditional front with wide horizontal slats for a grill, and based on market research, some Team Taurus members argued these should be used for the lower-priced models.

"We're not going with the slats—in any model," Veraldi declared to the team in his usual blunt manner. "This is what the car's gonna have. The Taurus deserves it." Bob Rewey, Lincoln-Mercury's representative on the Team, agreed with Risk and Veraldi that they should use the oval, but the research still pointed in the opposite direction.

"Don't you believe in research?" Lou Ross asked Veraldi. "If you don't believe in it, what do you have it for?"

"Research doesn't tell you everything, Lou," Veraldi said. "And in this case the research is wrong. We're going with the oval. That's final."

As Veraldi returned from the meeting, Terri Glowacki, Veraldi's secretary, couldn't help notice her boss's grumpy mood. She had become pretty convinced that his diabetes, not his passion for excellence, was causing it.

"Lew, have you been watching your diet? Do you think your sugar level's out of balance again?" she wanted to know.

"Don't bother me!" Veraldi yelled as he slammed his office door. "What the hell is this? I've got a Polack on my back at home and a Polack on my back at work!"

"Oh yeah?" Glowacki yelled back. "Well, that's what the dagos need, a good strong Polack!"

Job One, the date that the first production Taurus would roll off Atlanta's assembly line, was scheduled for July 1985. (The Chicago plant would not start producing cars until January 1986.) The Taurus would be formally introduced to the public at the beginning of October, although some dealers would have cars a week or two earlier.

Plant workers had been assembling prototype vehicles for several months prior to Job One, and everything seemed to be working well. The increase in the amount of automated equipment allowed the plant to raise hourly production from 55 to 68 cars per hour, utilizing the same 2,700-person work force. The automobile's level of fit and finish was now much more highly dependent on automation than it had ever been.

Production sheet metal began arriving at the plant in June. Shortly thereafter, Veraldi received a message from

Atlanta. "We've got a problem, Lew. Parts are not fitting correctly."

As the underbodies and side panels were being assembled, plant personnel had noticed that the variability between the panels was much greater than it had been with the prototype sheet metal that they had assembled just weeks before. The production vehicles were coming out all wrong. Large gaps were developing between the front and rear panels. Doors were not fitting properly. Trunks were not opening or closing easily.

"Stop production," Veraldi ordered. "Find the problem and get it fixed. We're postponing the launch."

If this had been 1975 instead of 1985, management would have argued that the production errors were not all that grievous. Tolerances were off and clearances were wrong, but Veraldi would have shipped those cars. In the present competitive market, though, he could no longer afford to do that.

"The problem was that we had certified all the moldings, the fit of the glass, the interior trim, using preproduction metal—that's metal produced from preproduction dies that aren't completely finished," Veraldi said. "And when the final dies arrived at the plant, there were differences in radii and corner structures. We had to do them all over again because things didn't fit just right. In the past we would have just pumped the cars out and said, 'Well, we'll get better later.'

"We learned that you have to plan your launch after the production process is complete. The Japanese plan their launch about three months after the production is certified. And we were doing it simultaneously. I used to joke that we never really got our production metal until three months after we started production."

To make matters worse, Ford had contracted with too many suppliers for the metal. With ten separate sources for one item, variability problems were likely to happen.[1] The Taurus launch was rescheduled from October 1985 to the first quarter of 1986. It seemed like a good time for a product introduction, since Ford would be able to tie in the premiere with the upcoming Chicago and Detroit auto shows. With those extra months the Atlanta assembly plant now had enough time to guarantee that the production process would be accurate.

Gumushian immediately protested. "If we launch in January or February, we'll miss Car of the Year." *Motor Trend*'s Car of the Year award was a highly valued prize, one manufacturers loved to promote in their advertising as proof that their car was superior to others. Car of the Year eligibility rules stated that a vehicle had to be in production before the end of the previous calendar year, and the car had to be on sale before the magazine's January issue hit the stands. A January launch meant that the Taurus, as a 1986 model, was forever disqualified. "We don't know if we'll win," Gumushian and others argued, "but at least let's not lose the chance to give it a shot."

The team agreed to change the premiere date again, but with the Christmas holidays looming, there weren't too many options. Launch in early December, and everyone would be busy shopping. Launch after Christmas, and people would be too busy paying bills. There was only one day when neither of those two events would occur: Thursday, December 26, 1985. The day was a holiday for many. Hopefully, people would have nothing to do, and some of them would decide to head down to a car showroom.

Prior to launch, the company continued to perform consumer evaluations and tests. Some were small, resembling efforts by a young importer struggling to gain a foothold in the U.S. But Ford was struggling to hold on to its market share and stem its financial losses.

In conjunction with Hertz, more than a thousand people were asked to drive and evaluate the car for several days. The program began in California, site of Ford's harshest critics. Consumers loved getting a brand-new car to drive for free. "All my neighbors came over at night asking me to give them a ride," said one participant. If one person liked the car, Ford executives figured, they could influence the buying interest of forty to fifty people. Ray Ablondi said, "All these people just got through telling us they were not going to buy Fords anymore, or even pay any attention to us. This is what you have to do when you're desperate."

The prelaunch publicity generated continued press coverage about the cars. Based on the mail coming into the office of Joel Pitcoff, Ford's ad hoc consumer advocate, Ford staff sensed that the Taurus and Sable were attracting a more knowledgeable consumer.

"Remember," Pitcoff pointed out, "I'm the marketing plans manager for this car, so all the mail gets funneled to me. And I start reading that people want to know how the car does in a crash test relative to a Volvo. Or whether it has this kind of feature that they have in the Saab. The world always said we were going after these imports. And the irony is, if I added up the volumes of all those imports that the world thought we were targeting this car on, we wouldn't have had enough volume to keep one of our plants running all year, let alone two of them.

"But that was the perception people had. We planned the car as a better than domestic midsize car. We said we had enough content in this car that we could stand a certain amount of premium pricing over the watermark that was established by the Chevrolet Celebrity, which was the planning target for the car. But what the world saw was not that this was a step up from Celebrity justified by added value. They saw the car had the near equivalent of a $25,000 import car that you could buy for $15,000."

The hint of strong initial interest in the car did not allay the concerns of conservative company executives. The uniqueness of the product still frightened them, and they remained wary about the car's potential. They continued to try to slow down the pace of change exemplified by Taurus.

Changes in the car product line were happening too fast, argued one top Ford executive in a summer 1985 meeting with the new Ford president, Red Poling. There was still a large reservoir of loyal customers who liked the traditional vehicles that Ford made, said the executive, including those that the Taurus and Sable were going to replace. By discontinuing those Taurus and Sable predecessors, Ford would alienate a loyal owner body and lose sales.

"Make Atlanta the only plant producing the new cars," Poling was advised. "Chicago should continue to make the LTD and Marquis for another year." Poling rejected the idea. The company had made a firm commitment to this new model, he said. True, the demographics of those LTD buyers were older than what was expected for the Taurus. But the public had to get used to the new look. The company needed to show direction. The Taurus and Sable would help people become accustomed to new styling, instead of sticking to their old ideas.

Dealers across the country were also nervous about the new cars. Although they had no say over the company's product mix, some believed the market would split between traditional LTD lovers and Taurus converts, and they continued to push the old models to their customers. After five years of working on the Taurus project, Joel Pitcoff knew otherwise. He was convinced that the product was going to destroy all other competition, including its own. "Within thirty days after we introduce Taurus and Sable," he predicted, "you won't be able to give away those leftover LTDs and Marquis'. They'll be deader than a mackerel in Lake Erie."

17

THE LEGACY OF TAURUS

Taurus and Sable launched, as scheduled, on December 26, 1985. In Nebraska, the initial showroom traffic was so strong that a dealer said, "This is the best response I've seen for a new car since the 1969 [Lincoln] Mark." In Minneapolis, the introduction became a media event, with the arrival of a television crew at the local Ford dealership to film the launch of the car in its city.[1]

In January 1986, *Motor Trend* awarded the Taurus its Car of the Year award. "If we were to describe the Taurus's design in a word, the word is *thoughtful*," wrote *Consumer Reports* in May 1986. "The automaker clearly studied the features of the world's cars and chose the best for its Taurus/Sable. . . . Overall, it scored the highest of any domestic car we've tested." *Car and Driver* said that the Taurus was "one of history's most radical new cars. . . . This is the gutsiest car of our time because it's aimed squarely at the middle of the market." Four years later, in May 1990, *Motor Trend* wrote that the Taurus LX "represents the established standard in the class. If you're simply shopping for the best all-around four-door, the choice remains the same as it was five years ago: the Ford Taurus LX."

Car and Driver put the Taurus on its Ten Best Cars list in 1986. It did it again in 1987, '88, '89, and 1990. "[Taurus makes] the most attractive station wagon in Detroit history," the magazine stated.[2]

"[It] stands out in the material landscape," *Business Week* reported in a cover story. "The sleek, elegant lines of a liquid black automobile as it slips around a curve. The difference is design, that elusive blend of form and function, quality and style, art and engineering. [Was this] product created in the famous design studios of Paris, Munich, Milan, or Turin? No. The car is a Ford Sable from Detroit."[3]

"Well, Terri," Veraldi said to his secretary after the initial sales reports and reviews were in, "it didn't turn out to be the perfect car. But it is the closest thing I've ever seen to one."

The Taurus project and its associated programs changed Ford, but did not revolutionize the company. Employee Involvement programs remain in place at all assembly plants. New car projects continue to be organized around the Team Taurus model, but the success of the approach depends on the personalities involved in the program. Ford's customer-driven philosophy has permeated the company.

Taurus/Sable sales never reached the predicted 550,000 units annually. Its earnings were high enough, however, to help the company generate record profits, and its unit sales were responsible for two-thirds of Ford's U.S. market-share increase. Thanks to the two cars, Ford captured an average 28.1 percent of the U.S. midsize segment between 1987–89, compared to 14.5 percent for its predecessor LTD/Marquis models in the years 1983–85.

In the first quarter of 1986, Ford had turned its billion-dollar annual loss around, making $728 million on $14 billion in sales. By the first quarter of 1987, Ford made more money than General Motors: $1.49 billion in profit compared to GM's $922 million. Sales jumped to $18 billion while GM's were steady at $26 billion. In 1986, Ford's profits totaled $3.28 billion. For 1987, the company made a profit of $4.6 billion. Profits rose further to $5.3 billion in 1988, then declined in 1989. "Ford's Taurus/Sable twins put the company back on the map and filled Ford's coffers, making it the big winner in the Detroit sweepstakes," noted the automotive columnist for the *New York Times* in an end-of-decade wrap-up.[4]

The cars also succeeded in lowering the demographics for Ford's midsize segment. The median age of 1985 Ford LTD buyers was sixty, that of Mercury Marquis, fifty-nine. In 1986, that dropped to fifty-one for Taurus (the LTD replacement), fifty-four for Sable. Taurus wagon buyers were on average nine years younger than their comparative LTD wagon purchasers.[5]

Taurus sales increased from 354,000 in 1987 to 374,000 in 1988, becoming the best-selling car in America. Sable sales rose from 104,000 to 119,000 in the same period. Taurus sales declined to 348,000 in 1989, while Sable dropped to 110,962. In that year, Taurus was the best-selling Big Three car in America, beating its sister Escort by 15,000 units.[6]

In late 1987, the Taurus's growing positive reputation was on the verge of being seriously damaged. On October 1, Clarence Ditlow III, executive director of the Center for Auto Safety, a nonprofit consumer organization founded by Ralph Nader, wrote Ford chairman Don Petersen, asking him to recall all Tauruses and Sables manufactured to date. "Based on the hoopla and the promise of a great car, initial Taurus and Sable sales were spectacular," Ditlow noted. "But the bloom fell quickly off the rose as poor quality and design problems led to recalls, extended warranties, bad crash-worthiness and general consumer dissatisfaction."

Ditlow cited several areas that needed particular attention, including widespread problems with stalling and steering binding, piston scuffing, rough downshifting, and electrical systems. Worst of all, he pointed out that the U.S. Department of Transportation's thirty-five-mile-per-hour crash-worthiness tests of the 1986 Taurus and Sable models showed that the drivers of both cars would likely suffer serious injury or death. "These Taurus/Sable problems belie Ford's advertising claims and make a mockery of the early reviews the car received in some publications," Ditlow said.

Veraldi was furious when the defect reports started coming into his office.

"This should never have happened!" he screamed. "I want to find out who didn't do their job. Damn it, we were striving for the perfect car. There's a problem and I want to see those things fixed."

Within months of learning about them, Ford had sent close to sixty engineers to each Taurus assembly plant, attempting to discover the bugs that had not turned up during vehicle testing. It took engineers twelve months to figure out necessary design changes to improve the car's quality. Joe Bobnar was happy to see the quality turned around at his Chicago plant, but he was mystified as to why these problems hadn't been rectified before the car went into production.

As far as Veraldi was concerned, customers were satisfied because Ford did not hesitate to fix things that didn't work. Hot lines were set up whereby he personally called customers with problems. When a customer reported that the engine in their new Taurus didn't work properly, Ford flew one down to the dealership. "That made the customer happy," Veraldi said. " 'As long as I can get it fixed,' they say, 'I'm happy.' That's what quality improvements are all about. The car we made in '87 was a lot better than in '86. And it keeps going that way."

The federal government refused to act on Clarence Ditlow's request for a recall of the cars. Despite the negative press and the poor reliability of many early models, Taurus and Sable sales continued to grow, and the build quality of the cars improved. It was another example of David Davis's belief that in the eyes of the American public, Ford simply remained unassailable.

Four years after launch, internal company research showed that the number of "things gone wrong" reported by Taurus owners declined 53 percent from 1986 to 1990. The figures were part of Ford's annual Competitive New Vehicle Quality study, a survey of 30,000 owners of competitive cars. The 180-question surveys became the basis for the company laying claim to producing "the best-built cars in America, from 1981–1989." This claim was upheld by the Better Business Bureau and the three broadcast networks, which declined, according to Ford market-research executives, to air Ford's commercials until the company could prove that its methodology and findings were accurate.

The efforts by Tom Page and the UAW to improve efficiency and thereby cut costs at Ford have worked. In 1988, Ford's Taurus/Sable plants in Atlanta and Chicago were the first and third most efficient automobile-assembly operations in America. Atlanta needed 2.72 workers to produce each car, while Chicago required 2.87. Among Japanese producers, Honda's Ohio Accord plant ranked 11th, with 3.61 workers/car, and Toyota's U.S. facility for the Camry came in 12th, with 3.65 workers/car, 34 percent more than Taurus's Atlanta operation.[7]

Through the decade the Taurus and Sable, as the Chevrolet Bel-Air and Ford Mustang before them, became synonymous with classic American automobile design. Four years after its launch, the car still looked modern enough to be used as the futuristic police vehicles in *Robocop*, yet the average American family found the car appealing, not strange. The Taurus raised the expectations of middle-class Americans who had still not been touched by the sweeping wave of Japanese automobiles. Thanks to the Taurus, as for no other American family car, U.S. consumers now expected a higher level of quality, performance, and convenience in their vehicles.

General Motors was said to have been forced to redesign its GM-10 cars because they looked too much like Taurus and Sable. "Ford's new cars look just like what we were going to be putting out two years from now," a GM staffer was quoted as saying.[8] Publicly, the corporation had little good to say of its competitor's design. "I remember GM claiming, 'We would never do such an ugly car, or we would never spring it on the public so fast,' " recalled Jerry Hirshberg, Buick's former head of design. " 'We would not be so rude as to spring something on the public without an evolutionary step.' "

"People did say that car was funny-looking," Lou Ross agreed. "Two years later they said, 'That car looks better to me.' And by the third year they're ready to buy it. When we launched the Taurus, Roger Smith said it looked like a jellybean. 'Roger's going to learn to like jelly beans,' I said at the time."

Three years after the Taurus introduction, GM launched the Chevrolet Lumina, its replacement for the GM-10 Celebrity. With the Lumina, the company retreated from any interest it may have previously had in imitating Taurus. Its looks, both inside and out, were conventional. The vehicle retained the traditional squared-off shape of American cars, tempered only by a slight softening of the edges surrounding the top of the trunk. On the inside was the same tired, unattractive, straight-across dash that Ford executives had wholly rejected for the Taurus, Lumina's direct competitor.

Lumina's looks were politely described as "conservative . . . a freshening of the Celebrity model it replaces. The conservative look is what carefully researched Chevrolet customers want," the company's chief engineer claimed.[9] But America's leading consumer magazine didn't think the Lumina was what the public should buy. "Chevrolet's new nameplate doesn't measure up," *Consumer Reports* decided about the Lumina. "Ride and seating were disappointing, and the reliability of new GM models hasn't been encouraging.[10]

By the end of the 1980s, the aerodynamic look pioneered in America by Taurus and Sable had become the company's established design. Whereas the Taurus had been a radical departure from the company's existing boxy shapes, all of Ford's new cars—the 1989 Ford Thunderbird and Mercury Cougar, the 1990 Continental and Town Car, the 1992 Crown Victoria/Mercury Grand Marquis—followed its lead. The 1991 Ford Escort station wagon looks just like a miniature Taurus wagon—a fact Ford proudly boasts of in its ads.

The Taurus was not planned to be reskinned until the 1992 model year, with major changes in sheet metal, taillights, and interior. A completely new Taurus was not scheduled to appear until 1996, ten years after the vehicle had been introduced. By mid-1990, that date had been pushed back even further, until 1997 or 1998. Originally, the next Taurus was to have been built on a platform that would be shared and developed in conjunction with Ford of Europe for its Scorpio model. By mid-1990, that idea had been abandoned. Ford of Europe reportedly wanted to keep its new Scorpio as a rear-wheel-drive car to better fight off its other European competitors.[11] The additional delay demonstrated an abandonment, at least in this vehicle segment, of the world-car concept so strongly favored by head designer Jack Telnack.

The public would have to wait close to an incredible twelve years for the next Taurus. And that gave Honda and other Japanese competitors a further wedge into the increasingly competitive family-car market. Honda has premiered a new Accord every four years, not every twelve. The company has worked on a much faster two-two-two year cycle than Ford has: two years after a new car was introduced, it received a face-lift. Two years later, it underwent a major redesign, and two years later, it was face-lifted again. Instead of moving rapidly ahead, Ford management stalled, unable to settle on a plan for the Taurus replacement, the size of its wheelbase, when it should appear in the company's cycle plan. As they slowed, others began to pick at Ford's success. Honda's sales rose, until by the end of the decade, the unthinkable happened: the Accord became the best-selling car in America. Honda sold 362,000 Accords compared to Taurus's 348,000. In 1990, the Accord remained America's most popular model.

The Japanese began to understand better than the Big Three what Americans wanted in their cars. Honda even picked up some of Ford's styling cues; the company's 1991 Accord station wagon, with its parallelogram-shaped side windows and slightly bulbous rear deck, bore an unmistakable resemblance to Ford's Taurus wagon. "Two kids, a cat or a dog, cable TV, a health club, a home in the suburbs, and a Honda in the driveway. It doesn't get any better than that for most Americans," said a *Washington Post* columnist.[12]

Some Ford officials pooh-poohed Honda's rapid changes. "When you spend $3 billion to develop a new program from the ground up," said Joel Pitcoff, "if you've done your job right, you goddamn well better make your $3 billion investment last longer than four years! It would be frivolous to throw away that investment."

Lou Ross, too, was annoyed at the public's perception of changes in Japan's cars. He knew that the alterations were often cosmetic, yet the public thought differently. "The Japanese seldom change over sixty percent of a car, for example, and everybody says, 'Oh, it's a new model!' Honda made their first change in twelve years when they resized the 1990 Honda. Then, it was 90 percent new. But for twelve years they had great interchangeability between models, and they changed the sheet metal very often. They do change their patterns frequently, but they do it to be competitive in Japan. The change frequency is in fact faster than Europe or the U.S. wants it."

Honda's incremental face-lifts may have been minor or too frequent, but Ford executives were missing the point. However superficial, Honda succeeded in creating an impression of a manufacturer that was always looking for improvements. The changes may even have sped up owner replacement, as buyers looked to shed their last Honda for the latest one. Ford's inability to move as quickly only perpetuated the sense that stodgy American car companies couldn't compete with forward-looking Japanese manufacturers. As with the development of sixteen-valve engines and the introduction of front-wheel drive, what truly mattered wasn't the improvements a customer needed, but what he had come to expect.

Chris Cedergren, J. D. Powers and Associates' chief auto analyst, noted that a remarkable and fundamental change occurred in the U.S. automobile industry during the 1980s. "To someone who is thirty years old, the names Chevy, Ford, and Oldsmobile are more foreign than Honda, Toyota, and Nissan," Cedergren said. "If you've bought a Toyota or a Honda now, you are likely to stay with a Japanese nameplate. The Japanese carmakers that had so captured the loyalty of young Americans in the 1970s and '80s are now 'upsizing' their vehicles in the '90s for their baby-boom customers who, with growing families and incomes, are getting ready to buy bigger cars.

"Preferences are generational," said Cedergren. "Someone who owns a Toyota and is approaching his fiftieth birthday and wants a bigger car is not going to look for a Buick. He'll look for a bigger Toyota. The Japanese are guaranteeing that as the baby boomers mature, they will continue to buy Japanese cars while still keeping a strong presence with younger customers as they start buying cars. That in itself spells tremendous trouble for the domestic manufacturers."

At least at the beginning of the 1990s, GM, Ford, and Chrysler could still claim the heartland of America as their own. To date, the Japanese sales success has come largely from the East and West coasts. But with an increasing number of Japanese cars now designed for and made in the United States, it is only a matter of time before the Big Three find themselves under attack there as well. "The Japanese right now plan on opening over 1,600 new dealerships just in the Midwest," Cedergren said. "With just conservative sales, that would yield an additional 600,000 units a year to the Japanese manufacturers. That translates into five to six percentage points [of sales]. And that's a big threat."

March 14, 1989, was a special day for Lew Veraldi. This day, he handed out his employees their bonus checks. He always liked to perform this ritual, and even though he had been feeling miserable all night, he still wanted to do it. It meant a lot to him to be able to congratulate his staff for good work. But Irene didn't want him to go to the office; he looked too ill. "I'll give them their checks and then I'll go to the doctor," Veraldi promised his wife.

Later that afternoon, he was carried out of his office on a stretcher, having suffered a massive heart attack. "It looks bad. I hope he makes it to the hospital," the company nurse said to Lew's secretary as the ambulance sped off.

Veraldi survived. Six months later, he was back to his normal twelve-hour workdays. But his severely weakened heart and diabetes quickly made that impossible, and the man who had lived to work for the Ford Motor Company was forced to take medical retirement. Without his beloved job, Veraldi soon deteriorated. By August 1990 his heart was so bad that he became exhausted walking from one room to the next. Only the presentation of the Taurus to the Greenfield Museum that month seemed to breathe any life into him.

Several weeks later, Lew lapsed into a coma. His good friend John Risk visited him often at the hospital, and when Lew periodically woke up, he only wanted to know what was happening at Ford.

"John, I feel like I've failed them," Veraldi told Risk on the last day of his life. "There are so many more things that I have to do for Ford that I can't now. I haven't done enough."

"Don't think that, Lew," John said. "You've done more than your share. You've accomplished more than most people would in three lifetimes." On October 13, 1990, Lew Veraldi died.

"Veraldi was the father of the Taurus," Chuck Gumushian said. "The company didn't like to call him that, because Iacocca used to be called the father of the Mustang. But that's what Lew was."

More than a decade after work first began on the Taurus, Ford's future was again open to question. Due to the beginnings of a recession and its increased reliance on rebates to sell cars, Ford's profits fell 78.7 percent in the third quarter of 1990 from a year earlier, to $102 million. In February 1991, the company announced further cost-cutting and layoffs. But unlike Henry Ford's strategy twenty years earlier, this time it wisely avoided cutbacks in new product expenditures.

Ford's turnaround of the 1980s has become the company's nemesis. "We got on fat street," Lou Ross said. "Everybody was saying we're the greatest people in the world, we make more money than GM. It goes to your head." With its increased financial strength and growing market share, the company has again grown fearful of taking a risk, because now there's too much to lose. As a result, Ford's successful aero look is replicated in all its new models; the once radical design has become the company's unwavering, neoconservative statement. The Japanese continue to make model changes every two years that are perceived by the public as improvements. Ford argues that rapid model changes are unnecessary, and undoable for a company as large as Ford, while it watches the sales of its competitive models decline.

The public is not interested in excuses. It wants cars

that come from companies that, as with the Taurus, have shown they can overcome the obstacles and produce something truly unique and special. Instead of innovations, the company continues to play catch-up, introducing such conveniences as cupholders, multi-valve engines, and ABS brakes only years after its competition has shown that people want them.

"Knockout punch one," said a Ford executive, "was the T-Bird. Knockout punch two, the Taurus. Knockout punch three, the Continental. We could have kept knocking GM on their butt, but we didn't. With the Taurus we even had the Japanese scared. But we sat there, saying, 'Isn't it nice?' Management sat back and said 'we're done.' Heck no, we're not done. The Japanese are never done, and neither should we."

It became the same old story: rather than leaving the designers alone to do what they did best, management was back to checking up on them. "We had freer rein with the Taurus than we ever had, and look at how successful it was," Mimi Vandermolen said. "Now, with our new models, the executives come in to review things—not every week but every day, every hour. It breaks down your morale. You feel 'Nobody trusts me.' "

The Taurus succeeded in the 1980s because the men in control of the Ford Motor Company were willing to gamble, to advance beyond their provincial ways of working and look for guidance from men and women who had broader, international experience. These people often did not fit into the corporate mold and were looking for ways to abolish it and create more equitable working relationships.

To move ahead in the 1990s, Ford must be willing to take the greatest chance of all: make radical changes even when things are going relatively well. Only by continually being innovators, by sacrificing financially now to reap greater rewards in the future, can the Ford Motor Company regain its stature of the 1980s as America's most innovative and customer-conscious automobile corporation.

If Ford is willing, as it did with the Taurus, to risk every-thing, it will find in the end that it has really risked noth-ing at all.

Notes

CHAPTER 1

1. Peter Collier and David Horowitz, *The Fords: An American Epic* (New York: Summit Books, 1987), p. 377.

CHAPTER 2

1. Allan Nevins and Frank Ernest Hill, *Ford: The Times, the Man, the Company* (New York: Charles Scribner's Sons, 1954), p. 234.

2. Robert Lacey, *Ford: The Men and the Machine* (Boston: Little, Brown, 1986), p. 6.

3. Lacey, p. 42.

4. *Ibid.*, p. 74.

5. Collier and Horowitz, p. 47.

6. As quoted in Lacey, p. 84.

7. Collier and Horowitz, p. 52.

8. Lacey, p. 100.

9. *Ibid.*, p. 121.

10. *Ibid.*, p. 120.

11. Carol Gelderman, *Henry Ford: The Wayward Capitalist* (New York: Dial Press, 1981), p. 220.

12. Allan Nevins and Frank E. Hill, *Ford: Expansion and Challenge* (New York: Charles Scribner's Sons, 1957), p. 410.

13. As quoted in Lacey, p. 296.

14. *Ibid.*, p. 299.

15. David Halberstam, *The Reckoning* (New York: William Morrow, 1986), p. 88.

16. Collier and Horowitz, p. 150.

17. Lacey, pp. 335–36.

18. *Ibid.*, pp. 362–63.

19. Allan Nevins and Frank Ernest Hill, *Ford: Decline and Rebirth* (New York: Charles Scribner's Sons, 1963), p. 137.

20. *Ibid.*, p. 139.

21. *Ibid.*, p. 138.

22. Reminiscences of Joe Golomb, as related in Collier and Horowitz, p. 197.

23. Nevins and Hill, *Ford: Decline and Rebirth*, p. 262.

24. *Ibid.*, p. 268.

25. *Ibid.*, p. 305.

26. The other three were the Model T, the Model A, and Ford V-8 (introduced in 1932).

27. As quoted in Collier and Horowitz, p. 251.

28. Halberstam, pp. 562–66.

CHAPTER 3

1. Lacey, p. 530.

2. In 1989, the Fiesta sold 478,300 units, 31 percent of its total European sales of 1.55 million, the best-selling

Ford nameplate in Europe *Automotive News*, March 19, 1990.

3. The 1991 Escort, a "C" class car developed in conjunction with Toyo Kogyo (Mazda) was designated "CT20." The larger-than-Taurus 1989 Thunderbird/Cougar received the codename "MN12." The 1992 restyled Crown Victoria has been designated EN53. The replacement for the Taurus, currently scheduled for 1997, is called the D-FC55, with the "C" indicating that development is being handled by "combined" North American and European teams.

4. Taurus and Sable/A History, unpublished manuscript commissioned by Ford Motor Company, chapter 2, p. 12.

CHAPTER 6

1. Scott L. Bottles, *Los Angeles and the Automobile: The Making of the Modern American City* (Los Angeles: University of California Press, 1987), pp. 2–4.

2. In 1974, a report to the Senate Judiciary Committee accused GM of actively conspiring to rid Los Angeles of its streetcars, in order to force residents to buy automobiles. It did so, legislative analyst Bradford Snell claimed, by purchasing its interest in National City Lines with the sole purpose of shutting down the railways and replacing them with inferior diesel buses. Residents would dislike the buses so much, they would then buy cars. (S1167, 93rd Congress, second session, 1974, part 4A.)

CHAPTER 7

1. "Hail and Farewell at Ford Design," *Automotive News*, June 1, 1987.

2. "Japan's Edge in Auto Quality," *Los Angeles Times*, January 14, 1990.

3. *Ibid.*

4. In 1989, Fiat sold 68 percent of its output in Italy, Renault sold 47 percent of its cars in France, and Peugeot

sold 44 percent to its own countrymen. Volkswagen (including Audi and SEAT), sold 39 percent of its output to Germans, while only 25 percent of Volvos were purchased by Swedes. (*Automotive News 1989 Market Data Book.*)

CHAPTER 8

1. *Automotive News 1990 Market Data Book.*

CHAPTER 9

1. The federal agency sets rules for various design aspects of vehicles which affect safety.

2. Patrick Bedard, "Ford Taurus LX: Mr. and Mrs. Middle America Aren't Gonna Believe This," *Car and Driver*, October 1985.

3. "Car Talk," National Public Radio, May 12, 1990.

CHAPTER 10

1. Lacey, p. 489.

CHAPTER 11

1. By the end of the decade, management would come to accept the notion that quality started at home. "In the late 1970s and early 1980s, attention seemed to be focused on the hourly worker as the cause of high costs and poor quality. As we now understand the reasons for poor quality, they have little to do with workers trying deliberately to produce a bad car. But just ten years ago it was convenient to blame them for all of the industry's problems." Mary Ann Keller, *UMTRI Research Review*, vol. 19, no. 2–3 (Ann Arbor, Mich.: University of Michigan Transportation Research Institute, September–October, November–December, 1988).

2. In 1989, profit sharing gave each Ford worker $1,025. Honda workers received $1,601, General Motors, $50, and Chrysler employees received nothing. *Automotive News*, July 2, 1990.

3. "UAW 1979–1989: A Decade of Decline." Pamphlet distributed by New Directions, Pontiac, Mich.

This position would continue to be raised at union meetings for many years to come. Some workers were opposed to wage and benefit compromises of any sort. In the late 1980s, New Directions, a dissident union faction, would accuse the UAW of selling out its workers by negotiating this settlement with Ford. "Even the large profit-sharing bonuses paid to Ford workers make up less than half of what we have lost by the sacrifice of annual wage increases," the faction proclaimed.

CHAPTER 13

1. Alton F. Doody and Ron Bingaman, *Reinventing the Wheels: Ford's Spectacular Comeback* (Cambridge, Mass.: Ballinger Publishing Co., 1988), p. 81.

CHAPTER 14

1. Ford's Atlanta facility was designated as the Taurus's first assembly plant.

2. Taurus introductory press conference, Los Angeles, January 29, 1985.

3. *Impact*, Chicago Assembly Plant, vol. 3, no. 6, Oct.–Nov. 1988.

CHAPTER 16

1. It was a good lesson for the company. When the restyled Lincoln Town Car began production in 1989, Ford ordered sheet metal delivered to the plants seven months before Job One. It reduced its suppliers of the metal from ten for the Taurus to one for the Town Car. Job One was not delayed.

CHAPTER 17

1. Richard Johnson, "Taurus, Sable Rocket onto Market," *Automotive News*, January 1986.

2. Patrick Bedard, "Ford Taurus LX: Mr. and Mrs. Middle America Aren't Gonna Believe This," *Car and Driver*, October 1985.

3. Jim Miller, "Chevrolet Lumina Euro Sedan vs. Ford Taurus LX vs. Eagle Premier ES Limited," *Motor Trend*, May 1990.

4. *Car and Driver*, January 1990.

5. Bruce Nussbaum, "Smart Design; Quality Is the New Style," *Business Week*, April 11, 1988.

6. Marshall Schuon, "About Cars," *New York Times*, section one, December 31, 1989.

7. *1989 National New Car Buyer Study*, J. D. Power and Associates.

8. *Automotive News Market Data Book*, 1989 and 1990.

9. Harbour and Associates, Inc. report, 1988.

10. "Taurus-Sable Styling a Problem for GM10," *Automotive News*, January 1986.

11. Laura Clark, "Redesigned Taurus Delayed; Front Wheel Drive Set for Big Ford Cars," *Automotive News*, August 20, 1990.

12. Jerry Knight, "Two Kids, a Cat or a Dog, Cable TV and a Honda Accord," *Automotive News*, April 2, 1990.

Index